BELIZE

Carlos Soldevila

ULYSSES
TRAVEL PUBLICATIONS
Travel better... enjoy more

Author Carlos Soldevila	**Project Supervisor** Daniel Desjardins	**Series Director** Claude Morneau
Translation Tracy Kendrick Sarah Kresh Danielle Gauthier	**Layout** Stephanie Heidenreich	**Production Director** Pascale Couture
Editing Tara Salman Stephanie Heidenreich	**Cartography** André Duchesne Assistants Patrick Thivierge Isabelle Lalonde	**Photography** *Cover Photo* Joseph Van Os (Image Bank)
	Illustrations Marie-Annick Viatour	**Design** Patrick Farei - Atoll Dir.

Thanks to Nelli Ivanovna and Laura Bari. Special thanks to SODEC (Québec) and the Department of Canadian Heritage for their financial Support.

DISTRIBUTORS

AUSTRALIA: Little Hills Press, 11/37-43 Alexander St., Crows Nest NSW 2065, ☎ (612) 437-6995, Fax: (612) 438-5762

BELGIUM AND LUXEMBOURG: Vander, Vrijwilligerlaan 321, B-1150 Brussel, ☎ (02) 762 98 04, Fax: (02) 762 06 62

CANADA: Ulysses Books & Maps, 4176 Saint-Denis, Montréal, Québec, H2W 2M5, ☎ (514) 843-9882, ext.2232, 800-748-9171, Fax: 514-843-9448, www.ulysses.ca

GERMANY AND AUSTRIA: Brettschneider, Fernreisebedarf, Feldfirchner Strasse 2, D-85551 Heimstetten, München, ☎ 89-99 02 03 30, Fax: 89-99 02 03 31

GREAT BRITAIN AND IRELAND: World Leisure Marketing, Unit 11, Newmarket Court, Newmartket Drive, Derby DE24 8NW, ☎ 1 332 57 37 37, Fax: 1 332 57 33 99

ITALY: Centro Cartografico del Riccio, Via di Soffiano 164/A, 50143 Firenze, ☎ (055) 71 33 33, Fax: (055) 71 63 50

NETHERLANDS: Nilsson & Lamm, Pampuslaan 212-214, 1380 AD Weesp (NL), ☎ 0294-494949, Fax: 0294-494455, E-mail: nilam@euronet.nl

PORTUGAL: Dinapress, Lg. Dr. Antonio de Sousa de Macedo, 2, Lisboa 1200, ☎ (1) 395 52 70, Fax: (1) 395 03 90

SCANDINAVIA: Scanvik, Esplanaden 8B, 1263 Copenhagen K, DK, ☎ (45) 33.12.77.66, Fax: (45) 33.91.28.82

SPAIN: Altaïr, Balmes 69, E-08007 Barcelona, ☎ 454 29 66, Fax: 451 25 59, altair@globalcom.es

SWITZERLAND: OLF, P.O. Box 1061, CH-1701 Fribourg, ☎ (026) 467.51.11, Fax: (026) 467.54.66

U.S.A.: The Globe Pequot Press, 6 Business Park Road, P.O. Box 833, Old Saybrook, CT 06475, ☎ 1-800-243-0495, Fax: 800-820-2329, sales@globe-pequot.com

Other countries, contact Ulysses Books & Maps (Montréal), Fax: (514) 843-9448

"British Honduras is not on the way from anywhere to anywhere else, has no strategic value, is all but uninhabited; if the world had any ends, British Honduras would surely be one of them."

Aldous Huxley,
Beyond the Mexique Bay, 1934

TABLE OF CONTENTS

CATALOGUING

Soldevila, Carlos, 1969-

    Belize

    (Ulysses Travel Guides)
    Translation of: Belize.
    Includes Index

    ISBN 2-89464-179-6
    1. Belize - Guidebooks I. Title II. Series.
F1443.5.S6413 1998   917.28204'5   C98-940809-4

WRITE TO US

The information contained in this guide was correct at press time.
However, mistakes can slip in, omissions are always possible, places
can disappear, etc. The authors and publisher hereby disclaim any
liability for loss or damage resulting from omissions or errors.

We value your comments, corrections and suggestions, as they allow
us to keep each guide up to date. The best contributions will be
rewarded with a free book from Ulysses Travel Publications. All you
have to do is write us at the following address and indicate which title
you would be interested in receiving (see the list at the end of guide).

Ulysses Travel Publications
4176 Rue Saint-Denis
Montréal, Québec
Canada H2W 2M5
www.ulysses.ca
E-mail: guiduly@ulysses.ca

MAP SYMBOLS

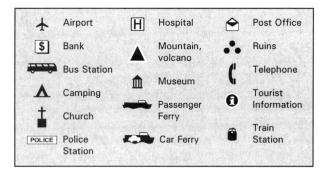

✈	Airport	Ⓗ	Hospital	✉	Post Office
$	Bank	▲	Mountain, volcano	•••	Ruins
🚌	Bus Station	🏛	Museum	(	Telephone
⛺	Camping	🚢	Passenger Ferry	❶	Tourist Information
✝	Church	🚗🚢	Car Ferry	💼	Train Station
POLICE	Police Station				

LIST OF MAPS

SYMBOLS

🌴	Ulysses' favourite
☎	Telephone number
⊷	Fax number
≡	Air conditioning
⊗	Fan
#	Screen
≈	Pool
ℜ	Restaurant
♿	Wheelchair access
⊛	Whirlpool
ℝ	Refrigerator
K	Kitchenette
△	Sauna
⊖	Exercise room
tv	Colour television
hw	Hot water
pb	Private bathroom
sb	Shared bathroom
ps	Private shower
bkfst	Breakfast
fb	Full board (lodging plus 3 meals)
½b	Half board (lodging plus 2 meals)

ATTRACTION CLASSIFICATION

★	Interesting
★★	Worth a visit
★★★	Not to be missed

HOTEL CLASSIFICATION

The prices in the guide are for one double occupancy room.

RESTAURANT CLASSIFICATION

$	BZ$20 or less
$$	BZ$20 to BZ$30
$$$	BZ$30 or more

The prices in the guide are for a meal for one person,
not including drinks and tip.

All prices in this guide are in Belizean dollars.

Where is Belize?

Belize

Capital: Belmopan
Main City: Belize City
Area: 22 962 km²
Population: 219 000 inhab.
Official languages: English and Spanish
Currency: Belizean Dollar

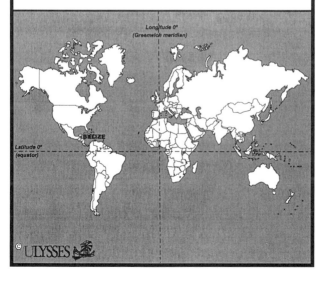

© ULYSSES

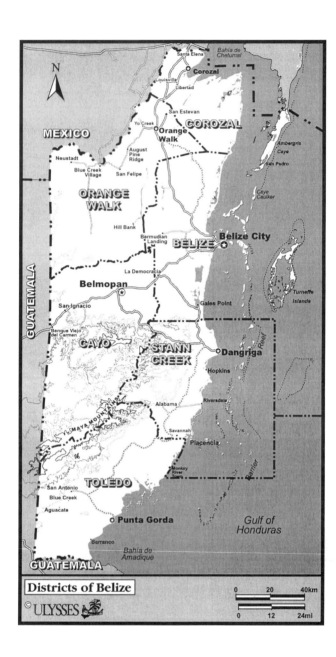

Districts of Belize
© ULYSSES

PORTRAIT

I n 1934, British author Aldous Huxley wryly remarked
that "if the world had any ends, British Honduras
would certainly be one of them." Belize was a British
colony called British Honduras before it acquired independence
in 1981. For centuries, this region was among the least
accessible in Central America. Its coast, protected by the
Barrier Reef, the second largest coral reef in the world, was the
site of many shipwrecks, one of which may have changed the
course of the region's history. According to one legend, the
country was founded in 1638 by a crew of shipwrecked English
sailors. Belize's western border with Guatemala adjoins the
Petén jungle, which is equally difficult to cross, allowing the
Mayan people who inhabited this forest resisted conquest
longer than any other indigenous group. In this "ends of the
Earth" environment, pockets of Englishmen, made up of
lumberjacks and buccaneers on the run, along with their slaves,
gradually created the nation that Belize is today. Its close to
200,000 citizens inhabit the youngest and least populated
country in Central America.

The same geographical features that once made Belize an
isolated, inaccessible country make it a traveller's paradise
today. Pirates and buccaneers were the first to benefit from the
thousands of islands and cays in the sea off the coast of Belize,
using them as hideouts between their attacks on Spanish ships.

On the mainland, numerous Mexicans found peace in the middle of the 19th century, when the War of the Castes raged in the Yucatán Peninsula. Garifuna people, expelled from the island of St. Vincent, found the land on the country's coasts suitable for a renewal of their culture. Finally, Mennonites migrated to parts of the country that were sufficiently isolated for them to live according to their habits and customs. Even the Maya, the first inhabitants of this land, lived in relative tranquillity, compared to the fate of their kin in Guatemala. Today the country is made up of myriad cultures and languages: Maya, blacks, Creoles, Garifunas, Spanish and Indians coexist in peace, a true blessing for the only Central American country that has not suffered the horrors of war in the last two centuries.

Today the hundreds of islands in the Caribbean Sea are favourite refuges of travellers and modern-day adventurers. Long the best-kept secret of experienced divers from all over the world, the underwater mysteries of the Barrier Reef and its dozens of virgin islands are now both accessible and well-known. Belize does not have the most beautiful beaches in the Caribbean, which may be the reason it remains unspoiled by mass tourism. But for every missing beach there is a quiet island dotted with typical wooden houses along palm-shaded sand roads, whose spirited, light-hearted inhabitants savour the hours between sunrise and sunset. One accessory visitors have little use for here is a watch!

The interior of the country is resplendent with idyllic landscapes and national parks, riches that remain under-recognized by travellers. In the south and west of the country, the Maya Mountains shelter Mopán and K'eckchi villages where aboriginal people still proudly display their traditional multicoloured clothing. In the west, nature reigns and you will find unspoiled rivers, caves and mountains. Eco-tourism is gaining ground in this land of jaguars, howler monkeys, toucans and iguanas.

Archaeology fans will not be disappointed in Belize. Home to a large number of sites including Cuello, the oldest-known Mayan settlement, and the superb ruins of Lamanaí, nestled in the northern tropical forest, which were inhabited up until the Conquest, Belize has no cause to envy its Central American neighbours.

Travellers visiting Belize for the first time will find that this small Central American country is like a Pandora's box. From the outside it appears to be little more than an unpopular nation of men and women abandoned to their fates by Spanish and British governments, which were uninspired by the land's natural treasures. For those who dare to open it, however, this box contains an amazing store of surprises.

GEOGRAPHY

Although it is the second-smallest nation in Central America, after El Salvador, Belize possesses such tremendous natural diversity that any other country in the world pales by comparison. Its 22,962-square-kilometre (8,866-square-mile) territory includes tall mountains, forests, lakes, rivers, marshes, islands, some of the largest caves in the Americas and the second-longest coral reef in the world.

Belize's coasts face east onto the Caribbean Sea and south onto the Gulf of Honduras. The country shares a northern border with Mexico (the Yucatán Peninsula) and western and southern borders with Guatemala. Distances in Belize are never very great, since the country is only 280 kilometres (173.6 miles) long from north to south and barely 109 kilometres (67.6 miles) wide from east to west.

A few million years ago, all of Belize rested on the ocean floor. Gradually, volcanoes rose form the sea, creating the Maya Mountains. Belize actually emerged from the water twice, with a period of submergence in between. Today, a large part of the country is barely above sea level, and if the ocean should rise again, Belize could be reduced to a series of islands.

The north of the country is characterized by two mountain chains. One runs along the Guatemalan border in the northwest of the country, to Blue Creek, the source of Río Hondo, which demarcates the northern border with Mexico. The other chain is more frequently visited and more accessible, because it runs along the Western Highway to the Maya Mountains. At the foot of these hills there are marshes, just above sea level, and broad, pine-covered plains that are suitable for sugar-cane and corn farming. Many rivers wind through this part of the country, including Belize River, which empties into the sea at Belize City. Río Hondo, New River and Sibun River, the three longest rivers in the country, also course through this ecosystem.

During the era of Mayan civilization, these fertile lands were rich in cocoa and were an integral part of the Mayan trade route. The Maya lived here for centuries and built temples that can still be admired today.

In the south, the **Maya Mountains** and the **Cockscomb Range** form the country's spine. The forest-covered Maya Mountains boast the highest summit in the country, Victoria Peak, which reaches an altitude of 1,121 metres (3,680 feet) above sea level. In addition to many rivers, the southern landscape includes the "Bald Mountains", Baldy Sibun and Baldy Beacon.

The superb landscapes of western Belize feature the **Mountain Pine Ridge**, the second-largest mountain chain in the country. The spectacular waterfalls of **Hidden Valley**, set amid lush vegetation, are over 300 metres (1,000 feet) tall.

Belize's Caribbean coast, abundant with mangroves and dotted by a few sandy beaches, stretches 280 kilometres (173.6 miles) from north to south. At sea, the **Barrier Reef**, the second-longest coral reef in the world after Australia's Great Barrier Reef, forms several islands.

FLORA

Belize possesses some of the most beautiful forests in Central America, which are home to over 4,000 plant species.

Belize is set in a region that is regularly ravaged by hurricanes, a factor that has had a definite impact on the type of tropical forest that grows in the country. Every forest is hit by these violent winds at least once every 100 years, which is often enough to influence its structure and composition. For this reason, the tropical forests of Belize are generally not as tall or dense as those of places like Costa Rica.

Ground vegetation has also had to adapt to the frequent flooding caused by heavy rains that swell rivers and streams beyond their banks. By contrast, the incidence of forest fires in certain regions, especially in the south, has favoured the development of pine trees, which are more fire resistant than other types. Caribbean pine (*Pinus caraibaea*) is the most common species in the country.

Belize has extremely varied dry and humid tropical forest with over 700 tree species. Mahogany, Belize's national tree, still grows in the country's interior, despite centuries of large-scale harvesting.

Mangroves are very common on the coast. As well, coconut trees and palms stand tall on the horizon, shading some of the most diverse aquatic vegetation in the world.

FAUNA

Belize's spectacular fauna offers visitors the opportunity to observe exotic wild animals, ranging from toucans, the national bird, to jaguars.

The tapir, the national animal of Belize, is more difficult to spot than the many other species of monkeys that live in the wet tropical forests. The distinctive cry of the howler monkey can often be heard at dusk and dawn, especially in the Baboon Sanctuary (see p 96).

Coati

Jabiru

The abundance of forests in Belize has created a safe environment for numerous animal species. There are over 150 mammal species, including 70 types of bats, jaguars, monkeys, pumas, coatis and tapirs, to name a few.

The jaguar, whose survival is threatened in other parts of the world, is protected in Belize. There is a wildlife reserve dedicated to jaguars at the Cockscomb Basin Wildlife Sanctuary (see p 180), where visitors can observe them. For the Mayans, the mysterious, dangerous jaguar was a deity called *balum*, and an integral part of the culture's pantheon. According to the Mayan creation myth, god created humans because jaguars already existed.

Of course, Belize is also home to many bird species, about 520 according to research conducted in the country. Ducks, eagles, falcons and owls share the skies and treetops with toucans, parrots, hummingbirds and jabirus.

POPULATION

The population of Belize is characterized by its great cultural and racial diversity, although different ethnic groups tend to be concentrated in different regions. Sixty-eight percent of the population of Belize City is Creole, and this group forms the dominant culture of the nation. Mestizos, of mixed Spanish and aboriginal descent, compose close to 70% of the population in the area of Orange Walk, in the north. In the south, in the district of Toledo, the Mopán and the K'eckchi' represent 63% of the population. In the area of Stann Creek, especially in the town of Dandriga, Garifunas make up 70% of the population. Garifunas, who are descended from runaway black slaves and Caribs, the indigenous people of northeastern South America and the Lesser Antilles who rebelled against the British, have developed a completely unique culture over the centuries (see p 179). Expelled from the island of St. Vincent in the 18th century, great numbers of Garifunas came and settled the southern coastal villages of Dandriga, Placencia, Hopkins and Punta Gorda.

Finally, East Indians, brought over as slaves and cheap labour by the British, live all over the country. There is also a fairly large Chinese community. Mennonites (see p 12) have settled far from urban centres in the areas of Orange Walk and Cayo.

Languages

Although English is the official language of Belize, the majority of the population in the north and west speak Spanish. In the south, Mopán, a Mayan language is predominant in the region of San Antonio (see p 185), and Garifuna, mostly spoken in coastal villages such as Hopkins (see p 177), are both current. While English is understood by everyone, it is Creole, a mixture of English, African and Spanish, that is the language of everyday life all over the country.

The First Peoples

Belize was once one of the main centres of Mayan civilization. Today, many important Mayan ruins can be visited, including those at Lamanaí, Cuello, Santa Rita, Altun Ha, Cerros, Xunatunich, Caracol, Pacbitun, Cahal Pech, Pilar, Maintzunun, Lubaatun, Nim Li Punit and Uxbenca. In fact, Cuello, the oldest Mayan site ever discovered, was found in the western part of the country. All evidence indicates that the Mayan civilization survived in Belize long after the post-classic period, especially at Lamanaí (see p 148), which served as a hub of trading activity.

The history of the Maya is one of discovery, deep knowledge of the order of things (astronomy, architecture, writing, etc.), and a relation with nature and a concept of time that are foreign to us. The history and culture of these "corn people" are unique to them. The Maya have been persistent in preserving their beliefs despite the 500-year-long presence of Europeans, and their history and culture continue to be a source of fascination to people all over the world. Vibrant as ever, Mayan culture is still there to be appreciated and literally uncovered in Belize.

Very little is certain about the history of the Mayans. Based on ruins and archaeological finds, many schools of thought have developed, espousing theories that are sometimes contradictory. The confusion seems to increase over the years and with each new find. Nonetheless, some time lines of Mayan civilization have been put forward by archeologists. Based in part on the results of carbon dating and in part on Mayan calendars, these chronologies are also subject to constant revision and even litigation among researchers.

To better describe the history of Central America and Mexico, archaeologists have designated the territory from the central Mexican plateau (Toltecs, Aztecs) to the Mayan lands in Central America as Mesoamerica. This division separates these civilizations from those of North America, which, at the time of the Spanish conquest, were still principally nomadic.

HISTORY

Prehistory

From 20,000 to 2000 BC, Siberian hunters and gatherers colonized the New World and Mesoamerica. They crossed the Bering Strait about 60,000 years ago and reached Central America 15,000 to 20,000 years before the beginning of the common era. **Clovis**, named for the archeologists that discovered it, was the first culture to exist in Mesoamerica, in about 9000 BC. Objects dating from this era, including spearheads, have been excavated in the Guatemalan highlands.

Over the course of what some archeologists refer to as the archaic period, from 8000 to 2000 BC, some aboriginal groups passed from nomadic to sedentary life thanks to the development of agriculture. Most of the edible plants found in the region were eventually domesticated, most importantly corn. The first permanent settlement also appeared in this era, as did art forms associated with sedentary life such as pottery and weaving.

The Early Maya

According to archaeologists, the earliest roots of Olmec, Zapotec and Mayan civilizations emerged during the preclassic or formative period, from 2000 BC to AD 250, which was crucial to the evolution of Mesoamerican cultures. There is evidence from this era of the production of vases and more elaborate ceramics, which were painted or engraved with motifs representing rather realistic faces. The oldest pieces that have come to light, were discovered in Cuello, in northern Belize, and date from between 2000 and 1500 BC. In addition, the discovery of stones used to grind corn indicates that these population had also mastered agriculture.

The discovery of numerous architectural remains from 1000 BC in the territories inhabited by the Maya point to a significant population increase in this period. The area of Orange Walk is rich in archaeological evidence from this era, including ruins at

Cuello (see p 146), Lamanaí (see p 148) and Kichpanha. The ruins at Cerros (see p 155), in the region of Corozal, also date from this period.

The Golden Age of Mayan Civilization

The golden age, or classic period, of Mesoamerican cultures, from AD 250 to 900, is characterized by the prominence of the great city of Teotihuacán, on the central Mexican plateau, and of the Mayan cities to the southeast. This period has also bequeathed to us the most important vestiges of Mayan civilization, which was then at its peak.

To fully understand this period, one must examine the time around 300 BC, when the Maya introduced the calendar and writing and their civilization began its lightning-speed development. Hieroglyphs discovered on temples include dates and tell the stories of chiefs, battles and of the succession of Mayan dynasties.

In the fifth century of our era, the great temples, such as those of Tikal and Kaminaljuyú in Guatemala, acquired their significant scale. In Belize, the temples of Altun ha, Lubaatun, Nim Li Punit and Xunantunich (see p 219) testify to the grandeur of the Maya's golden age. As the population increased, great numbers of Maya chose to live in these urban religious centres. The great Mayan cities, the ruins of which can be appreciated today, had become the centres of Mayan culture. Tikal, in the northern part of the Petén, was the largest of these cities. With close to 3,000 buildings, including huge pyramids, Tikal had an estimated population of about 10,000, and probably close to 75,000 people lived in its surroundings.

Of the 3,000 Mayan sites discovered by archaeologists in Mesoamerica, about 50 are considered important centres. North of the Petén, there are the great cities of Uaxactún, El Naranjo, Nakum and Holmul. Copán, in Honduras, and Quirigua are two significant southern sites. The ceremonial centres of Piedras Negras, Yaxchilán and Palenque are found on the shores of the Usumacinta river, which has its source in the highlands of Guatemala, and empties into the Gulf of Mexico. Río Bec, Uxmal and Kabah, of Puuc inspiration, stand in the surroundings of the Yucatán Peninsula, while the peninsula

The Birth of the "Corn People"

According to the *Popol Vuh*, the sacred book of the Quiché, Cakchiquel and Tzutuhil Mayan peoples, there were three creations. In the first creation, humans were made from mud. But, to paraphrase the original text, the people dissolved, became soft, had no movement, no strength, they fell, were aqueous, didn't move their heads, their faces collapsed on one side, they could not see. At first they spoke, but they had no consciousness. Soon it became humid and they could not hold together. Disappointed, the gods destroyed their work.

For the second creation, a couple of older gods decided to make men of wood and women of reeds. These people saw, spoke and reproduced like humans, but they possessed no souls, their physical traits were unexpressive, and their skin was yellow. Because they did not remember their creators, they were destroyed in their turn, drowned in a flood or devoured by demons. Those who survived turned into monkeys.

In the third creation, four men and four women were created from white and yellow corn. The gods were pleased because the men thanked their creators, but they found them to be too intelligent and there was a danger that they might become the intellectual equals of the gods. From the heavens a fog was blown into their eyes, and their wisdom diminished. The "corn people" became the ancestors of the Maya.

itself is home to the sites of Chichén Itzá and Tulum. Finally, Tikal is located in the Petén jungle.

The influence of the great city of Teotihuacán, near present-day Mexico City, was a determining factor in the rapid evolution of these Mayan religious centres. Stele 31 at Tikal depicts a Mayan nobleman richly adorned with jade ornaments with two Teotihuacán warriors at his sides. The latter wear shields emblazoned with the effigy of Tlaloc, the Teotihuacano god of rain. This Mayan nobleman may even have been a "puppet" of the Teotihuacano empire, which began to decline toward the end of the sixth century.

Agriculture and Trade

As the Maya became increasingly urbanized, agricultural progress became essential to the survival of the civilization. The Maya, who possessed a fairly advanced knowledge of agriculture, mainly cultivated corn, beans and squash. They cleared land of brush and bushes, which were burned, and then planted seeds one at a time at the beginning of the rainy season. Recently, terraces created by stone walls were discovered in the Yucatán, evidence of even more advanced drainage techniques.

Although subsistence was the principal preoccupation of the Maya, they maintained links with the rest of Mesoamerica through trade. Obsidian from Cerro de las Navajas, on the central Mexican plateau, has been found at Tikal and Uaxactún in the Petén, at Altun Há in Belize, and in other Mayan villages. Another highland product, volcanic ash from the area of present-day El Salvador, was used in the creation of Mayan pottery. Finally, highland regions furnished jade, one of the era's most prized materials for jewellery-making. Members of the elite were often buried with jade beads in their mouths.

Cocoa was the most important export from the lowlands to the highlands, where it was much in demand, as much for ritual use and as currency. Cocoa was imported from El Salvador and later cultivated by the Maya of Belize. Salt, found in lakes, wells and the sea, was also a valuable export to the highlands, and cotton was certainly an important commodity as well.

From the tropical-forest centres of Tikal, Caracol (see p 222) and Xunantunich (see p 219), among others, exotic items such as jaguar skins and toucan, parrot and hummingbird feathers were exported to the highlands, while the superb feathers of the mystical highland quetzal travelled in the opposite direction.

More than a means of subsistence and enrichment, trade among the various cultures and urban centres of Mesoamerica also permitted these peoples to share their knowledge of

Quetzal

astronomy, mathematics, writing, the arts, and architecture, as well as of different forms of social and religious organization.

The Mayan Calendar

Mayan codices and hieroglyphic inscriptions on temples illustrate the civilization's fascination with the concept of time. This pronounced interest has evoked two general interpretations among archaeologists. One purports that it demonstrates the Maya's dedication to the expansion of their knowledge of astronomy. The other, more widely accepted theory states that these texts indicate a marked interest in astrology and the prediction of future events. According to archeologist Muriel Porter Weaver, "it was only by being able to predict with certainty eclipses, seasonal changes, the movement of the sun and of the other planets, the ends of periods, and cyclical events that these people could prepare themselves to negotiate with the gods and the forces of good and evil by making the offerings and sacrifices necessary to ensure their support."

Although the Mayan calendar was based on other existing Mesoamerican calendars, the Maya perfected it as a tool for recording important astronomical information. The Mayan system of time is made up of three parts:

1) The sacred year, consisting of 260 days (*tzolkin*) and divided into 13 months, or numbers (from 1 to 13), and a strict order of 20 named days per month.

2) The solar year (*haab*), divided into 18 months (*uinal*) of 20 days each, numbered from zero to 19, followed by a period of five days of misfortune (*uayeb*), for a total of 365 days.

3) Based on this system, there is a series of temporal cycles: the *uinal* (20 days or *kins*); the *tun* (360 days); the *katun* (7,200 days); the *baktun* (144,000 days); and finally, the largest cycle is the *alautun* (23,040,000,000 days), a period of 63 million years!

Every period of 20 days makes up a month (*uinal*), and each month has a name and a corresponding hieroglyph. Every temporal cycle is also designated by a hieroglyph.

Like the Roman calendar, the Mayan calendar begins at a year zero, which corresponds to 3113 BC. This mythical date, which marks the beginning of the Mayan era, is doubtless earlier than the actual appearance of the Maya. Mayan inscriptions enumerate the cycles that have passed from the year zero.

Today, like in the golden age of Mayan civilization, the sacred year of 260 days (*tzolkin*) is the highest tool of divination. Priests knew the esoteric significance of every day and number and could thereby predict the beneficial or malevolent influences on each of these periods. Central American Mayan towns and villages still respect these calendars.

Mathematics

The calendar is grounded in an elaborate arithmetic system based on vigesimal numeration, in which numbers increase in sets of twenty, as opposed to our own decimal number system. The Maya's greatest accomplishment in this area of knowledge is unquestionably the discovery of zero, an achievement reached only by the world's most brilliant early civilizations.

For calculation, the Maya used very simple symbols. The shell had a value of zero, the dot had a value of one, and the dash had a value of five. Numbers between one and four were designated with the corresponding number of dots; five with a dash; six to nine with a dash on top of which were placed the corresponding number of dots; 10 with two dashes; 11 to 14 with two dashes under one to four dots, and so on to twenty. Twenty constituted a second set of numbers. Every set of twenty was represented by a dot above the other dots and dashes.

Writing

According to Spanish testimony from the 14th century, only a small proportion of the Mayan population could read and write, and only the nobles could truly understand the scientific foundations of Mayan texts. Nonetheless, there must have existed hundreds, if not thousands, of books, which were destroyed by the effects of the tropical climate and, more significantly, the Spanish Inquisition.

Today, written records of the pre-Columbian period are very rare. Only three precolumbian codices and fragments of a fourth survived the Spanish conquest and the climate. Of these, the Dresden codex is the most interesting and the most useful to archaeologists. This well-preserved document, an almanac of tables for consultation, is kept in the German town after which it is named.

The Peresiano codex, conserved in Paris, deals with predictions, prophecies, and the cycle of 52 years. Unfortunately, the archaeological value of this document is diminished by the fact that two passages are missing from it and it is in very poor condition. The Tro-Cortesiano codex, stored in Madrid, is very incomplete. Finally, the authenticity of the fragments of the Grolier codex, which is preserved in New York, is still in doubt.

These codices are scrapbooks of drawings made up of many pages glued together that unfold to a length of about 10 metres or longer. The pages were made from the inner layers of tree bark. Once the bark was pulped, the threads were pounded to create a flat surface. The page was then soaked, dried, and finally coated with a thin layer of calcium carbonate.

Important Mayan documents were also produced after the Spanish conquest, including the *Popul Vuh* and the books of Chilam Balam, which were written in the Spanish alphabet. Chilam is derived from "Cilan", a famous Mayan prophet, and Balam means "jaguar". In addition to calendars, it contains songs, magic formulas, and medical knowledge.

The *Popul Vuh*, the sacred book of the Quiché Maya, offers a mythical interpretation of Mayan history. The tale divides the saga of the Maya into four long cycles. The first three are part of "prehistory". The last cycle represents history and civilization. These ages are simultaneously separate and unified in a single whole, so that readers can establish links among the different periods described.

Art and Architecture

Heavily ornamented and expressive, Mayan art at the height of their civilization is different from the more austere styles than that of other Mesoamerican peoples. Unfortunately, much Mayan artwork has disappeared over time, since the Mayans painted on wood and bark, using bird feathers as decorative elements, and none of these materials can be preserved for very long in a tropical climate. Some wooden objects have nonetheless survived, especially at Tikal, where visitors can admire scenes representing noblemen and their guards, as well as long hieroglyphic texts. In addition to pottery used in burial rituals, carefully worked jade pieces displaying superb reliefs have been found.

Mayan architecture is the modern era's most vibrant relic of this civilization. The typical Mayan ceremonial constructions consisted of a small, closed temple covered by a vault, atop a large pyramid. The vault was supported by the junction of two parallel walls that thickened toward the bottom and were sealed off by a flat slab. A stone ridge the same width as the temple rose above this vault, usually on the back wall. The rooms, which were rather cramped because of the shape of the walls that created the vault, were covered with stucco.

Mayan palaces were smaller and, more significantly, less elevated than temples. However, unlike the temples, they contained many rooms, though the purpose of these rooms remains a mystery. They seem to have been too humid to have served as bedrooms, and no trace of their function has yet been uncovered. The temples and palaces towered above squares and courtyards in which stood magnificent steles and religious altars that weighed several tons. These were engraved with hieroglyphic inscriptions and drawings, especially in sites in central Belize. A large stone alley, which led directly to the temple, occupied the centre of these squares. Sometimes there were also ball courts and saunas on these squares.

World View

The Maya believed that 13 heavens were layered above the Earth, which itself rested on a giant reptile floating in water. One god presided over each of these heavens, and collectively these were called the Oaxlahunticu gods. The underworld is made up of nine successive layers governed by nine Bolontiku gods.

Sacrifices

Sacrifices made to obtain the favour of the gods took many forms, from the donation of jade or flowers to animal sacrifice, and even the sacrifice of humans or parts of the human body. The most common form of "self-sacrifice" involved making small incisions in the skin with a flint blade. Many examples of these flint blades are displayed in Belize's archaeological museums.

Social Organization

For many years, the prevailing theory held that the Maya were a religious, peaceful people whose main preoccupation was scientific inquiry. Without belittling the importance of religion in Mayan culture, some archaeological discoveries indicate that the Maya were actually competitive and aggressive, and often involved in local conflicts. Battle scenes, portraits of warriors, depictions of torture and prisoners all seem to confirm this new interpretation. The idea that the Maya were a society of priests and devout farmers has changed considerably. During the classic period, the Maya were governed by "semi-divine" leaders whose histories were chronicled by court sculptors.

At the height of their civilization, the Maya undoubtedly formed a complex society with a powerful, "semi-divine" elite. The members of this elite wore elegant clothing and were buried, along with their jewellery, in sumptuous tombs. To this elite were added a class of scribes, accountants and sculptors, then a class of potters and tool-makers, and, finally, farmers, at the bottom of the social scale. Of course, this theory of Mayan social structure is hypothetical, reminding us just how incomplete our knowledge of this great American civilization remains.

The Collapse of Mayan Civilization

Toward AD 790, the Maya abruptly stopped erecting temples and steles. The last dates to appear on Mayan temples, according to our calendar, are: Copán, 820; Naranjo, 849; Caracol, 859; Tikal, 879. Finally, the year AD 889 was the last inscribed in the Mayan calendar of Uaxactún.

American archeologist Muriel Porter Weaver sums up a few factors of the sudden erosion of Mayan civilization as follows:

- There was rapid population decline and sites were abandoned.
- The arrival of outsiders, although it undoubtedly precipitated the decline, did not cause it.
- A new trade route skirted the Yucatán Peninsula instead of passing through Mayan centres.
- The quality of ceramics deteriorated.
- Finally, the collapse of Mayan civilization was real and unequivocal.

What could have caused the Mayan civilization, which reached its peak between 680 and 780, to witness the collapse of one after the other of its ceremonial centres? Speculation on the subject is rampant, but unfortunately data explaining these events is rare. Despite the multitude of theories advanced, the collapse of Mayan civilization remains a mystery.

Among the many hypotheses put forward, which range from possible natural cataclysms to more outlandish explanations involving extraterrestrials and other phenomena, two theories are most widely accepted. One posits that farmers revolted in Mayan centres, overthrowing the class of elites. The second speculates that increases in urban populations created excessive demand for agricultural production, which in turn impoverished the soil, causing the downfall of the elite and unproductive classes. A combination of these two explanations is also highly likely.

PORTRAIT

From the Mayan Decline to the Spanish Conquest

A period characterized by militarism followed the collapse of Mayan civilization. The Toltecs dominated Mesoamerica from that time until 1200, followed by the Aztecs, who controlled practically all of the lands not occupied by the Maya. Until the Spanish conquest, the territory of Guatemala and Belize was populated by a myriad of aboriginal peoples, most claiming Toltec descent, illustrating the significant impact of the Toltec occupation.

The Quiché, who dominated the zone formerly occupied by the Maya until the arrival of the Spanish, were a warrior culture. They penetrated the highlands of Guatemala around 1250, in the period when Chichén Itzá was abandoned. Gradually, they established themselves, monopolized fertile land, and completed the conquest of the Guatemalan highlands around 1400. They founded their capital at Utatlán, which has the remains of four temples, four ball courts and many platforms for houses.

People of Mayan origin were numerous in the area of Belize at the time of the Spanish conquest, especially in the region of Chetumal, Mexico, just north of Belize.

The Spanish Conquerors

The arrival in the 16th century of the first Europeans in the territory of Belize, then simply called the Bay of Honduras, profoundly transformed the landscape. The Spanish were the first to set foot on this land, although they never established a colony in the area. In fact, the very first European to arrive in Belize was none other than Hernán Cortés, who, in all likelihood, landed in the area of Toledo in the southern part of the country, where he was met by the indigenous Mopán people.

In 1528, a few years after the conquest of the Yucatán by Pedro de Alvarado, the *adelantado* Francisco de Montejo left the villa of Salamanca, near Cozumel, and navigated the southern coast of the Yucatán in search of a more appropriate setting for a Spanish settlement. His lieutenant, Alfonso Dávila, travelled overland, but he was soon repelled by a Mayan attack and never reached his destination. Francisco de Montejo had more luck and reached the old Mayan village of Chetumal, then probably located on the Bay of Corozal, in northern Belize. What a surprise it was for the conqueror when he was told that a Spaniard, Gonzalo Guerrero, lived with the Maya of Chetumal! Guerrero, who had been shipwrecked, had become a prominent member of Chetumal's Mayan society and refused to join the Spanish in combat against his adoptive people. Rather, Guerrero fought alongside the Maya. Legend has it that he succeeded in convincing Montejo that Dávila and his men were killed, and sent word to Dávila that the same fate had befallen Montejo. The latter retreated from Chetumal, and Guerrero used the respite to organize Mayan defences.

It was not until 1531 that Dávila again crossed the Yucatán overland with the aim of establishing a colony in Chetumal. When he arrived, he found Chetumal abandoned by the Maya, who were advised by Guerrero, and well aware of his adversaries' military power. Dávila changed the name of Chetumal to Villa Real. He wanted to "pacify" the region in order to develop it as a shipping route. However, the Maya on the outskirts of the settlement resisted, ambushing the Spanish whenever they strayed from Villa Real. Gradually, the Spanish found themselves under siege and had to retreat, abandoning Villa Real in 1532. For a second time, the Spanish had failed to establish a colony in the Bay of Corozal.

The Spanish returned to Belize about 10 years later. In 1544, Gaspar Pacheco, his son, Melchor Pacheco, and his nephew Alonso undertook to reconquer the region. They were sent by Montejo, who ordered them to take the territory from Chetumal to Golfo Dulce, which corresponds to the borders of Belize today. To achieve this end, the Pacheco family relentlessly terrorized local populations as they passed through the region.

In 1548, Fray Lorenzo de Bienvenida wrote the following about Nero Pacheco. This text, which is of tremendous historical value, was sent to the Spanish crown:

"Nero was a man of a cruelty altogether comparable to that of [Alphonso Pacheco]. He pushed ahead into the province called Chetumal, which was then at peace. And while the natives had demonstrated no belligerence toward him, he cooly pillaged their territory and appropriated their provisions, even going so far as to set his dogs on all those he succeeded in capturing. The fear that the Spanish inspired in them soon incited local populations to flee into the brush and abandon their crops, with the result that they were decimated by famine. And this completely, because while the *pueblos* once regrouped from 500 to 1,000 houses, it is now difficult to find one that numbers as many as 100.

"This same captain is personally responsible for many outrages. Clubbing more than one native with his bare hands, he had the habit of saying: "This is absolutely the best instrument with which to punish these infidels." Then, after finishing them off, he added, "It serves them right!" He tied them to posts, cut off the hands, noses and ears of the men, sliced the breasts of many women, then tied gourds to their feet, and threw them into marshes for the pleasure of seeing them drown. He committed numerous other cruelties which I will abstain from describing here for lack of space."

The *Encomienda* System

The Pacheco family used the same tactics to conquer Belize as did the Spanish in Guatemala, although in more moderate degree. The strategy of "pacification" of territory entailed subduing the people they encountered by force. Once villages were taken, the land and its inhabitants were distributed among the conquistadors, who used conversion to Christianity as a pretext for subjugating the indigenous peoples. Thus the Pacheco family, after reducing the region's Mayan population to slavery, were granted several *encomiendas*. The *encomienda* was the system by which the Spanish distributed land and the enslaved natives who lived on it. In 1544, the Pacheco family founded Villa Salamanca de Bacalar near the Mayan village of Bakhalal, in the southern part of the Yucatán Peninsula.

In 1567 and 1568, another Spaniard, Juan Garzón, made several *entradas* to southern Belize from Villa Salamanca. On his way, he razed Mayan villages, proceeding with the so-called pacification of the territory before establishing several *encomiendas* in it. The Spanish *encomiendas*, however, were subjected to repeated attacks by the Maya. Finally, very few Spaniards settled the actual territory of Belize. Their numbers were fewer than 250 in 1582. In 1618, missionaries explored the country on the New River, the Belize River, the Macal Branch and the Sibun River, but they did not establish any lasting religious missions. The Spaniards' lack of interest in this area opened the door to English adventurers, who saw ways to profit from the weakness of Spanish authority in the neglected region.

The Arrival of English Colonists

In 1604, Spain and Great Britain signed the Treaty of London, which would have a deciding impact on the English presence in the Americas. The treaty stipulated that the English could colonize territories unoccupied by the Spanish. The English had certainly visited the Bay of Honduras at the end of the 15th century, but it was not until 1629 that they established the first British colony in the western Antilles, on the island of Old Providence, off the coast of Nicaragua. They subsequently established themselves of the island of Ruatan, in the Bay of Honduras, and probably on the mainland south of Belize. From their two posts, British buccaneers (see p 35) engaged in their favourite pastime, attacking Spanish ships, under the authority of the mother country. Ultimately, the British were expelled by the Spanish from Old Providence and Ruatan, in 1641 and 1642 respectively.

English adventurers and pirates also established themselves at the mouth of the Belize River, but the scarcity of historical records from this era makes it impossible to say exactly where and when the British first arrived. There were definitely already

English here in the 1640s. Oral tradition stipulates that Belize was founded between 1638 and 1640 by Scottish buccaneer George Wallace. In fact, the word "Belize" is a Spanish corruption of "Wallace". Another legend states that the first English colonists were shipwrecked off the region's coast.

Whatever the origins of the British colonists, a record dating from 1670 offers the earliest confirmation of an English presence on the shores of the Bay of Honduras. This document, a journal written by a Spanish priest, Fray José Delgado, indicates the presence of the English on the Mullins River. It was also in 1670 that Spain and England signed a second treaty, the Treaty of Godolphin. This pact recognized the legitimacy of British settlements in the Caribbean, but not of those in Belize. This treaty had an additional impact, the prohibition by a joint accord between Spain and Britain of buccaneering. Some buccaneers became pirates, but most of them chose to work in the logwood lumber industry, especially in the "Bay of Honduras", as Belize was known. The first English to land on the shores of Belize were not, therefore, the most dignified representatives of the British crown...

The logwood industry was flourishing in the 17th and 18th centuries. Logwood is a small tree that grows in marshy regions of the Yucatán Peninsula and Belize. It was used to make dye in the British textile industry, principally in the 18th century. It could be used in the production of various colours, from black to gray, red, blue, green and purple.

Lumberjacks only established small logging camps and, undoubtedly because they were illiterate, left no written records of their stay, unlike the Spanish missionaries. In 1672, the Spanish, who were already exploiting logwood in the Yucatán Peninsula, banned foreigners from cutting and trading the resource. In the hopes of preserving good relations with Spain, the British tried to reduce logging in the Bay of Honduras but had little success. Ex-buccaneer lumberjacks had plenty of experience evading authority.

The Hesitation of the Spanish

The Spanish threat hung like a Sword of Damocles over the heads of the Bay of Honduras lumberjacks, who were known as Baymen. In 1683, the governor of Jamaica, then the largest British colony in the Caribbean, was at the point of evacuating the English from Belize, because of the imminence of a Spanish attack. For their part, the Spanish were aware of the English presence, but did very little to expel them from their territory, despite the obvious weakness of the little British lumber camps. What could explain this attitude on the part of the Spanish? For one thing, the territory of Belize was under the authority of the governor of the Yucatán, who lacked both the interest and the funds to hire an expeditionary force. Also, the marshy topography of Belize and the difficulty of reaching its coast by sea made the task that much more arduous.

Nonetheless, there were several Spanish expeditions to dislodge the British, especially in the 18th century. The first was organized in 1716 by Governor Juan José Vertiz y Ontanón. The second, a larger one which almost rousted the English for good, was led by Antonio de Figueroa y Silva in 1730. Figueroa had been preparing a large-scale invasion by way of the Belize River. Like the expedition that preceded him about 15 years earlier, his won several battles. However, his dream of establishing a permanent colony in Belize evaporated when he died of a fever. His men did not take advantage of the momentum and were defeated by the Baymen. Finally, authorities set about to unite the governor of the Yucatán and the Audiencia de Guatemala in an alliance combining their forces to put a definitive end to the territorial pretensions of the English in the Bay of Honduras. Although Belize was twice evacuated by the British between 1739 and 1748, during the war between Spain and Britain, the Spanish never capitalized on these opportunities to establish a permanent colony. Content to see the governor of the Yucatán struggle with his own problems, the powerful Audiencia de Guatemala preferred to engage in a rivalry with its peninsular New World confederate, giving the British some respite.

Despite the efforts of the English's during the 17th century to prevent Baymen from cutting wood in Belize because of the

Buccaneers' Old Habits

At the end of the 17th century, British buccaneers in the West Indies found a new use for their axes. No longer supported in their piracy by the crown, great numbers of them gave up the practice of cutting the moorings of Spanish ships for the wood-cutting business. Famous buccaneers like Blackbeard (Edward Teach), Nicholas van Horn and William Benbow spent time in the lumber camps of Belize, which served both as hideouts and new sources of income.

The work was no vacation, though, especially for sailors who were used to making easy gains. Logwood lumbering was carried out in mosquito-infested marshes. During the rainy season, the camps had to be moved to higher ground and rebuilt from scratch. Despite the exhausting labour, ex-buccaneers preserved an old habit: drink.

The first recorded description of the Baymen of Belize, written by an Englishman named Dampier and reproduced in *Readings in Belizean History*, portrays rather vividly the habits of these hard-living, faithless and lawless men:

"The lumberjacks are a tough, inebriated lot... Their greatest pleasure is drink, and when they open a cask of wine they rarely leave it until it is completely dry. However, they most often water on rum punch, and it happens occasionally that they devote several days to this pastime. It goes without saying that most of their work is done when there are no spirits at hand, since as long as their preferred elixirs are flowing, nothing and no one can distract them."

Spanish threat, their attitude changed over time as the industry developed. Beginning in 1760, successive Jamaican governors defended the Baymen of Belize at all costs. In 1765, Admiral Sir William Burnaby left Jamaica for Belize with several ships and hundreds of soldiers. He discovered that the Baymen lived peacefully with their Spanish neighbours and, before returning to Jamaica, he outlined the constitution that would govern their lives until 1862, when Belize officially became a British colony. The Burnaby Code permitted the establishment of the Public

Meeting, the Baymen's legislative body. Only land owners and whites were eligible to vote. The British crown's support of the lumberjacks of Belize ensured the Baymen's domination of the trade in logwood and mahogany. These precious woods fetched high prices and soon became the lumberjacks' preferred merchandise. Many lumber agreements were signed between the British and the Spanish between 1763 (Treaty of Paris) and 1786, but Spain continued to claim sovereignty over the territory.

The Battle of St. George's Caye

In the 18th century, the majority of English colonists in Belize lived on the island of St. George's Caye, which would ultimately be where the country's fate was decided by battle. On September 15, 1779, the Spanish captured 140 prisoners and 250 slaves on the island and sent them to Havana, but they did not occupy the settlement on St. George's Caye. Four years later, the British returned and colonize the island anew.

On September 10, 1798, the fate of Belize was finally determined by another battle on St. George's Caye. A very strong Spanish contingent of 32 warships and 2,500 soldiers attempted once again to capture the island. The Baymen had only five sailboats and one warship, the *H.M.S. Merlin*, but they knew the deep waters of the bay better than their opponents did, and forced their slaves to join them in battle. Miraculously, they repelled Spanish attacks. Today, September 10 is a holiday and the occasion of celebrations all over the country. Although the British of Belize lived in relative tranquillity from this time on, England never demonstrated any particular interest in the region.

The independence of Central American countries from the yoke of the Spanish crown in 1821 provoked a dangerous situation. Although Spain no longer claimed sovereignty over the area of Belize, Guatemala was not about to pass up an opportunity to increase its territory, and the dispute between Britain and Guatemala over Belize would remain one of the principle preoccupations of Belizeans throughout the 19th and 20th centuries.

Nonetheless, the British crown did not make Belize an official colony until half a century after Guatemala gained independence. The cause of this change in policy was the War of the Castes, which raged in the Yucatán Peninsula for almost 60 years. This war, which pitted the Maya against the mestizos of Mexico, created an unprecedented wave of immigration to Belize. In a short time, the country's population doubled; mestizos, Maya, and Spaniards established themselves in the area of Corozal, in the north. They transformed the country's demographics, planted sugar cane, and their presence led to many conflicts. The Baymen decided to call on the British crown and request the status of a colony so that their lands would be protected. Many of their petitions went unheeded before Queen Victoria finally accorded them the status they sought in 1862. The colony was named British Honduras, an assembly was instituted, and the Queen sent a bill for the expenses of the British army, provoking the first dispute between herself and her colonists...

The English and the Maya

The first Mayan uprisings began shortly after Belize acquired colonial status. However, for the first century of the English presence in Belize, there is no indication that the English and the Maya even encountered one another. Entire generations of colonists propagated the myth that the Maya had abandoned the region before the English arrived, and Belizean histories generally start off with this hypothesis. Of course, this theory is false. In its early stages, the logwood industry was undertaken in coastal regions, and it seems that the Maya left these settlers in peace. However, when forest resources were exhausted on the coast, the English colonists travelled inland. The end of the logwood industry also marked the beginning of large-scale cutting of mahogany, demand for which was rapidly increasing in England. The English presence in the country's interior was a threat to Mayan territory, and lumberjacks were repeatedly attacked. During the 18th and 19th centuries, there were numerous skirmishes, and on more than one occasion the British sent in troops to overpower the Maya, who retreated to the region of San Ignacio.

The most important battles between the Maya and the British occurred between 1866 and 1872 in the Orange Walk area (see p 146). Marcos Canul, a Mayan rebel, spread panic in the lumber camps and often challenged the British army. In 1870, he even succeeded in taking Corozal Town (see p 160), and in 1872, he attacked the English barracks at Orange Walk. During this last battle, Canul was fatally wounded and the Maya retreated for good.

Slavery

In many ways, Belize has more characteristics of a Caribbean country than a Central American one. The importation of African slaves to the country was not unusual. Belizeans' popular belief holds that slaves were treated better in their country than in Caribbean British colonies, but records of slave rebellions suggest the opposite. Slaves were, after all, the property of their masters, who decided their fates. In fact, a report dated 1820 reveals that some colonists treated their slaves with "extreme inhumanity". Later it would also be reported that a "horrible barbarism [was] practised" toward slaves all over the country.

However, slavery in Belize was different in many respects. Slaves were used to work in forestry and not in sugar cane fields, as they were in other colonies. The men lived in lumber camps in groups of 10 to 50, while their families lived in Belize City, where they were employed as domestic labourers.

In the second half of the 18th century, during a period when the mahogany industry was growing rapidly, the importation of slaves was at its height. The majority of these slaves were bought from markets in Jamaica, but some were purchased in the United States and a few came directly from Africa. In 1790, a census indicated that slaves represented three quarters of the population of Belize; one tenth of the population was white, and the rest was made up of free blacks and other ethnic groups. However, the slave population diminished over the years, especially when the slave trade was abolished in 1807. One quarter of a century after the 1790 census, slaves accounted for just half the population. At the end of the 18th century, about 20 British families possessed both the majority of the land in the country and more than half of the slaves.

There were three major slave revolts in Belize. Two of them occurred between 1765 and 1768, but the most serious one occurred in 1773, lasted several months, and was only put down by a contingent of the British army. The majority of the rebels were captured, but about 10 of them fled north to the Mexican border.

Slavery was abolished in 1838, but the lot of freed slaves did not improve very much since British colonists still owned the land and governed matters of labour law.

PORTRAIT

Racial Stratification

As in all of Britain's Caribbean colonies, a rigid racial hierarchy was instated in Belize. Although black slaves and indigenous populations received the worst treatment, Creoles were also subjected to the condescension of British citizens. *The Honduras Almanack* of 1830, quoted in *Readings in Belizean History*, describes the country's racial stratification as follows: "...the law decrees that there are seven or eight formal gradations between blacks and whites, which one must transcend by blood lineage, supported by proof, before enjoying the same privileges as do Europeans." Blacks, even free ones, were considered former slaves or children of slaves. Therefore, the almanac continues, "few of them prove to be completely free of the base propensity for barbarism."

Beginning in the late 1820s, a movement of "coloured people", or Creoles, arose to lay claim to equal rights. In 1831, the Public Meeting, under pressure from the British Colonial Office, was forced to grant "coloured people" the same rights that whites enjoyed; however, these were not extended to free blacks.

Half a Century of Poverty

The 20th century got off to a rough start for the young English colony. The First World War put an end to the lucrative mahogany trade, and the colony fell into a state of ongoing poverty that would last decades. The first half of the 20th century was also marked by an increased presence of American interests, to the detriment of British interests. Mahogany merchants and chicle traders alike depended more and more on American buyers. Finally, a Creole merchant elite was beginning to form, setting its sights on the United States rather than on England. All of these factors combined to create the basis for a nascent nationalism.

Unemployment and chronic poverty provoked numerous popular demonstrations, which, in the long run, also fed the sense of Belizean nationalism. The first riot sparked by racial and economic issues occurred in Belize City in 1919. Most of the demonstrators were black veterans of the British West Indies Regiment who were unhappy with this situation. Together with other sectors of the black population, they provoked several incidents of violence.

In the 1930s, the depression and the hurricane of 1931 further destabilized the precarious conditions in which inhabitants of the colony lived. On February 15, 1934, a group called the Unemployed Brigade marched on Belize City. One month later, Antonio Soberanis formed the Labour and Unemployed Association. He launched strikes and numerous protests at a time when unions were prohibited in the nation, casting doubt yet again on colonial authority. He opened his ranks and expanded his ideology to include mestizos, Maya and Garifunas, in addition to the black and Creole populations. His movement became the first union in the country – the General Workers Union – when labour laws were modified in 1943. From these beginnings, the nation's first political party was born, the People's United Party (PUP).

Toward Independence

George Price, who would become the dominant figure of Belizean politics in the second half of the 20th century when independence was achieved, founded the People's United Party (PUP) on September 29, 1950. Political self-determination was the new party's main demand. In 1954, Price and his party successfully won the majority of seats in the National Assembly, but executive power still resided in the hands of the governor, the representative of the British crown, and three other crown-appointed members. In March of 1961, PUP took every seat in the legislature, forcing the governor to name Price prime minister of Belize.

Price finally obtained independent parliamentary authority for Belize in 1965, and he remained in power himself until 1984, three years after the nation gained its independence. In 1984, Price and his party were defeated in legislative elections by the United Democratic Party (UDP) and its leader, Manuel Esquivel. Price was restored in the next elections, in 1989. Finally, in 1993, Esquivel again won the electoral battle, proving that the Belizean electorate enjoys seeing its two major political parties share power.

POLITICS

The main body of the British-inspired parliamentary system is the National Assembly, which is composed of a House of Representatives (28 elected seats) and a Senate (five members appointed by the prime minister, two chosen by the opposition, and one selected by the governor general).

ECONOMY

Agriculture is the most important sector of the economy, and its products, including sugar, citrus fruit, and bananas, constitute 75% of the country's total exports. Paradoxically, Belize must import over 20% of the food consumed in the country. Corn, cocoa, beans, and rice are also cultivated.

Tourism is the second most important sector of the nation's economy. Increasing from about 80,000 visitors in 1991 to almost 150,000 in 1997, tourism has become an important source of foreign currency. Over 60% of visitors come from the United States and about 20% travel from Europe.

Unfortunately, Belize is a major drug-trafficking centre. The United States includes Belize on its list of the main countries grappling with this difficult issue. The fight against the drug trade in Belize is complicated by the phenomenon of drug-money bribes corrupting the highest reaches of political power.

The nation's economic indicators are somewhat disturbing. Between 1985 and 1995, Belize only generated 5.2% growth of its gross domestic product. In 1996, the GDP actually fell by 0.8%. Belize's foreign debt is 3.8 billion dollars and the country must spend 16.4% of its revenue to service this debt. Moreover, because most of the country is developing, runaway inflation (the rate of inflation in Belize was 13.8% in 1996) remains a primary cause of economic strife, and assails the population and the government alike.

PRACTICAL INFORMATION

Whether alone or with a group, it is easy to travel anywhere in Belize. In order to make the most of your stay, it is important to be well prepared. This chapter is intended to help you plan your trip; it also provides information on local customs.

ENTRANCE FORMALITIES

Make sure you bring all the necessary papers to enter and exit the country. Though requirements are not very strict, you will need certain documents to travel in Belize. You should therefore keep your important papers safe at all times.

Passport

To enter Belize, citizens of Canada, the United States and the European Union are advised to bring their passport, making sure it is valid for the length of their stay. It is also possible to enter the country with an official birth certificate or a citizenship card. Be reminded, though, that in case of problems with the authorities, the most official proof of your identity is your passport.

It is a good idea to keep a photocopy of the key pages of your passport, and to write down your passport number and its expiry date. This way, in case it is lost or stolen, it will be much easier to replace (do the same with your birth certificate or citizenship card). Should this occur, contact your country's consulate or embassy to have a new one issued.

Visas

A visa is not required for visitors from Canada, the United States or Great Britain. Citizens of other countries must contact the nearest Belizean embassy or consulate to obtain a visa.

Departure Tax

Each person leaving Belize must pay a departure tax of $15 US. The tax is collected at the airport when you check in for your return flight. Remember to keep this amount in cash, as credit cards are not accepted.

Customs

Visitors may enter the country with up to one litre of alcohol, 200 cigarettes and up to $100 US worth of goods (not counting personal belongings). Bringing in illegal drugs and firearms is, of course, prohibited.

FOREIGN EMBASSIES AND CONSULATES IN BELIZE

Embassies and consulates can be an invaluable source of help to visitors who find themselves in trouble. For example, consulates can provide names of doctors or lawyers in the case of death or serious injury. However, only urgent cases are handled. It should also be noted that the cost of these services is not absorbed by the consulates.

Austria
Honorary Consul: 16 Regent Street, Belize City, ☎02-77070, ⌨75593.

Belgium
Honorary Consul: Queen corner of North Front Street, Belize City, ☎02-45773 or 45769, ⌨31946.

Canada
Honorary Consul: 83 North Front Street, Belize City, ☎02-31060, ⌨30060.

Denmark
Honorary Consul: 13 Southern Foreshore, Belize City, ☎02-72172, ⌨77280.

Guatemala
Embassy: 8A Street, Belize City, ☎02-33150 or 33314, ⌨35240.

Germany
Honorary Consul: Princess Margaret Drive, Belize City, ☎02-35940, ⌨35413.

Great Britain
High Commission: Embassy Square, Belmopan, ☎08-22146 or 22717, ⌨22761.

Honduras
Embassy: 91 North Front Street, Belize City, ☎02-45889, ⌨30562.

Italy
Honorary Consul: 18 Albert Street, Belize City, ☎02-78449, ⌨73056.

Israel
Honorary Consul: 4 Albert Street, Belize City, ☎02-73991 or 73150, ⌨30463.

Mexico
Embassy: 20 North Park Street, Belize City, ☎02-30194, ⌨78742.

PRACTICAL INFORMATION

Netherlands
Honorary Consul: 14 Central American Boulevard, Belize City, ☎02-75663, ⬏75936.

Norway
Honorary Consul: 1 King Street, Belize City, ☎02-77031, ⬏77031.

Sweden
Honorary Consul: 11 Princess Margaret Drive, Belize City, ☎02-30623.

United States
Embassy: Hutson, corner of Eyre Street, Belize City, ☎02-77161, ⬏30802.

BELIZEAN EMBASSIES AND CONSULATES ABROAD

Austria
Consulate: Franz Josefs - Kai, 13/5/16, A-1010 Vienna, ☎(43-1) 533-7663, ⬏(43-1) 533-8114.

Canada
Honorary Consul: 1080 Beaver Hall Hill, suite 1720, Montréal, Québec H2Z 1S8, ☎(514) 871-4741, ⬏(514) 397-0816.

Honorary Consul: Royal Bank Plaza, Suite 3800, South Tower, Toronto, Ontario M5J 2J7, ☎(416) 865-7000, ⬏(416) 865-7048.

Germany
Consulate: Libenstrasse 46-48, 7120 Bietithiem, Bissingen, ☎(49-71) 423-924, ⬏(49-71) 423-225.

Great Britain
High Commission to London: 10 Harcourt House, 16A Cavendish Square, London W1M 9AD, ☎(44-171) 499-9728, ⬏(44-171) 491-4139.

Guatemala
Embassy: Avenida de La Reforma 1-50, Zona 9, Edificio El Reformador, suite 803, ☎334-5531, ⬏334-5536.

Italy
Consulate: Via Emilio de Cavalieri 12, 00198 Rome, ☎(39-6) 841-7907, ⊷(39-6) 841-5496.

Mexico
Consulate: Avenida Alvaro Obregon 226A, Chetumal, QR., ☎24908.

Embassy: Calle Bernardo de Gálvez, no. 215, Colonia Las Lomas, Chapultepec, México DF 11000, ☎520-1214, ⊷520-6089.

Spain
Consulate: Avda. Diagonal 469, 4th floor 2A, 08036 Barcelona, ☎(34-3) 430-3044, ⊷(34-3), 405-3883.

Switzerland
Consulate: 1 Rue Pedro-Meylan, PO Box 106, 1211 Geneva 17, ☎(41-22) 786-3883, 736-8611 or 736-8882, ⊷736-9939 or 786-3720.

United States
Embassy: 2535 Massachusetts Avenue, NW, Washington, DC 20008, ☎(202) 332-9636, ⊷(202) 332-6888.

Tourist Board: 421 Seventh Avenue, Suite 701, New York, NY 10001, ☎(212) 563-6011, ⊷(212)563-6033.

Consulate: 862 NE 2nd Avenue, Miami, FL 33138, ☎(305) 751-5655.

PRACTICAL INFORMATION

GETTING TO BELIZE

By Plane

International

There is only one international airport in Belize; **Goldson International Airport** in Belize City. The following airline companies serve the country:

Aerovias de Guatemala *(Goldson International Airport,*
☎*02-75745)* offers daily flights between Belize City and Flores.

American Airlines *(New Rd., corner of Queen St.,* ☎*02-32522,*
⊶*02-31730; USA:* ☎*800-624-6262; Canada:* ☎*800-433-7300)*.

Continental Airlines *(32 Albert St.,* ☎*02-78309,* ⊶*02-78114,*
USA ☎*800-231-0856; Canada* ☎*800-525-0280)*.

TACA International Airline *(41 Albert St.,* ☎*02-77185,*
⊶*02-75213; USA:* ☎*800-535-8780; Canada:* ☎*416-968-2222,*
⊶*416-968-0563; London, UK: Ocean House, Hazelwick Ave.,*
Three Bridges, Crawley West, Sussex RH10 1NP,
☎*(44-1293) 553-330,* ⊶*(44-1293) 553-321)*.

Domestic Flights

Larger towns and cities generally have airports that serve local
flights and small planes. These include Belize City, Corozal, San
Pedro, Placencia, Dandriga and Punta Gorda.

Here is a list of some of the domestic airlines:

Island Air *(*☎*02-31140)*
Maya Airways *(Municipal Airstrip,* ☎*02-77215,* ⊶*02-30585;*
USA and Canada, ☎*800-552-3419)*
Tropic Air *(Municipal Airstrip;* ☎*02-24567; USA and Canada*
☎*800-422-3435; Belize* ⊶*02-62338; tropicair@btl.net)*
Caribee Air Service *(*☎*02-44253)*
Javier's Flying Service *(*☎*02-45332)* offers flights aboard
Cessnas.

FINDING YOUR WAY AROUND

Distances in Belize are rather short, but roads are unpaved in
certain areas, which can make for long trips, especially in the
rainy season.

By Car

Renting a car is the easiest way to get around in Belize. Rental cars are generally in good condition. It costs anywhere between $60 to $90 US a day for a compact car, not including insurance ($15 US). The minimum age for renting a car is 25. Choose a vehicle that is in good condition, preferably a new one. Most local companies offer similar competitive prices. It is strongly recommended that you take out sufficient automobile insurance to cover all costs in case of an accident. Before signing any rental contract, make sure the methods of payment are clearly indicated. Finally, remember that your credit card must cover both the rental fees and the deductible in case of an accident. While some credit cards insure you automatically, you should check if the coverage is complete. A valid driver's license from your country is accepted in Belize.

It is strongly recommended to rent a vehicle with four-wheel drive, especially during the rainy season (May to November). It is well worth the extra cost if you go to the south or more rugged parts of the country.

PRACTICAL INFORMATION

Driving and the Highway Code

In general, the main roads and highways in the Belize are in good condition, especially the Western Highway and Northern Highway. However, Hummingbird Highway and Manatee Highway, which run through the southern part of the country, are not completely paved. Therefore, it is strongly recommended that you drive an all-terrain vehicle when travelling in the south. Each of the country's four main highways has only one lane in either direction and no shoulder. Nonetheless, it is usually possible to drive at a reasonable speed since there is little traffic.

Road signs are inadequate in many areas, for both traffic control (there are only three stoplights in the entire country!) and orientation. Asking for directions is often the only way to find your way around, but residents are generally very helpful in this regard.

Table of Distances (km)
Via the Shortest Route

1 mile = 1.62 kilometres
1 kilometre = 0.62 miles

							Belize City	Belize City
						Belmopan	80	Belmopan
					Corozal	214	134	Corozal
				Dangriga	233	79	99	Dangriga
		Orange Walk	189	44	170	90		Orange Walk
	Punta Gorda	337	168	381	227	247		Punta Gorda
San Ignacio	276	206	115	250	36	116		San Ignacio

Example : The distance between Orange Walk and Belmopan is 170 km.

© ULYSSES

Due to the lack of signs and street lights on Belizean roads, driving at night is strongly discouraged. If your car breaks down you will be stranded.

Flat Tires

Flat tires are fairly common in the south and on unpaved roads. Before you leave, be sure that you are equipped with a spare tire in good condition and all of the tools necessary for changing a tire. In case of a flat tire, stop at the first garage you encounter to repair it so that you will have a spare when you need it again.

Car Watchers

Throughout Belize, especially in villages, youths will offer to wash or keep an eye on your car — for a small fee, of course. Sometimes they will even perform these services without asking, and still expect to get paid. To avoid a touchy situation, agree on a price ahead of time.

The Police

Police officers are posted all along Belizean highways. In general, they are approachable and ready to help if you have problems on the road.

Gasoline (Petrol)

There are gas stations all over the country. However, if you plan to venture off the beaten path, or travel in the south, be sure to fill up before you leave. Since distances are very short, you should not run out of gasoline. Gas prices are slightly higher than in North America, but less than Europe, at 80¢ US. Most stations are open until 10pm, and many stay open 24 hours. More and more stations now accept credit cards, but always carry cash on you just in case.

Scooter and Golf-Cart Rental

In most vacation areas, such as Ambergris Caye, it is possible to rent scooters or the very popular golf carts. Your passport or another valid piece of identification will be requested as a deposit, and sometimes you will be asked to show a driver's license. Remember to drive carefully, especially in the Cayes, since the sandy roads are often busy with pedestrian traffic. Always determine the price and conditions of payment before leaving with your rental.

By Taxi

Taxi services are offered in every resort area and moderate-sized city. The cars tend to be large American family sedans. The rates are fairly high, and are usually posted at the taxi stand. Make sure to agree on the fare with the driver before starting out. Some cities, including Belize City, have fixed fares for trips within city limits (see the corresponding section for each city).

By Bus

Many busses travel the roads of Belize, constituting the most economical and practical means of transportation throughout the country. Tickets must be purchased at the offices of the various companies, since there are no central bus stations. Here are the addresses of the major companies, each of which specializes in a particular region:

PRACTICAL INFORMATION

The North

Batty Brothers: 54 East Collet Canal, Belize City, ☎02-77146.

The South

Z-Line: Magazine Rd, Belize City, ☎02-73937.

The West

Novelos Bus Service: West Collet Canal, Belize City, ☎02-77372.

INSURANCE

Health Insurance

Health insurance is the most important type of insurance for travellers and should be purchased before your departure. A comprehensive health insurance policy that provides a level of coverage sufficient to pay for hospitalization, nursing care and doctor's fees is recommended. Keep in mind that health care costs are rising quickly everywhere. The policy should also have a repatriation clause in case the required care is not available in Belize. As patients are sometimes asked to pay for medical services up front, find out what provisions your policy makes in this case. Always carry your health insurance policy with you when travelling to avoid problems if you are in an accident, and get receipts for any expenses incurred.

Theft Insurance

Most residential insurance policies in North America protect some of your goods from theft, even if the theft occurs in a foreign country. To make a claim, you must fill out a police report. Usually the coverage for a theft abroad is 10% of your total coverage. If you plan to travel with valuable objects, check your policy or with an insurance agency to see if additional baggage insurance is necessary. European visitors should take out baggage insurance.

Cancellation Insurance

This type of insurance is usually offered by your travel agent when you purchase your air ticket or tour package. It covers any non-refundable payments to travel suppliers such as airlines, and must be purchased at the time of initial payment for the air tickets or tour packages. This insurance allows you to be reimbursed for the ticket or package deal if your trip must be cancelled due to serious illness or death. This type of insurance can be useful, but weigh the likelihood of your using it against the price.

Life Insurance

By purchasing your tickets with certain credit cards you will get life insurance. Several airline companies offer a life insurance plan included in the price of the airplane ticket. However, many travellers already have another form of life insurance and do not need extra insurance.

PRACTICAL
INFORMATION

HEALTH

Belize is a wonderful country to explore; however, travellers should be aware of and protect themselves from a number of health risks associated with the region, including malaria, typhoid, diphtheria, tetanus, polio and hepatitis A. Cases of these diseases are rare but there is a risk. **Travellers are therefore advised to consult a doctor (or travellers' clinic) for advice on what precautions to take.** Remember that it is much easier to prevent these illnesses than it is to cure them and that a vaccination is not a substitute for cautious travel.

Identity and Culture Shock

Before going on vacation, we prepare our luggage and get the necessary vaccinations and travel documents, but rarely do we prepare for culture shock. The following text explains what culture shock is and how to deal with it.

In a nutshell, culture shock can be defined as a certain anxiety that may be experienced upon arriving in another country where everything is different, including the culture and language, making communication as you know it very difficult. Combined with jetlag and fatigue, the strain of orienting yourself in a new cultural context can lead to psychological stress that may throw you off track.

Culture shock is a frustrating phenomenon that can easily turn travellers setting out with the best of intentions into intolerant, racist and ethnocentric ones – they may come to believe that their society is better than the new, and seemingly incomprehensible, one. This type of reaction detracts from the whole travel experience.

People in other countries have different customs and lifestyles that are sometimes hard for us to understand or accept. We might even find ourselves wondering how people can live the way they do when their customs run contrary to what we deem to be "normal". In the end, however, it is easier to adapt to them than to criticize or disregard them.

Even though this is the era of globalization and cultural homogenization, we still live in a world of many "worlds", such as the sports world, the business world, the worlds of different continents, suburbia, and the world of the rich and the poor. Of course, these worlds intersect, but each has its own characteristic set of ideas and cultural values. Furthermore, even if they are not in direct contact, each has at least an image of the other, which might be distorted and wrong, or accurate, but in either case is ultimately nothing more than an image. If a picture is worth a thousand words, then our world contains million upon millions of them. Sometimes it is hard to tell what is real and what isn't, but one thing is certain: what you see on television about a place is not the same as when you travel there.

When people interact with each other, they inevitably make sense of each other through their differences. The strength of a group, human or animal, lies in its diversity, whether it be in genetics or ideas. Can you imagine how boring the world would be if everyone were the same?

Travelling can be seen as a way of developing a more holistic, or global, vision of the world; this means accepting that our cultural fabric is complex and woven with many different ethnicities, and that all have something to teach us, be it a philosophy of life, medical knowledge, or a culinary dish, which adds to the richness of our personal experience.

Remember that culture is relative, and that people's social, technological and financial situation shape their way of being and looking at the world. It takes more than curiosity and tolerance to be open minded: it is a matter of learning to see the world anew, through a different cultural perspective.

When travelling abroad, don't spend too much energy looking for the familiar, and don't try to see the place as you would like it to be – go with the flow instead. And though a foreign country might be difficult to understand and even seem unwelcoming at times, remember that there are people who find happiness and satisfaction in life everywhere. When you get involved in their daily lives, you will begin to see things differently – things which at first seemed exotic and mystifying are easily understood after having been explained. It always helps to know the rules before playing a game, and it goes without saying that learning the language will help you better understand what's going on. But be careful about communicating with your hands, since certain gestures might mean the opposite of what you are trying to say!

Prepare yourself for culture shock as early as possible. Libraries and bookstores are good places for information about the cultures you are interested in. Reading about them is like a journey in itself, and will leave you with even more cherished memories of your trip.

Written by Jean-Étienne Poirier

PRACTICAL
INFORMATION

Illnesses

Please note that this section is intended to provide general information only.

Malaria

Malaria (paludism) is caused by a parasite in the blood called *Plasmodium sp.* This parasite is transmitted by anopheles mosquitoes, which bite from nightfall until dawn. In Belize, the risk is minimal and anti-malaria drugs are not necessary for short stays in resort areas. It is nevertheless a good idea to take measures to prevent mosquito bites (see the section on mosquitoes, p 59).

The symptoms of malaria include high fever, chills, extreme fatigue and headaches as well as stomach and muscle aches. There are several forms of malaria, including one serious type caused by *P. falciparum*. The disease can take hold while you are still on holiday or up to 12 weeks following your return; in some cases the symptoms can appear months later.

Hepatitis A

This disease is generally transmitted by ingesting food or water that has been contaminated by faecal matter. The symptoms include fever, yellowing of the skin, loss of appetite and fatigue, and can appear between 15 to 50 days after infection. An effective vaccination by injection is available. Besides the recommended vaccine, good hygiene is important. Wash your hands before every meal, and ensure that the food and preparation area are clean.

Hepatits B

Hepatitis B, like hepatitis A, affects the liver, but is transmitted through direct contact of body fluids. The symptoms are flu-like, and similar to those of hepatitis A. A vaccination exists but must be administered over an extended period of time, so be sure to check with your doctor several weeks in advance.

Dengue

Also called "breakbone fever", Dengue is transmitted by mosquitoes. In its most benign form it can cause flu-like symptoms such as headaches, chills and sweating, aching muscles and nausea. In its haemorrhagic form, which is the rarest and the most serious, it can be fatal. There is no vaccine for the virus, so take the usual precautions to avoid mosquito bites.

Typhoid

This illness is caused by ingesting food that has come in contact (direct or indirect) with an infected person's stool. Common symptoms include high fever, loss of appetite, headaches, constipation and occasionally diarrhea, as well as the appearance of red spots on the skin. These symptoms will appear one to three weeks after infection. Which vaccination you get (it exists in two forms, oral and by injection) will depend on your trip. Once again, it is always a good idea to visit a travellers' clinic a few weeks before your departure.

Diphtheria and Tetanus

These two illnesses, against which most people are vaccinated during their childhood, can have serious consequences. Thus, before leaving, check that your vaccinations are up to date; you may need a booster shot. Diphtheria is a bacterial infection that is transmitted by nose and throat secretions or by skin lesions on an infected person. Symptoms include sore throat, high fever, general aches and pains and occasionally skin infections. Tetanus is caused by a bacteria that enters your body through an open wound that comes in contact with contaminated dust or rusty metal.

PRACTICAL
INFORMATION

Other Health Tips

Cases of illnesses like hepatitis B, AIDS and certain venereal diseases have been reported; it is therefore a good idea to be careful.

Remember that consuming too much alcohol, particularly during prolonged exposure to the sun, can cause severe dehydration and lead to health problems.

Due to a lack of financial resources, Belizean medical facilities may not be as up-to-date as those in your own country. Therefore, if you need medical services, expect them to be different from what you are used to. The clinics outside large urban centres might seem modest to you. Before a blood transfusion, be sure (when possible) that quality control tests have been carried out on the blood.

Insufficiently treated water, which can contain disease-causing bacteria, is the source of most of the health problems travellers are likely to encounter, such as stomach upset, diarrhea or fever. Throughout the country, it is a good idea to drink bottled water (when buying bottled water, make sure the bottle is properly sealed), or to purify your own with iodine or a water purifier. Most major hotels treat their water, but always ask first. Ice cubes should be avoided, as they may be made from contaminated water. In addition, fresh fruits and vegetables that have been washed but not peeled can also pose a health risk. Make sure that the vegetables you eat are well-cooked and peel your own fruit. Do not eat lettuce, unless it has been hydroponically grown (some vegetarian restaurants serve this type of lettuce; ask). Remember: cook it, peel it or forget it.

If you do get diarrhea, soothe your stomach by avoiding solids; instead, drink carbonated beverages, bottled water, or weak tea (avoid milk) until you recover. As dehydration can be dangerous, drinking sufficient quantities of liquid is crucial. Pharmacies sell various preparations for the treatment of diarrhea, with different effects. Pepto Bismol and Imodium will stop the diarrhea by slowing the loss of fluids, but they should be avoided if you have a fever, as they will prevent the necessary elimination of bacteria. Oral rehydration products, such as Gastrolyte, will replace the minerals and electrolytes which your body has lost as a result of the diarrhea. In a pinch, you can make your own rehydration solution by mixing one litre of pure water with one teaspoon of sugar and two or three teaspoons of salt. Afterwards, eat easily digested foods like rice to give your stomach time to adjust. If symptoms become more serious (high fever, persistent diarrhea), see a doctor as antibiotics may be necessary.

Food and climate can also cause problems. Pay attention to the food's freshness, and the cleanliness of the preparation area. Good hygiene (wash your hands often) will help avoid undesirable situations.

It is best not to walk around bare-foot as parasites and insects can cause a variety of problems, the least of which is athlete's foot.

PRACTICAL INFORMATION

Mosquitoes

A nuisance common to many countries, mosquitoes are no strangers to Belize. They are particularly numerous during the rainy season. Protect yourself with a good insect repellent. Repellents with DEET are the most effective. The concentration of DEET varies from one product to the next; the higher the concentration, the longer the protection. In rare cases, the use of repellents with high concentrations (35% or more) of DEET has been associated with convulsions in young children; it is therefore important to apply these products sparingly, on exposed surfaces, and to wash it off once back inside. A concentration of 35% DEET will protect for four to six hours, while 95% will last from 10 to 12 hours. New formulas with lesser concentrations of DEET, but which last just as long, are available.

To further reduce the possibility of getting bitten, do not wear perfume or bright colours. Sundown is an especially active time for insects. When walking in wooded areas, cover your legs and ankles well. Insect coils can help provide a better night's sleep. Before bed, apply insect repellent to your skin and to the headboard and baseboard of your bed. If possible, get an air-conditioned room, or bring a mosquito net.

Lastly, since it is impossible to completely avoid contact with mosquitoes, bring along a cream to soothe the bites you will invariably get.

The Sun

Its benefits are many, but so are its harms. Always wear sunscreen (SPF 15 for adults and SPF 30 for children) and apply it 20 to 30 minutes before exposure. Many creams on the market do not offer adequate protection; ask a pharmacist. Too much sun can cause sunstroke (dizziness, vomiting, fever, etc.). Be careful, especially during the first few days, as it takes time to get used to the sun. Take sun in small doses and protect yourself with a hat and sunglasses.

First Aid Kit

A small first-aid kit can prove very useful. Bring along sufficient amounts of any medications you take regularly as well as a valid prescription in case you lose your supply; it can be difficult to find certain medications in small towns in Belize. Other medications such as anti-malaria pills and Imodium (or an equivalent), can also be hard to find. Finally, don't forget self-adhesive bandages, disinfectant cream or ointment, analgesics (pain-killers), antihistamines (for allergies), an extra pair of sunglasses or contact lenses, contact lens solution, and medicine for upset stomach. Though these items are all available in Belize, they might be difficult to find in remote villages.

CLIMATE

The average temperatures in the temperate subtropical climate of Belize are very pleasant: 26°C on the coast and 21°C in the Maya Mountains. The sea breeze significantly affects temperatures, so coastal regions are cooler while temperatures in the interior of the country can sometimes reach 38°C.

Belize has two seasons; a rainy season from May to November and a dry season from late November to April. Rain is abundant n the southern part of the country: the central and northern parts of Belize receive an annual average of 1,295 millimetres of rain, while the south receives almost four times as much, over 4,445 millimetres. During the rainy season, the daily showers generally last only a few minutes.

PACKING

The type of clothing required does not vary much from season to season. In general, loose-fitting, comfortable cotton or linen clothes are best. When exploring urban areas, wear closed shoes that cover the entire foot rather than sandals, as they will protect against cuts that could become infected. Bring a sweater or long-sleeved shirt for cool evenings, and rubber sandals (thongs or flip-flops) to wear at the beach and in the shower. During the rainy season, an umbrella is useful for staying dry during brief tropical showers. To visit certain attractions you must wear a skirt that covers the knees or long pants. For evenings out, you might need more formal clothes, as a number of places have dress codes. Finally, if you expect to go hiking in the mountains, bring along some good hiking boots and a sweater.

PRACTICAL INFORMATION

SAFETY AND SECURITY

Crime is especially common in Belize City and Orange Walk. During the day, travellers are generally not bothered, except by craft sellers or beggars. At night, however, it is strongly recommended to avoid walking alone in Belize City and Orange Walk. A degree of caution can help avoid problems. For example, do not wear too much jewellery, keep your electronic equipment in a nondescript shoulder bag slung across your chest, and avoid revealing the contents of your wallet when paying for something. Be doubly careful at night, and stay away from dark streets, especially if there are strangers lurking about.

A money belt can be used to conceal cash, traveller's cheques and your passport. If your bags should happen to be stolen, you will at least have the money and documents necessary to get by. Remember that the less attention you draw to yourself the less chance you have of being robbed.

If you bring valuables to the beach, you are strongly recommended to keep a constant eye on them. It is best to keep your valuables in the small safes available at most hotels.

MONEY AND BANKING

Currency

The national currency is the Belizean dollar, which is made up of 100 cents. All bills bear the image of the Queen of England.

Banks

Banks are open Monday to Friday, from 8am to 1pm, and some close later on Fridays. They can be found in all large and medium-sized cities. All banks exchange US and foreign currencies at competitive rates, especially for American dollars. It is best to carry some cash with you at all times. Credit card cash advances can also be made at major bank branches, including Barclay's Bank, Scotia Bank and Belize Bank.

Exchanging Money

The exchange rate with the American dollar has remained steady over the years, generally hovering at about two Belizean dollars to one American dollar (BZ$1 = US$0.50). The American dollar is accepted throughout the country, in shops and businesses as well as in hotels and restaurants. For other foreign currencies, travellers must go to banks, preferably in Belize City. All prices in this guide are in Belizean dollars, except for the chapter on Tikal, Guatemala, in which prices are quoted in American dollars.

Exchange Rates

Belizean Dollar

$1 CAN	= BZ$1.35	BZ$1	= $0.74 CAN
$1 US	= BZ$2	BZ$1	= $0.50 US
1 EURO	= BZ$2.21	BZ$1	= 0.45 EURO
1FF	= BZ$0.33	BZ$1	= 3.03 FF
1SF	= BZ$1.33	BZ$1	= 0.75 SF
10 BF	= BZ$0.54	BZ$1	= 18.52 BF
100 PTA	= BZ$1.09	BZ$1	= 91.74 PTA
1000 ITL	= BZ$1.14	BZ$1	= 877.19 ITL

American Dollar

$1 CAN	= $0.68 US	$1 US	= $1.46 CAN
1 EURO	= $1.09 US	$1 US	= 0.92 EURO
1 FF	= $0.16 US	$1 US	= 6.03 FF
1 SF	= $0.65 US	$1 US	= 1.54 SF
10 BF	= $0.28 US	$1 US	= 36.15 BF
100 PTA	= $0.54 US	$1 US	= 185.19 PTA
1000 ITL	= $0.59 US	$1 US	= 1706.74 ITL

PRACTICAL INFORMATION

Travellers' Cheques

It is always best to keep most of your money in travellers' cheques, which are accepted in some restaurants, hotels and shops (if they are in American dollars). They are also easy to cash in at banks and exchange offices. Always keep a copy of the serial numbers of your cheques in a separate place; that way, if the cheques are lost, the company can replace them quickly and easily. Do not rely solely on travellers' cheques, always carry some cash as well.

Credit Cards

Most credit cards, especially Visa and MasterCard, are accepted in a large number of businesses. However, a surcharge of 5% is applied to every purchase. Most branches of Barclay's Bank, Scotia Bank and Belize Bank offer credit card advances.

Bank Cards

Bank cards, or automatic teller machine (ATM) cards, are not commonly used in Belize. Only the Belize Bank issues these cards. Travellers can obtain Belize Bank cards buy making a deposit, which will correspond to the amount they may withdraw during their stay in the country. However, since there are very few Belize Bank automatic teller machines, this is not a very practical option. International bank cards are not accepted in Belize for the time being.

TELECOMMUNICATIONS

Mail

There are post offices in every city. They are generally open from 8am to noon and from 1pm to 4pm. They sell stamps, which make great collectors items with their depictions of Belize's natural wonders. Most hotels offer mailing services. It takes 15 days for your package or letter to reach its destination in North America, and three to four weeks for Europe. If you have something important to send, you are better off using a fax machine, available at most of the larger hotels in Belize. To send something by courrier, go to **D-H Worldwide Express** *(38 New Rd., Belize City, ☎02-34350)*.

Telephone and Fax

Domestic and international calls can be made from hotels or from the few international telephone offices of Belize Telecommunication Limited (BTL). The rate for calls to North America is about US$2 per minute and the rate for calls to Europe is about US$4 per minute.

To reach the **international operator**, dial 115.
To reach the **domestic operator**, dial 114.
To reach **directory assistance**, dial 113.
To reach the **police**, dial 911.

Each region of the country has its own area code, which must be dialled before all long-distance numbers. Here are the area codes for the various regions of the country:

Belize City : (02)
Belmopan : (08)
Benque Viejo : (093)
Caye Caulker : (022)
Corozal : (04)
Dandriga : (07)

Ladyville : (025)
Orange Walk : (03)
Placencia : (06)
Punta Gorda : (07)
San Ignacio : (092)
San Pedro : (026)

To call Belize from outside of the country, dial 011-501 from North America or 00-501 from Europe and omit the first zero of the Belizean area code. For example, to call Belize City from Canada, dial 011-501-2 and then the number, or from Europe, dial 00-501-2 and then the number.

To reach a Canadian operator and charge a call to your home account, use **Canada Direct**: dial 558 from a hotel or 816 from a public telephone.

Internet

The Internet is becoming increasingly popular throughout the country. Many establishments offer their guests access to the World Wide Web and electronic mail, especially hotels and travel agencies. These services are available mostly in the capital, Belmopan, and in vacation areas such as Belize City, San Pedro, Caye Caulker, Placencia and San Ignacio.

PRACTICAL INFORMATION

ACCOMMODATIONS

Hotels

Compared to other Central American countries, accommodation expenses are relatively high in Belize. The rates of the most affordable establishments range from US$10 to US$15 for double occupancy. In this price category, hot water is normally not available and washrooms are usually shared. Generally, the rooms in these hotels are equipped with ceiling or table fans. Because hygiene standards in these establishments are occasionally doubtful, it is preferable to travel with your own sleeping bag or sheets.

Hotel rooms in the medium price range offer basic comfort and are occasionally air conditioned. Rates vary between US$25 and US$60 for double occupancy. These establishments are generally very inviting and friendly. The owners often live on the premises and, whether they are Belizean or from outside the country, they strive to make your stay as enjoyable as possible. Hotels and inns on the seaside or in the countryside are usually made up of small, rustic *cabañas* with thatched roofs. Some of these establishments have private bathrooms with hot water.

Finally, luxury hotels, found in in San Pedro, Belize City and Placencia, all boast exceptional sites and try to surpass each other in comfort and luxury. Some of these hotels have a very select family atmosphere, while others belong to international hotel chains. Most offer all-inclusive packages, which usually include two or three meals a day, all locally produced drinks and the service charge. When a package deal is available, it will be indicated next to the room rate in the hotel listings.

Youth Hostels

There are no youth hostels in Belize, but many of the country's small hotels and inns offer very good rates.

Camping

There are no official campsites in Belize, but in most parts of the country, especially near nature reserves, inn-keepers and restaurant owners let travellers camp on their property. Of course, this is the most economical type of accommodations. There are very few places that offer electricity or specialised services for recreational vehicles.

RESTAURANTS AND FINE FOOD

There are many small restaurants that serve local cuisine in Belize. These are popular and mainly target a local clientele. They feature economical menus that don't sacrifice quality and are excellent places to meet residents and taste their favourite meals. Rice & beans is the most common dish, especially for lunch. American, Mexican and Chinese cuisine also appear on the menus of these establishments.

A meal for two costs about BZ$20, including non-alcoholic beverages.

$	Bz$20 and less
$$	Bz$20 to Bz$30
$$$	Bz$30 and more

The choice is more varied in larger towns like San Pedro, San Ignacio, Placencia and Caye Calker. The best chefs in the country concoct the most original dishes, especially fish and seafood. Some hotel restaurants are excellent.

Service is usually friendly and attentive in both small and large restaurants.

Belizean Cuisine

You'll soon grow to love rice & beans, the national dish, because it is served everywhere in Belize! It consists of a base of boiled rice with black or red beans, accompanied by chicken, pork or beef.

PRACTICAL
INFORMATION

Although rice & beans has been embraced by every culture in the country, each group has its own specialty. For example, the classic of Belizean mestizo cuisine is cow soup, which is composed of beef, cow's feet, tripe, potatoes, carrots and pumpkin. Traditional corn tortillas, which are sometimes fried, are also served.

Chinese restaurants are plentiful all over the country, but especially in Belize City and in the north. Various fried rice dishes, seafood, and traditional Chinese dishes have been adapted to the spices, vegetables, and fruit grown in Belize. These restaurants are very popular with Belizeans, and with anyone who wants a break from the ever-popular rice & beans.

Tipping

A 10% to 15% tip should be left in restaurants.

SHOPPING

Travellers who love to shop will find their options very limited in Belize, and will probably want to visit neighbouring Guatemala or Mexico to purchase crafts. Belize is not known for its markets or its craft tradition, but mahogany sculptures of animals, birds and tropical fish are available here. In terms of clothing, there is very little to choose from aside from American-style T-shirts.

Jewellery made from various types of coral, including black coral, is much coveted. However, this industry endangers the survival of the reef, so try not to buy any.

Opening Hours

Most stores are open from 9am to 5pm. Stores rarely close at lunchtime, especially in resort areas.

HOLIDAYS

January 1	New Year's Day
March 9	Baron Bliss Day
April 21	Queen's Birthday
May 1	Labour Day
May 24	Commonwealth Day
September 10	St. George's Caye Day
September 21	Independence Day
October 12	Columbus Day (Pan-American Day)
November 19	Garifuna Settlement Day
December 25	Christmas Day
December 26	Boxing Day

Calender of Events

Feb. 26-28:	San Pedro Carnaval, Ambergris Caye.
March 9:	Baron Bliss Day. Regatta in Belize City.
March 19:	San José Succotz Day (Mayan village).
April 15:	Holy Saturday Cross Country Classic. Bike race between Belize City and San Ignacio.
April 19-23:	San José Succotz Village's patron saint day.
May 22:	Numerous festivities take place throughout the country on Commonwealth Day: Cashew Festival in Crooked Tree, Cayo Expo in San Ignacio, Coconut Festival in Caye Caulker and Toledo Festival of Arts in Punta Gorda.
June 29:	Dia de San Pedro (patron saint), Ambergris Caye.
Aug. 13-18:	International Sea and Air Festival, San Pedro, Ambergris Caye.
Sept. 16-25:	Deer Dance Festival, San Antonio.
October 12:	Pan-American Day.
November 19:	Garifuna Settlement Day. Celebrations in Dangriga, Punta Gorda and other parts of the country.

PRACTICAL INFORMATION

MISCELLANEOUS

Alcohol

Alcohol, most often rum and beer, is sold in all little grocery stores (*mercados*).

Duty-Free Shops

There are duty-free shops in the airports. Most of the products sold are foreign. All purchases must be paid for in American dollars.

Electricity

Like in North America, wall sockets take plugs with two flat pins and work on an alternating current of 110 volts (60 cycles). European visitors with electric appliances will therefore need both an adaptor and a converter.

Women Travellers

Women travelling alone should not encounter any problems. For the most part, people are friendly and not aggressive. Generally, men are respectful toward women, and harassment is uncommon, although Belizean males do have a tendency to flirt. Of course, a certain level of caution should be exercised; avoid making eye contact, ignore any advances or comments and do not walk around alone in poorly-lit areas at night.

Smokers

There are no restrictions with respect to smokers. Cigarettes are not expensive, and smoking is allowed in all public places.

Gay Life

The situation of gays and lesbians in Belize is similar to that found in other Latin American countries. Gays still suffer from a certain form of repression, which stems from old family and chauvinistic values and politics. Homosexuality is better tolerated in certain resort towns and in the Cayes.

Time Change

Belize is in the same time zone as eastern North America (EST), six hours behind Europe.

Weights and Measures

Belize uses the imperial system:

Weights
1 pound (lb) = 454 grams (g)
1 kilogram (kg) = 2.2 pounds (lbs)

Linear Measure
1 inch = 2.2 centimetres (cm)
1 foot (ft) = 30 centimetres (cm)
1 mile = 1.6 kilometres (km)
1 kilometres (km) = 0.63 miles
1 metre (m) = 39.37 inches

Land Measure
1 acre = 0.4 hectare
1 hectare = 2.471 acres

Volume Measure
1 U.S. gallon (gal) = 3.79 litres
1 U.S. gallon (gal) = 0.83 imperial gallon

Temperature
To convert °F into °C: subtract 32, divide by 9, multiply by 5
To convert °C into °F: multiply by 9, divide by 5, add 32

PRACTICAL
INFORMATION

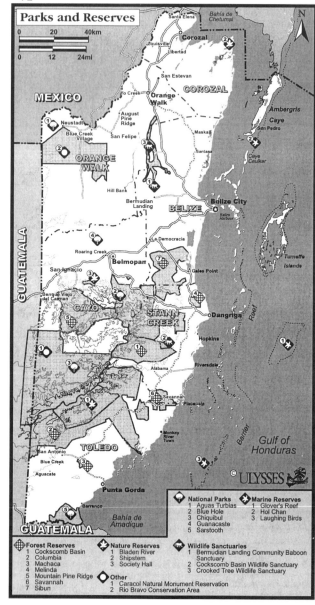

Parks and Reserves

| 0 | 20 | 40km |
| 0 | 12 | 24mi |

MEXICO

Santa Elena
Bahía de Chetumal
Corozal
Louisville
Libertad
San Estevan
Yo Creek
COROZAL
Orange Walk
Neustadt
August Pine Ridge
Maskall
Blue Creek Village
San Felipe
Ambergris Caye
San Pedro
ORANGE WALK
Santana
Caye Caulker
Hill Bank
Bermudian Landing
BELIZE
Belize City
Belize Harbour

GUATEMALA

Roaring Creek
Belmopan
La Democracia
Turneffe Islands
San Ignacio
Benque Viejo del Carmen
CAYO
STANN CREEK
Gales Point
Dangriga
Hopkins
Alabama
Riversdale
Reef
Savannah
Placencia
Gulf of Honduras
San Antonio
TOLEDO
Monkey River Town
Blue Creek
Aguacate
Barrier
© ULYSSES
Punta Gorda
Barranco
Bahía de Amadique
GUATEMALA

National Parks
1 Aguas Turbias
2 Blue Hole
3 Chiquibul
4 Guanacaste
5 Sarstooth

Marine Reserves
1 Glover's Reef
2 Hol Chan
3 Laughing Birds

Forest Reserves
1 Cockscomb Basin
2 Columbia
3 Machaca
4 Melinda
5 Mountain Pine Ridge
6 Savannah
7 Sibun

Nature Reserves
1 Bladen River
2 Shipstern
3 Society Hall

Wildlife Sanctuaries
1 Bermudian Landing Community Baboon Sanctuary
2 Cockscomb Basin Wildlife Sanctuary
3 Crooked Tree Wildlife Sanctuary

Other
1 Caracol Natural Monument Reservation
2 Rio Bravo Conservation Area

OUTDOORS

Belize has a wide range of exceptionally beautiful natural attractions, most notably its coral reefs. The Barrier Reef, second largest in the world, attracts a vibrant variety of plant and animal life that can be observed by scuba divers and snorkellers alike. The interior of the country also has its share of breathtaking scenery: there are mountain ranges blanketed with alternately lush and sparse forests which are protected by national parks and perfect for hikes and horseback-riding excursions.

 SWIMMING

Swimming is the preferred sport of Belizeans in summer and tourists year-round, though there are very few sandy beaches in the country.

Generally, tourist beaches are well kept, so you should respect the natural environment.

 SCUBA DIVING

Several diving centres take visitors to see the wonders of the Barrier Reef.

Certified divers can explore the secrets of the Belizean coastline to their heart's content. Others can still experience underwater breathing, but must be accompanied by a qualified guide, who will supervise their descent (to a depth of 5 m). There is little danger; however, be sure that you are properly supervised. Before diving for the first time, it is very important to at least take an introductory course in order to learn basic safety skills: how to clear the water from your mask, equalize the pressure in your ears and sinuses, breathe underwater (don't hold your breath), adjust to the change in pressure underwater, and become familiar with the equipment. Many hotels offer a one-hour resort course before first-timers take the plunge. Equipment can easily be rented from the different centres along the coasts.

Scuba diving makes it possible to discover fascinating sights like coral reefs, schools of multi-coloured fish and amazing underwater plants. Don't forget that this ecosystem is fragile and deserves special attention. All divers must respect a few basic **safety guidelines** in order to protect these natural sites: do not touch anything (especially not urchins – their long spikes can harm you); do not take pieces of coral (it is much prettier in the water than out, where it becomes discoloured); do not disturb any living creatures; do not hunt; do not feed the fish; be careful not to disturb anything with your flippers and, of course, do not litter. If you want a souvenir of your underwater experience, disposable underwater cameras are available.

 SNORKELLING

It doesn't take much to snorkel: a mask, a snorkel and some flippers. Anyone can enjoy this activity, which is a great way to admire the riches of the underwater world. Coral reefs inhabited by various underwater species are accessible from certain beaches. Some companies organize snorkelling trips. Remember that the basic rules for protecting the underwater environment (see scuba diving section) must also be respected when snorkelling.

SURFING AND WINDSURFING

Some beaches in Belize have calm waters suitable to boarding activities. If you would like to try these sports, you can rent equipment at the hotels.

If this is your first time, a few safety pointers should be followed before hitting the waves: choose a beach where the surf is not too rough; steer clear of swimmers; don't head too far out (make a distress signal by waving your arms in the air if you need to) and wear shoes to avoid cutting your feet on the rocks.

SAILING

Excursions aboard sailboats and yachts offer another enchanting way to ride the sea's sparkling waves. Some centres organize trips, while others rent sailboats to experienced skippers. A few addresses are provided throughout the guide.

DEEP-SEA FISHING

Deep-sea fishing enthusiasts will be pleased to know that several places offer fishing excursions, mostly out of San Pedro and Placencia. Whether you want to catch big fish (like marlin, for example) or smaller ones will determine how far offshore you go. These trips usually last about 3 hours and are quite expensive. Equipment and advice are provided. Even if you come back empty-handed, this is still a great way to spend the day.

PARKS

Belize's natural beauty is protected by several national parks and reserves managed by the Audubon Society. They are found

OUTDOORS

throughout the country and each one protects a different plant or animal species. Efforts have been made to attract visitors to these parks, but not all of them are easily accessible. The ones near the larger towns are easier to get to and have hiking trails. If you decide to set out on one of these, make sure to take the necessary precautions discussed in the "Hiking" section bellow.

 ## HIKING

Hiking and walking are undoubtedly the easiest activities to do. However, parks with well-marked trails are hard to find, so anyone heading off on them must be well prepared. A few trails near the resort towns are worth a quick visit; just be sure to bring along everything you might need during your outing.

There are a few things to keep in mind when hiking. Before taking any trail, try to find out its length and level of difficulty. Remember: there are no maps available at the parks, and if you get lost, there are no rescue teams.

You will have to be well prepared and bring along anything you might need during your hike. The longer the hike, the better prepared you must be. First of all, bring a lot of water (you won't find any along the way) and sufficient food. Remember that the sun sets between 6pm and 7pm, and hiking is dangerous in the dark, so return before sundown. Ideally, you should start out early in the morning; that way you can avoid hiking when the sun is at its hottest, and get back before the day is done.

Sunstroke

Some trails include long sections in the open, with no shade. Anyone hiking in the tropics has a greater risk of getting sunstroke. Cramps, goose bumps, nausea and loss of balance are the first signs of sunstroke. If these symptoms arise, the affected person needs immediate shade, water and ventilation.

To avoid this problem, always wear a hat and a good sunscreen. By getting an early start, you'll have time to hike in cooler temperatures.

Clothing

Dressing properly is one of the best ways to avoid the little inconveniences of the outdoors. In light of that, remember to wear lightweight and light-coloured clothing; long pants to protect your legs from underbrush, thorny bushes and bug bites, and thick-soled hiking boots that are lightweight but solid, with good traction. Downpours are frequent, especially in the rainforest, so bring water-resistant clothing, and don't forget your bathing suit if you plan on cooling off in one of the many waterfalls in the mountains.

What to Bring

To be prepared in any eventuality, it is a good idea to bring along a few necessities, including a water bottle, a pocketknife, antiseptic, bandages (both adhesive and non-adhesive), scissors, aspirin, sunscreen, insect repellent, food and above all enough water for the trip.

 BICYCLING

The road system in Belize is made up mostly of one-lane highways with no shoulders and unpaved secondary roads strewn with potholes. Not exactly a cyclist's dream. Caution is advised as people drive fast. Despite this, cycling can still be a very pleasant way to see the countryside outside the large cities. Bicycles can be rented in most of the larger cities for a few dollars.

 HORSEBACK RIDING

Horseback riding is another interesting way to see the country. In certain regions where the roads are often unpaved and narrow, horses are the main means of transportation. Many hotels organize guided horseback rides.

OUTDOORS

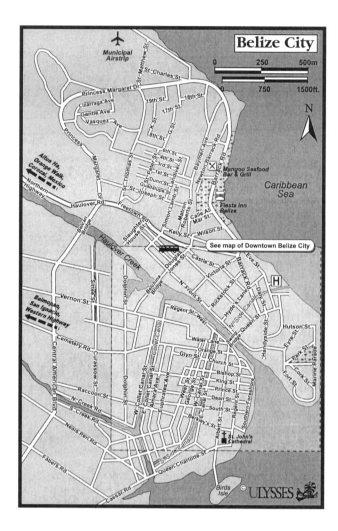

Belize City

Municipal Airstrip

Princess Margaret Dr.
St-Matthew-St.
St-Charles-St.
Lizarraga-Ave.
19th-St.
17th-St.
18th-St.
Gentle-Ave.
Vásquez-Ave.
K-St.
G-St.
8th-St.
8th-St.
6th-St.
4th-St.
Baymen-Ave.
Newton-Barrack-Rd.
3rd-St.
1st-St.
Dunn-St.
St-Thomas-St.
Landivar-St.
Guadalupe-St.
St-Joseph-St.
Matron-Roberts-Ave.
Calle-Al-Mar-St.
Simon-Lamb-St.
Kelly-St.
Wilson-St.

Princess Margaret Dr.
Margaret-Dr.

Northern Highway
Altun Ha,
Orange Walk,
Corozal, Mexico

Haulover-Rd.
Freetown-Rd.
Belcan Bridge

Haulover Creek
Slaughter-House-St.

Mangoo Seafood
Bar & Grill

Caribbean Sea

Fiesta Inn Belize

See map of Downtown Belize City

Castle-St.
Eve-St.
Douglas-Jones-St.
Victoria-St.
Barrack-Rd.
N.-Front-St.
Rickstock-St.
Hyde's-Lane
Daly-St.

H

Belmopan,
San Ignacio,
Western Highway

Vernon-St.
Sittee-St.
Dolphin-St.
Bechma Bridge

Regent-St.-West
Swing-Bridge
N.-Side-Canal
Queen-St.
Handyside-St.
Hutson-St.
Eyre-St.

Water-Lane
Orange-St.
Glyn-St.
Church-St.
Bishop-St.
Park-St.
Cork-St.
Cemetery-Rd.
Curassow-St.
Dolphin-St.
W.-Collet-Canal-St.
Collet-Canal-St.
Amara-Ave.
Euphates-Ave.
West-St.
George-St.
Canal-St.
King-St.
Prince-St.
Dean-St.
South-St.
Regent-St.
Fort-St.
Marine-Parade
Southern-Foreshore

Central-American-Blvd.
Raccoon-St.
N-Creek-Rd.
S-Creek-Rd.
Neais-Pen-Rd.
Berkley's-St.
Albert-St.
St. John's Cathedral
Fabers-Rd.
S.-Side-Canal
Queen-Charlotte-St.
Caesar-Rd.

Birds Isle

© ULYSSES

N

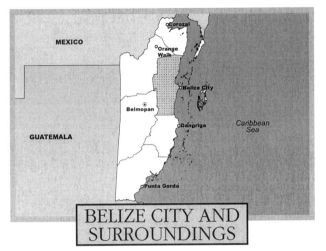

BELIZE CITY AND SURROUNDINGS

With a population of less than 90,000, the largest city in Belize is a must for travellers setting off to explore the country. In fact, all roads lead to Belize City. Not only does the city have an international airport, but it connects the country's main roads and waterways. Nevertheless, very few travellers stay in the city for long, because it has relatively few attractions to offer.

Belize City is a blend of the old and the new: several colonial-era houses have managed to withstand devastating hurricanes — including Hattie in 1981, which resulted in the death of close to 300 people. Surrounded by the sea, the city rests on a small low-lying peninsula shaped like a bird's open beak. It is divided by Haliver Creek, a branch of the Belize River.

On my first visit to the country's metropolis, for lack of anything better to do, I watched passers-by making their way through the winding streets. In addition to the many races living side by side in apparent harmony within the commercial hub, I noticed that some seemed to be heading toward a specific destination: wage-earners going to work, shopkeepers taking care of business and others running errands. Just as many were simply killing time: unemployed people hanging out on street corners and drifters knocking about to the languid pace of the Caribbean, as well as the penniless who have nothing to do but to watch time go by. Then, suddenly, torrential rain poured down on the city. For a brief moment, a hurried and fitful dance wound its way through the streets. The unemployed and workers alike came running, seeking shelter beneath the porches of banks and the doorways of shops as the water ran like rivers through the avenues. The downpour and resulting flood stopped time for everyone. Standing in a doorway, a vagrant took the opportunity to politely request a cigarette from a shopkeeper, who kindly acquiesced to his fellow friend in need. This rain suddenly put everyone on equal footing, as if it were Judgment Day.

Unfortunately, although visitors may be taken with its urban charm, Belize City has been particularly hit by poverty and unemployment, and has the highest crime rate in the country. By day, you will have to take the necessary precautions. By night, be sure to be accompanied by someone from the area or take a taxi to your destination.

Though Belize City may not be the preferred destination of travellers, its neighbouring regions prove to be very interesting. North of the city, the ruins of Altun Ha are a most enriching one-day excursion. Also, the Baboon Sanctuary and Crooked Tree Sanctuary nature reserves offer visitors a complete change of scene and are wonderful gateways to the country's flora and fauna.

 FINDING YOUR WAY AROUND

Belize City

Transfer to Belize City

There are numerous taxis at the various exits of **Goldson International Airport**, located approximately fifteen kilometres from the town centre. The fare to the downtown area is BZ$30.

If you're on a limited budget, it takes a good half-hour to walk from the air terminal to the Northern Highway, where you won't have any trouble finding a bus (BZ$1). **Chan Bus Service**

```
                    Logos
             1117 Pacific Ave.
             Santa Cruz CA 95060
                (831)427-5100
             Transaction No: 0599529
                Customer ID:


                   Station: 6
2/08/02  15:20:41          CLERK:CY


1 @   7.80 U                           7.80
   Used Book
UBTOTAL                                7.80
AX @ 8.000%                            0.62
OTAL                                   8.42
ASH                                   20.00
otal Tendered          $             20.00
ASH Credit (amount)                   11.58


                  THANK YOU!
ew & Used Books, Records, CDs, Tapes

         Open 10:00AM-10:00PM 7days
```

(BZ$1; every hour; Pound Yard, near the Novelos offices) offers decent bus service to the airport.

International Flights

A BZ$30 tax must be paid at the airport check-in desk upon your return. This tax must be paid in cash after checking in at your airline's counter.

Tropic Air (☎02-45671; USA and Canada, ☎800-422-3435, Belize ≈02-62338; tropicair@btl.net) offers regular flights to **Flores** from Goldson International Airport. **Aerovias de Guate-mala** (Goldson International Airport, ☎75745) provides daily flights between Belize City and Flores.

American Airlines (New Road at Queen St., ☎02-32522, ≈02-31730, USA ☎800-624-6262, Canada ☎800-433-7300).

Continental Airlines *(32 Albert St., ☎02-78309, ⌐02-78114, USA ☎800-231-0856, Canada ☎800-525-0280, France ☎01.42.99.09.09).*

TACA International Airline *(41 Albert St., ☎02-77185, ⌐02-75213, USA ☎800-535-8780, Canada: Quebec ☎800-263-4063, Ontario ☎800-263-4039; in Paris, E.C.R.I.T. ☎01.44.51.01.64, ⌐01.42.86.96.96).*

Domestic Flights

The plane is the best way to travel to the southern part of the country, and the rates are quite affordable. Though Belize is a small country, the southbound highway is not entirely paved, which makes the trip longer. Moreover, San Pedro, in the Cayes, and Tikal, in Guatemala, are often reached by air. There are several daily flights from Belize City to the country's other major cities.

Tickets can be purchased a day to a few days in advance, or even on the day of departure, at various travel agencies or directly from the airlines at the small municipal airport, from which the majority of domestic flights depart.

The municipal airport is on the northernmost edge of the city. By taxi, the standard inner-city fare (BZ$5 to BZ$16) is charged according to the number of passengers.

Scheduled Flights

Tropic Air *(Municipal Airstrip, ☎02-45671; USA and Canada ☎800-422-3435, Belize ☎02-62338; tropicair@btl.net):*

To **Dangriga**: *(departures at 8:30am, 11am, 1:30pm and 4:30pm; flight time: 20 min.; fare: BZ$60).*

To **Placencia** *(departures at 8:30am, 11am, 1:30pm and 4:30pm; flight time: 30 min.; fare: BZ$100).*

To **Punta Gorda** *(departures at 8:30am, 11am, 1:30am and 4:30pm; flight time: 1 hour; fare: BZ$130).*

To **San Pedro** *(departures at 7:40am, 8:40am, 9:40am, 10:40am, 11:40am, 12:30pm, 1:30pm, 2:30pm, 3:30pm, 4:30pm and 5:30pm; flight time: 20 min.; fare: BZ$60).*

Planes flying to San Pedro will stop at **Caye Caulker** and **Caye Chapel** upon request.

Maya Airways *(Municipal Airstrip, ☎02-35794; USA and Canada ☎800-552-3419)* and **Island Air** *(☎02-31140)* merged in 1997. These airlines offer numerous daily flights to San Pedro and Corozal.

Charters

In addition to scheduled flights, the **Caribee Air Service** *(☎02-44253)* and **Javier's Flying Service** *(☎02-45332)* charter companies offer tailored flights aboard Cessnas.

By Bus

Belize City does not have a central bus station for all local bus companies.

Batty Brothers *(54 East Collet Canal, ☎02-77146)* departs many times a day to northern Belize, with connections to Chetumal (Mexico).

To **Corozal** *(10 departures daily; fare: BZ$8; travel time: 2 hours, 30 min).*

To **Orange Walk** *(10 departures daily; fare: BZ$4.50; travel time: 2 hours).*

Z-Line *(Magazine Rd., ☎02-73937)* runs to Belmopan and southern Belize. To get to San Ignacio with Z-Line, you will have to transfer at Belmopan. Passengers can also transfer from Punta Gorda to Guatemala by boat.

To **Belmopan** *(departures: 8am, 10am, noon, 2pm, 3pm, 4pm and 5pm; fare: BZ$4; travel time: 1 hour, 15 min).*

To **Dangriga** *(departures: 8am, 10am, noon, 2pm, 3pm, 4pm and 5pm; fare: BZ$10; travel time: 3 hours, 30 min)*: Z-Line offers many connections from Dangriga to Hopkins, Placencia and Punta Gorda.

To **Placencia**: there are two ways of getting to Placencia. You can leave directly from Belize City *(BZ$18; departures at 9:30am and 1:30pm; travel time: 6 hours)*, or transfer at Belmopan (see p 212).

To **Punta Gorda** *(fare: BZ$22; travel time: 8 hours)*.

James Bus Line *(West Collet Canal St.)* has buses leaving Belize City for **Punta Gorda** every Monday, Tuesday, Thursday, Saturday and Sunday at 5pm. James Bus Line is faster than Z-Line; the journey takes eight hours instead of nine.

Ritchie's *(departures from Belize City at Pound Yard, ☎05-23132 in Dangriga)* goes to the southern part of the country. Their buses are faster, since they take the Southern Highway instead of the road to Belmopan. Only two departures a day are offered, however. The 2:30pm bus travels to **Dangriga** *(BZ$9; travel time: 1 hour, 45 min)*, **Hopkins** *(BZ$13; travel time: 2 hours, 30 min)* and **Placencia** *(BZ$17; travel time: 4 hours)*. A second bus leaves for Dangriga at 4:30pm.

Novelos Bus Service *(West Collet Canal, ☎02-77372)* travels to the western part of the country. Departures every hour to **San Ignacio** *(BZ$5)*. Novelos also offers express-service departures at 11am, 3pm and 5:30pm to San Ignacio, and many connections to Flores, Guatemala.

Jax & Sons Bus Service *(BZ$3.50; Mon to Sat, departures at 4pm, 4:30pm, 5pm and 5:15pm; travel time: 1 hour; ☎02-52032)* provides service to **Crooked Tree** from Pound Yard Park. Other buses leave for Crooked Tree from the corner of Regent Street West and Southside Canal *(BZ$3.50; Mon to Sat, departure at 10:55am; travel time: 1 hour)*.

Russel Bus operates a shuttle service to the **Baboon Sanctuary** from Cairo Street at Euphritis Avenue. Departures: 12:15pm and 4:15pm; fare: BZ$3; travel time: 1 hour, 30 minutes.

By Boat

Several high-speed shuttle boats leave Belize City for the Cayes. Be sure to bring sun screen and rain wear, because the boats have no roofs. If the weather is good, you can make the most of the Caribbean's crystal-clear waters whilst arriving safe and sound. You can also make many acquaintances aboard.

The best place to catch a boat from is the **Marine Terminal & Museum** *(10 North Front St., ☎02-31969)*, a modern, clean and safe terminal with several benches, a cafeteria and a small souvenir shop. The boats are affiliated with the Caye Caulker Water Association. It is best to reserve a day in advance for departures, especially on weekends, when many residents visit the islands. You can always get there on the same day, but this may entail a few hours' wait.

To **Caye Caulker**: daily departures, every two hours between 9am and 5pm; 40-minute crossing; fare: BZ$15.

To **San Pedro**: departure at 9am; 90-minute crossing; fare: BZ$30. Since there is only one departure to San Pedro, you can take a boat to Caye Caulker, then transfer to San Pedro.

Triple J *(5182 Baymen Ave., ☎02-44375)* offers a daily departure at 9am to Caye Caulker *(BZ$15)* and San Pedro *(BZ$25)* from its offices behind the supreme court, at the mouth of the Belize River. The **Ferry Boat Yarra Andrea** *(☎02-48204)* goes to these places from Monday to Saturday at 3pm for the same fare as its competitor.

Rental Cars

Many car-rental agencies are set up in Goldson International Airport in Belize City. You can also call one of the agencies from your hotel and have them deliver the car to you there.

Avis *(Municipal Airstrip, ☎02-34619; Goldson International Airport, ☎02-52385)*.

Budget *(771 Bella Vista Northern Highway, ☎02-32435 or ☎02-33986, ☎02-30237)*.

BELIZE CITY & SURROUNDINGS

National *(☎02-31600;   Goldson   International   Airport,*
☎02-52139, ⌐02-31586). Rental cars for Tikal also available.
Excellent rates.

Jaribu   Auto   Rental *(5576   Princess   Margaret   Drive,*
☎02-44680).

Jaguar Eco Tours & Rental *(Goldson International Airport,*
☎02-73142, ⌐02-70397).

Taxis

Taxis must charge a flat rate for fares within the city limits,
from BZ$5 to BZ$16 according to the number of passengers.
All taxis are easily identifiable.

Crooked Tree Wildlife Sanctuary

By Car

The entrance to the Crooked Tree Wildlife Sanctuary is at
Kilometre 50 on the Northern Highway. The exit, to the west,
is fairly well-indicated. The wildlife reserve's reception centre
is 4 kilometres after the turnoff from the Northern Highway.

By Bus

Batty Brothers and **Jax & Sons Bus Service** both offer departures to Belize City from Crooked Tree Village. To get to
Orange Walk, Corozal or Chetumal, go to the park's entrance
at the Northern Highway and take one of the many buses
travelling between Belize City and the northern part of the
country.

To Belize City

Batty Brothers Bus Service: departures: every day at 6am;
fare: BZ$3.50.
Jax & Sons Bus Service: departures: 5:50am, 6:30am and
7am; fare: BZ$3.50.

Altun Ha

Because no buses go directly to the ruins, visitors are strongly advised to visit Altun Ha by rental car, taxi or through an organized excursion. You can also get there by boat from the Crooked Tree Wildlife Sanctuary.

If you choose to take the bus from Belize City anyway, there are two options. The first is to take a bus travelling along the Northern Highway and ask the driver to drop you off at the intersection of the road leading to Rockstone Pound. You will then have to hitchhike to Rockstone Pound, then the ruins.

Your second option is to take a bus from Belize City *(Cinderella Plaza, BZ$3; every day, 1pm, 3:30pm, 5:30pm)* to Maskal (the closest village to Altun Ha). Ask to be dropped off at Rockstone Pound, located at the intersection of the road leading to the Altun Ha archaeological site, 3 kilometres farther. You will then have to walk the rest of the way or try hitchhiking. Unfortunately, you'll have to sleep here, because the only departures from Maskal and Rockstone Pound to Belize City are early in the morning *(BZ$3; every day, 6:15am and 6:45am)*.

Bermudian Landing Community Baboon Sanctuary

To **Belize City**: departures between 5am and 6:30am (BZ$3.50).

The Belize Zoo and Tropical Education Center

The Belize Zoo is situated on the Western Highway, at Kilometre 47. You can get there by bus (running toward Belmopan), but you will have to ask the driver to stop at the entrance. Count on spending BZ$3.

BELIZE CITY & SURROUNDINGS

Monkey Bay Wildlife Sanctuary

This wildlife sanctuary is also on the Western Highway, approximately two kilometres west of the Belize Zoo.

 PRACTICAL INFORMATION

Belize City

Tourist Information Office

The staff at the **Belize Tourist Board** *(Mon to Fri 8am to noon and 1pm to 5pm; 83 North Front St., ☎02-77213, ⊷02-77490; www.belizenet.com)* can answer your questions concerning your trip to the country. Maps of Belize, a few practical guide books, numerous tourist brochures and more are available here.

Foreign Exchange Office

Barclays Bank *(Mon to Thu 8am to 2:30pm; Fri 8am to 4:30pm; 21 Albert St., ☎02-77211 or 02-77054, ⊷02-35893)* is the best place to exchange currency and obtain a cash advance on your credit card.

The **Bank of Nova Scotia** *(Albert St. at Bishop St., ☎029-77027, ⊷02-77416)* is another option.

Post Office

The **Post Office** *(Mon to Sat 8am to noon and 1pm to 4pm; Queen St. at North Front St.)* is right on the north side of the Swing Bridge.

For fast courier service, head to **DHL Worldwide Express** *(38 New Rd., ☎02-34350)*. Not affordable for everyone.

Telephone

BTL *(Belize Telecommunications Ltd.)*: Mon to Fri 8am to 5pm;
1 Church Street.

Police

Emergencies: ☎911
Police Station: 9 Queen Street, ☎02-72222.

Hospital

Ambulance: ☎90
Belize City Hospital: Princess Margaret Street, ☎02-31548.

 EXPLORING

Belize City

The history of Belize City was shaped over the years by
buccaneers, pirates, merchants and farmers. Not so long ago,
wealthy English merchants unloaded their cargo here, at the
country's greatest seaport, then went in their funny feathered
hats to have tea at the sumptuous governor general's house
surrounded by palm groves. The sailors obviously had something altogether different in mind after such a long voyage and
had no trouble finding it. Those days are gone: modern-day
visitors mostly arrive by air, are virtually all middle-class, and
the city has changed accordingly. What remains of the governor general's residence, a museum since the country's independence, is nothing more than a small reflection of those
prosperous years. Even the "ladies of the night", who still walk
the streets, seem to miss the dashing sailors of the past.
Tourists now make a beeline for the harbour when they get off
the plane. Then, much like a chase scene from *Miami Vice*,
they zip across the crystal-clear turquoise waters to the islands
on the coral barrier reef in 45 minutes, on high-speed cigar-
shaped boats.

Belize City, the capital of this small nascent country, is hardly a great cultural metropolis. There are very few museums, art galleries or major cultural activities. Nevertheless, a great number of painters, sculptors, dancers and artists of all kinds ply their trade here, despite the few public spaces allotted to them.

Belize City is hardly lacking in charm and solitary strollers will be richly rewarded as they wander through the city on a sunny afternoon. The now famous **Swing Bridge**, the city's architectural symbol, dates from the turn of the century and is the best landmark from which to start a tour of the city.

The Northeastern District

On the northeast side of Haulover Creek, which divides the city, the bridge leads to the **Fort George** peninsula, formerly a peaceful seaside residential district. Opposite the post office is the **Marine Terminal & Museum** *(BZ$4; every day 8am to 5pm; 10 North Front St., ☎02-31969, ⇔02-78710)*, a small museum adjacent to the boarding pier for boats heading to Caye Caulker and San Pedro. You can kill two birds with one stone by visiting this exhibition hall and reserving your tickets for these destinations. The 2nd floor is devoted to marine wildlife and the Barrier Reef. Upstairs, there is an exhibition about colonial-era boats. The whole is presented in a very educational manner, with some photographs and texts.

Head southeast along **Front Street** and stop by the **Old Market**, dating from the 19th century and still bustling with activity, even though a new market has been built in the city's commercial centre. On the headland of the peninsula stands the **lighthouse**, rising up like a thin needle at the mouth of the bay. Before the lighthouse lies the tomb of **Baron Bliss**, a wealthy Englishman who bequeathed part of his fortune to the city, which was used to build the Bliss Institute (see p 92) on the Southern Foreshore.

Head north along **Marine Parade**, which runs past the seaside **Fort George Hotel**. Farther north is **Barrack Road**, which runs along the sea before entering the city. This main thoroughfare was once lined with the British army's barracks — hence the name. This is the coast on which the famous American aviator

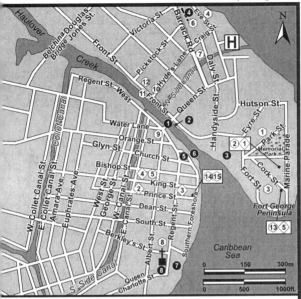

Downtown Belize City

● ATTRACTIONS

1. Swing Bridge
2. Marine Terminal & Museum
3. Old Market
4. Mexican Cultural Center
5. Court House
6. Bliss Institute
7. Government House Museum
8. St. John's Cathedral

○ ACCOMMODATIONS

1. Bon Aventure Hotel
2. Chateau Caribbean Hotel
3. Colton House
4. Downtown Guesthouse
5. El Centro Hotel
6. Freddie's Guesthouse
7. Glenthorne Manor
8. Hotel Mopan
9. Isabel Guest House
10. Kiss Hotel
11. Mira Rio
12. North Front Street Guesthouse
13. Radisson Fort George Hotel
14. Seaside Guesthouse
15. The Bellevue Hotel

◇ RESTAURANTS

1. Chateau Caribbean Hotel
2. Dit's Restaurant
3. GG's Cafe & Patio
4. Macy's Café
5. Radisson Fort George Hotel

BELIZE CITY & SURROUNDINGS

Charles Lindbergh grounded the *Spirit of St. Louis*, the first plane to land in the country in the thirties. Today, Barrack Road is a fairly busy thoroughfare, flanked by the **Mexican Cultural Center** *(Barrack Rd. at Wilson St.)* (see p 108), a few good restaurants and the Fiesta Inn, the biggest hotel in the country (see p 103).

The Southern District

The commercial and historic centre of Belize City lies south of the Swing Bridge. Belize City's urban layout is a veritable labyrinth and is wonderful to explore if you don't mind getting lost in its maze. At the foot of the Swing Bridge are numerous shops, restaurants, banks and travel agencies. A few streets are crowded with passers-by and cars, the latter lining up before one of the city's three (!) traffic lights.

The historic centre stretches mainly along **Regent Street**, where numerous colonial wooden houses and a few administrative buildings dating from various periods can be found. The **Court House**, built in 1926, is flanked by two cannons and faces the city's old main square.

Behind the Court House is the **Bliss Institute** *(free admission; Mon to Fri 9am to noon and 2pm to 8pm, Sat 8:30am to noon)*, founded in honour of the British baron who came to the coast of Belize to fish and died before he could return to his mother country. Bliss left his fortune to the Belizean people, who thanked him by making March 9, the day of his death, a public holiday. The institute houses the national library and the National Arts Council, which organizes exhibitions and cultural activities of all kinds.

The **Government House Museum** *(BZ$5; Mon to Fri 8:30am to 4:30pm)* is in the magnificent Governor's House. Built in 1840, this large wooden British colonial-style house is surrounded by splendid seafront gardens. The terrace and pergola are peaceful places to relax and enjoy the delightful breeze. The centrepiece inside the house is a long mahogany staircase, and there are several well-preserved rooms and lounges. This was the governor of Belize's private residence in colonial times, and the true centre of political power, where all decisions concerning the country were made. The somewhat disappointing museum

Frigate

features a permanent collection of historical photographs. Unfortunately, there are no guided tours.

Right nearby, on Regent Street, stands **St. John's Cathedral**, built in the 19th century entirely from stones from England. The church, whose ceiling is made of mahogany, is the oldest Anglican church in Central America and one of the oldest buildings in the country.

Altun Ha ★★★

The **Altun Ha** *(BZ$5; every day 9am to 5pm)* Mayan site lies 48 kilometres north of Belize City. It is one of the best preserved in the country, thanks to the extensive archaeological excavations and restoration work carried out here. Because the ruins are in the midst of dense tropical vegetation similar to a jungle, a host of film-production companies have shot movies here. The wildlife is abundant and, with a little luck, you'll catch sight of armadillos, foxes, and many other animal species. Numerous trails run deep into the jungle, which enables you to better observe the region's flora and fauna.

Guides are not always available to explore the ruins. However, you may get the chance to meet Richard Wallace, who has been working on the site since 1976. Creole-born Wallace was quite willing to relate a few vivid legends about Altun Ha. *"There is a running legend claiming that spirits inhabit the*

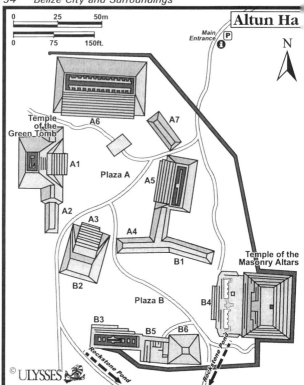

Altun Ha

summit of the main Temple. There are even people who refuse
to climb it," he asserts.

According to the tale, there are still spirits at Altun Ha, which
once contained the largest carved jade head in Central America.

"There definitely is another jade head somewhere on the site,
probably the mate of the other one, though many claim the
Maya did not believe in even numbers. But if there was really
was a second head buried here, wouldn't it be Altun Ha's
spirit?", he adds.

Altun Ha has undergone archaeological excavations since its
discovery in 1957. Archaeologists quickly saw that the site
was unique in many respects. Altun Ha was apparently used as

a burial ground for the tombs of the great ancient Mayan priests. The site is composed of two major plazas, surrounded by 13 temples. The temple of the Sun God towers above the others, at a height of 18 metres; the largest carving in the Mayan world was uncovered here, and has since become a national symbol. The piece appears on Belize-dollar bills. The carved head represents the Sun God, Kinich Ahau.

As related by archaeologist David Pendergast in the book *Warlords and Maize Men*, the Maya practised a very particular form of sacrifice on the B-4 structure at Altun Ha. The offerings — necklaces and pieces of jade — on the altar were thrown into a fire. Archaeologists found these items spread out on the ground here, undoubtedly marking the period in which the last ceremony took place.

Crooked Tree Wildlife Sanctuary

Located 45 kilometres north of Belize City on the Northern Highway, the **Crooked Tree Wildlife Sanctuary** *(BZ$8; every day 8am to 4pm; ☎02-22084)* covers 2,400-hectares of forests, swamps and waterways. Managed by the Belize Audubon Society, this nature reserve is home to more than 300 species of birds, including the Jabiru stork. This large white bird attracts many travellers and ornithologists between the months of January and April. Moreover, Crooked Tree Village innkeepers offer many boating excursions (see p 99) on the reserve's lagoon, so visitors can observe iguanas and crocodiles as well as the many birds.

A small village of scarcely 900 inhabitants developed inside the wildlife reserve well before the arrival of the Audubon Society. Crooked Tree Village lies on highlands surrounded by the sanctuary's lagoon and swamps. You can find accommodation here (see p 103) and get the chance to meet the interesting and colourful locals. The small dirt roads of the subsistence-farming village lead to the numerous inns. You could lose yourself in the warm colours of the sun setting over the swamps, the lagoon and the small plots of land. Unfortunately, unless you decide on camping, both the accommodations and excursions are somewhat expensive.

Bermudian Landing Community
Baboon Sanctuary ★ ★

Reaching the **Bermudian Landing Community Baboon Sanctuary**
(BZ$10; every day 8am to 5pm) is an adventure in itself. The
dirt roads run into the forest as far as the eye can see, over
many streams and a metal bridge crossing the Belize River. I
heading there by car, take the Northern Highway 20 kilometres
north of Belize City, then turn left and head west for
13 kilometres. The wildlife reserve is so named because
Belizeans call black howler monkeys "baboons", despite the
fact that they have little in common with their African cousins.

The wildlife reserve, which covers a 32-square-kilometre
stretch of land along the Belize River, offers visitors a wonderful opportunity to view animals living in their natural habitats.
Thanks to the efforts of environmental groups and local
residents, part of Belize's virgin territory is safeguarded for the
study and protection of black howler monkeys. The howler
monkey population has grown so much here that a number of
them are transferred to similar reserves in the country. Sadly,
once out of the reserves, these monkeys are either hunted for
their meat or domesticated. Though they are very hard to spot
in other regions, you can hear them at dusk and dawn, in Tikal
(see p 239) or the Cockscomb Sanctuary (see p 180).

Watching these primates roam freely is something to experience in Belize. These mischievous creatures will not hesitate to
screech at the top of their voice to startle you as soon as they
see you. A guide will help you coax them down from the
treetops. It's fun to play Dr. Doolittle with these animals: if you
can mimic their sounds, they will be quick to respond.

Though the observation of howler monkeys is the highlight of
a visit to the refuge, many other activities are offered by village
residents. The joint efforts of the region's inhabitants and
environmental groups have turned this reserve project into a
good example of sustainable development. The residents of
some twenty small villages have all agreed to refrain from
hunting the monkeys and cutting down the trees in which they
live and get their food. There are close to 2,000 black howler
monkeys in and around the reserve.

The reserve's administration has set up a few *cabañas* for visitors, and other organizations and businesses have followed suit, providing both accommodations and various excursions on the Belize River. Be sure to drop by the **Jungle Drift Lodge** (see p 105), whose cheerful proprietors have laid out a very easy-to-follow and informative nature interpretation trail. They also offer canoe excursions on the Belize River.

The Belize Zoo and Tropical Education Center ★

The **Belize Zoo** *(BZ$12; every day 9am to 4:30pm; Western Hwy., ☎08-13004)* is a must for anyone visiting the country. It is mainly frequented by groups of schoolchildren who flood in every day. All the animals of Belize are found in their natural habitats, though within the confines of cages. Various wild cats, including jaguars, pumas and ocelots, vie with the howler monkeys and the tapir, Belize's national animal, to be the most popular creatures at the zoo.

This zoo got its start in a rather unexpected way. It was founded in 1983 by Sharon Matola, who had been hired by a film-maker to tend to the animals assembled for a shoot about Belize's wildlife. Matola was taken by surprise when the film-maker did not receive the necessary funding to carry the

Pumas

project through. Because the animals had been living in captivity for some time, they had become ill-equipped to survive in the wild. So she decided to open a zoo and, little by

little, it grew. Ten years later, in 1993, the zoo moved to its current location, a 400-hectare site about forty kilometres north of Belize City. This new site has everything for visitors, including picnic tables, an outdoor amphitheatre, a bookshop and a souvenir shop.

Monkey Bay Wildlife Sanctuary

The **Monkey Bay Wildlife Sanctuary** *(free admission; every day; Western Hwy., approx. 2.5 km west of the Belize Zoo)* is located in a birdwatching paradise, and is home to more than 200 species of birds that live here year round. Toucans, parrots and storks nest in an ecosystem of pine forests and savannah, spread over a 400-hectare property with the Sibun River running through it. Those with luck (or patience) on their side might catch sight of pumas, crocodiles, iguanas and stags.

The reserve is managed by a private environmental protection fund; camping is permitted here for about BZ$8.

 OUTDOOR ACTIVITIES

 Bird-Watching

The great majority of hotels and inns at the **Crooked Tree Wildlife Sanctuary** (see p 103) offer birdwatching and local wildlife-observation excursions.

Sam Tillit Hotel & Tours (see p 104) organizes boat rides on the lake for BZ$140 per boat, for one to four people; BZ$30 for every additional person.

The **Bird's Eye View Lodge** (see p 104) also offers boating excursions for the same rate as above.

The lake excursions offered by the **Paradise Inn** (see p 104) are highly recommended. Same rates as above.

Canoeing

The **Bird's Eye View Lodge** (see p 104) at the **Crooked Tree Wildlife Sanctuary** rents out canoes.

Canoes can also be rented at the **Monkey Bay Wildlife Sanctuary** (see p 98). Rates vary according to the season. Further inquiries can be made at the sanctuary.

Horseback Riding

The **Bird's Eye View Lodge** (see p 104) at the **Crooked Tree Wildlife Sanctuary** offers various kinds of horseback-riding excursions.

ACCOMMODATIONS

Belize City

The **Seaside Guesthouse** (BZ$20-48; ⊗, sb; 3 Prince St., ☎02-78339) offers excellent value for the price. Moreover, all profits garnered by the six-room establishment, which is run by a Quaker organization, are donated to charitable institutions. If you are interested in social and environmental issues, the staff can be of help: they can give you practical advice as well. There are double-occupancy (BZ$48) and single-occupancy rooms with shared bathrooms, as well as a dormitory (BZ$20 per person). Rooms are simple and clean. Good ambiance and breakfast service if requested in advance.

The **Bon Aventure Hotel** (BZ$25, BZ$35 with pb; 122 North Front St., ☎02-44248 or 02-44134, ≈02-31134) is one of the city's better budget hotels, and is right downtown. From the upstairs terrace, you can get a view of the Belize River across the street. The Chinese-born family that owns the

Ulysses' Favourites

Accommodations

For colonial charm: **Chateau Caribbean Hotel** (see p 102)
For homey comfort: **Glenthorne Manor** (see p 101)
For howler monkeys: **Jungle Drift Lodge** (see p 105)

Restaurants

For rice & beans: **GG's Café & Patio** (see p 105)

hotel will be happy to provide you with information about the region. The rooms are small but clean. There are also less expensive rooms to share or for groups of five to seven people.

At the **Mira Río** hotel *(BZ$27; ⊗, ℜ, bar; 59 North Front St., ☎02-34147)*, baths are shared and there is no hot water. Nevertheless, it is centrally located and right by the Belize River. You can take a breather from the hectic pace of the city on the communal balcony overlooking the city. The rooms are rather simple, with old floors and humming ceiling fans. Get a room overlooking the river, because the street side ones are rather noisy. There is also a bar with a terrace and pool table on the main floor.

Unquestionably the most popular establishment with hikers, the **North Front Street Guesthouse** *(BZ$27; ⊗; 124 North Front St., ☎02-77595)* has a friendly and relaxed ambiance. The hotel has maps and tourist brochures in the common rooms, where guests can read or chat with their fellow boarders. The hotel's 13 rooms, all on the 3rd floor, are fairly large and clean. Ask for a room at the back; again, these are less noisy than the ones facing the street.

Run by a Mestizo family, the **Isabel Guesthouse** *(BZ$45; pb, hw, ⊗; 3 Albert St., ☎02-31139)* stands out for its enthusiastic family ambiance. The establishment boasts a pleasant common room. There are only three guestrooms, but they are large, comfortable, charming and all equipped with a private bath.

The Isabel Guesthouse is a bit difficult to find: go around the back of the Central Drugstore.

One of the most comfortable and modern establishments of its kind in the country, **Freddie's Guesthouse** *(BZ$50; hw, sb; 86 Eve St., ☎02-33851)* has but three rooms. It is therefore best to reserve in advance. Though there are no private baths, you'll only have to share the one with two other rooms. Freddie's is fairly well located on the northernmost edge of the city, within walking distance of Belize City's various attractions. One of the best places in town in terms of value for your money.

The centrally located **Downtown Guesthouse** *(BZ$50, BZ$70 with pb and ⊛; 5 Eve St.)* is easy to spot with its Maya-inspired murals on the exterior of the building. This fairly popular establishment offers rooms that are rather small and devoid of charm considering the prices asked, but it serves breakfast and provides a laundry service.

Glenthorne Manor *(BZ$80 bkfst incl.; pb, hw, ≡; 27 Barrack Rd., ☎02-44212)* is one of the most charming bed-and-breakfasts in the city. This old colonial wooden house exudes the old-fashioned charm of a bygone era. Though a bit disorganized — ultimately making it all the more charming — the house has a pleasant living room for guests. The beds are a little too soft, but the rooms are clean and the whole place has a lot of character. Some rooms have private balconies. Very warm and friendly staff. A great place to meet Belizeans and other travellers.

A colonial-style establishment located in the city's historic district, the **Hotel Mopán** *(BZ$80; pb, ⊛, ≡; 55 Regent St., ☎02-73356)* boasts a pleasant rustic dining room and a communal terrace, ideal for reading or simply whiling away the time. The rooms, though air conditioned, are small and offer nothing more than basic comfort considering the price.

Mostly business people from Belize and Central America stay at the centrally-located **El Centro Hotel** *(BZ$90; ⊛, tv, pb, hw; 4 Bishop St., ☎02-72413)*. The rooms here are comfortable, air-conditioned and furnished with large double beds. Though somewhat outdated and lacking in charm, the hotel is clean and practical.

The **Kiss Hotel** *(BZ$90; pb, hw, ⊗, tv; 8 Map St., ☎02-32916)* is aptly named, since it has a rather tacky candy-pink interior. Although this place is not so popular with tourists, it is a good idea to stay here during a heat wave, because its large rooms are air conditioned. Lacking in charm and rather poor value for the price.

For a moderately-priced hotel, **Colton House** *(BZ$100; pb, ⊗; 9 Cork St., ☎02-44666, ⊷02-30451)* has many advantages over its competitors. Though all are colonial wooden houses, Colton House is the loveliest of the bunch! Moreover, its rooms are tastefully decorated and, with a little imagination, you will get the impression of being in a British colonial-era house. The bathrooms are also stylish. There is an air-conditioned dining room with a satellite television. The management is very friendly and obliging. Only tea and coffee are served in the morning.

The **Bellevue Hotel** *(BZ$130; ⊗, tv, hw, pb, ≈; 5 Southern Foreshore)* is located in the southern part of the city. Though its charming rooms are in the colonial style, the hotel has all the modern comforts, including air conditioning, a satellite television and decent bathrooms, not to mention a swimming pool and gardens. A pleasant upstairs bar, which faces the sea, turns into a popular discotheque (see p 108) on weekends.

Part of the Best Western chain, the **Belize Biltmore Plaza** *(BZ$150; hw, pb, ≈, △, ℜ; Northern Highway Mile 3, ☎02-32302, ⊷02-32301)* is not within walking distance at 4.8 kilometres from the town centre. It is, however, close to Goldson International Airport. Opinions of the hotel vary widely. Although it is impressive from the outside and has decent rates, the hotel's interior is rather badly kept. Moreover, guests frequently complain about humidity problems. On the plus side, each of the air-conditioned rooms is large and has two double beds.

🏨 Definitely try to stay at the large colonial seafront residence now housing the **Chateau Caribbean Hotel** *(BZ$160; hw,* *pb, ℜ, ≡, ◌; 6 Marine Parade, ☎02-30800, ⌐02-30900)*. The attentive and professional staff will see to it that you feel right at home during your stay here. On the main floor there is a pleasant lounge with wicker seats and a small terrace facing the sea. Upstairs, the corridors with slightly slanted floors are typical of an old wooden house that has managed to withstand numerous hurricanes over the years. The rooms are rather small, but charming. The place is well air-conditioned, but it would be even more pleasant if there were windows that opened to let in the delightful breeze. The decor of the restaurant (see p 106) leaves something to be desired, but it has a wonderful view of the sea and you can enjoy a romantic tête-à-tête here come nightfall, or take the opportunity to jot down a few thoughts in your diary.

The biggest hotel in the country, the **Fiesta Inn Belize** *(BZ$200 -250; hw, pb, ≡, ≈, ◌, ◌, ℜ; Barrack Rd., ☎02-32670, ⌐02-32660)* is the typical of the type of modern establishment owned by North American chains. This large building faces the sea and has a lovely swimming pool, a volleyball court, a fitness centre and playgrounds for children. The rooms are sizable and have two double beds. The hotel also has a decent restaurant, a popular bar, The Calypso (see p 108), and a seafront bar-terrace, Lindbergh's Landing, which hosts Latin evenings. This former Ramada Inn was built in 1981 and is now managed by Posadas de México, Mexico's largest hotel chain.

The most famous luxury hotel in Belize is the **Radisson Fort George Hotel** *(BZ$320-360; hw, pb, ≡, tv, ≈, ◌, ℜ; 2 Marine Parade, ☎02-33333; ⌐02-73820)*. This seaside hotel complex has a comfortable and relaxed ambiance and a superb swimming pool. Like other Radissons, the rooms are spacious and come with queen-size beds, a satellite television, a mini bar, a small desk and a modern bathroom. The hotel also has a private dock. In short, worry-free accommodation!

Crooked Tree Wildlife Sanctuary

The **Paradise Inn** and the **Sam Tillit Hotel & Tours** permit camping on their grounds, which is the cheapest form of accommodation on the reserve. If you do not have the necessary equipment, B&Bs are the best alternative.

Molly's Place *(BZ$15 per person)* offers simple and clean rooms equipped with mosquito nets. Shared bathrooms and outdoor shower. Pleasant and hospitable. Breakfast is served for BZ$3. In the same category, the **Rhaburn Rooms**, located in the village centre, has comparable rates and features.

The **Sam Tillit Hotel & Tours** *(BZ$20-60; ⊗, pb, hw, ℛ; ☎02-12026)* has four double rooms *(BZ$60)* and the management permits camping on the palm tree-lined grounds for as little as BZ$10. The BZ$20 rooms are modest, and have shared bathrooms. All rooms are clean, and their palm-thatched roofs exude rustic charm and fit in perfectly with the reserve's environment. The hotel has a good restaurant (see p 108) and organizes boat rides on the lake (see p 98).

The best hotel in Crooked Tree, the **Bird's Eye View Lodge** *(BZ$80; pb, hw, ⊗, ℛ; ☎02-32040, ⬈02-24869)* offers large, rustic and cosy upstairs rooms, with an unparalleled view of the lake. You'll have to walk through the pleasant restaurant's kitchens to get to the rooms, which gives the hotel a family-like touch. There is a large terrace facing the lake, and boating and canoe rentals, as well as horseback riding excursions (see p 98, 99), are offered.

The *cabañas* of the **Paradise Inn** *(BZ$96; pb, hw, ⊗, ℛ, ⊚; ☎02-12084)* are spread around the lake with a dock and a promenade. Rates are a little high, but the *cabañas* are comfortable and cosy. Best place to camp in Crooked Tree *(BZ$10 per site)*. Excellent excursions available (see p 99).

Bermudian Landing Community Baboon Sanctuary

Staying in a private home *(BZ$25 per room)* is the cheapest form of accommodation on the reserve. The small museum here has more information. The small old houses have no hot water, and the bathrooms are outside.

The five guestrooms of the **Baboon Sanctuary** *(BZ$40 bkfst incl.)* are often occupied for long periods of time by researchers and students. The establishment operates like a B&B. Hammocks are at guests' disposal. A little pricey considering the service and the quality of the rooms.

The best hotel in the area, the **Jungle Drift Lodge** *(BZ$40; pb, ⊗; ☎02-49578, ⌐02-78160; jungled@btl.net)* offers first-rate *cabañas* in a family and community ambiance. The very affable owners, who built all the *cabañas* and laid out the surrounding tropical gardens themselves, do their utmost to make every day of your stay here a festive one. The kitchen, a rustic wooden cabin, is open as long as they are there preparing the excellent food served. What better place than the kitchen to discuss everything and anything? The meals, served on two large wooden tables, are shared by guests and hosts alike. The *cabañas* are very comfortable and well decorated. Every one of them has a small balcony, where you can sling a hammock or sit and contemplate the Belize River. A late-night walk trough the gardens, with flashlight in hand, will introduce you to the jungle's abundant insect life. The cries of the howler monkeys fill the air at dawn and dusk. In short, a real treat for nature lovers! Guests can also rent canoes or explore the nature interpretation trail.

RESTAURANTS

Belize City

Unfortunately, the biggest city in the country cannot be said to boast the best restaurants. The renowned chefs are generally found in the country's most touristy places, such as Ambergis Caye. On the other hand, there are a few good little lunchtime restaurants that are popular with workers and the few travellers who venture there. Like neighbourhood bistros, these restaurants tend to offer generous portions of good, simple ethnic fare for very little money.

Among these, **Dit's Restaurant** *($; King St., near Albert St.)* is a favourite with the local population for its low-priced regional fare. Particularly popular at lunchtime, Dit's offers rice & beans and a daily menu. Unpretentious, clean and friendly place with relaxed ambiance and good desserts.

 Right next door, **GG's Café & Patio** *($; 2-B King St., ☎02-74378)* is even more pleasant than its neighbour. This

BELIZE CITY & SURROUNDINGS

lovely house with arches has a very relaxed ambiance and a pleasant decor. The varied menu of regional fare offered here is as popular at lunch as it is at dinner. The restaurant serves the requisite rice & beans in hearty portions, but also prides itself on making the best burgers in town.

Judith's Pastries & Deli *($; 1 Queen St.)* prepares good sandwiches *(BZ$2.75)*, cakes and various pastries ideal for take-out or enjoying at the small counter or one of two tables. The modern and spotless bakery also offers a daily menu, generally featuring rice & beans.

A must for the quintessential rice & beans, served with pork or fish, the small **Macy's Café** *($; 18 Bishop St., ☎02-73419)* has a pleasant ambiance and a wide variety of local and international dishes. Those with a taste for adventure will want to try the local wild game, including armadillos.

The little **Pastry Hut** *($; 27 Eve Ave., ☎02-44731)* bakery serves traditional Mexican food. The place is very clean and located in the heart of downtown. In addition to various kinds of bread and pastries, you can sample the *salbutes*, fried corn tortillas garnished with chicken, tomatoes, lettuce and cheese; the *panadas*, or *empanadas*, corn-based "pastry" pockets stuffed with beans and fish; or the *garnaches*, tacos topped with melted cheese.

Porky's *($; 154 Haulover Rd., near the rotunda at the city's entrance)* barbecues a variety of grilled meats, including chicken, lamb and beef, in its gardens between 10am and 3pm. People come here for the food and simplicity, but other than that there is little to recommend the place. Local clientele.

As its name indicates, the **El Centro** restaurant *($-$$; Bishop St.)* is located right in the centre of town. If you want a break from regional cuisine, you've come to the right place: this small restaurant serves mainly pizza. Try the bacon-and-mushroom or the vegetarian one. Regional fare is also available. The restaurant has an air-conditioned dining room that is rather drab but very inviting when the sun reaches its zenith in hot weather.

Come nightfall, the restaurant of the **Chateau Caribbean Hotel** *($$-$$$; 6 Marine Parade, ☎02-30800, ≈02-30900)* is just the place for a daydream or a romantic tête-à-tête. Housed on the top floor of a large colonial residence, the restaurant's charm lies in its big open windows, which allow diners to enjoy the ocean breeze and the moon shimmering on the sea. Though the interior decor leaves something to be desired, the place serves a tempting selection of Chinese fried rice (vegetable, beef, pork or seafood fried rice), the house specialty. Also on the menu are an excellent filet mignon for meat-lover, and a variety of international dishes.

Finally, something other than rice & beans! The **Fort Street Restaurant** *($$-$$$; 4 Fort St., ☎02-30116)* has both a desirable location and a menu featuring nouvelle Californian and Brazilian cuisine. The Cajun shrimp or the lobster with garlic butter adds to the seaside atmosphere. Also on the menu are innovative vegetarian dishes and various salads. If you prefer dining at your hotel, the establishment delivers a simpler menu and lighter meals for lunch. Even the most unromantic types will succumb to the ambiance of the chandelier-adorned veranda.

The chic and trendy **Mango Seafood Bar & Grill** *($$$; 164 Newton Barrack Rd., ☎02-34201)* is one the city's better — and definitely pricier — restaurants. The intimate dining room has a Latin and tropical flair as well as an ocean view. You can sample an excellent selection of seafood in season, including scampi, lobster and grilled fish, as well as innovatively presented steaks or burgers. The menu changes on a regular basis.

The restaurant at the **Radisson Fort George Hotel** *($$$; 2 Marine Parade, ☎02-33333, ≈02-73820)* is another of the city's finer dining establishments. A meat lover's paradise, the place serves grilled meats, filet mignon and fresh lobster in a spacious air-conditioned dining room with a view of the city scape. There is also a private dock where you can enjoy a walk under the stars. Not only will you be able to savour the nighttime breeze while contemplating the soothing waves lapping the shore, but it will help you digest your lavish meal. The restaurant owners are justifiably proud of the establishment's reputation for impeccable and courteous service.

Crooked Tree Wildlife Sanctuary

The **Lakeview Restaurant** *($; by the lake; ☎02-12069)* is one of the most inexpensive eateries in the village. Housed in an old lakeside residence, the small restaurant offers a cafeteria-style menu featuring burgers, burritos and more. The place also has a bar and a pool table. The very friendly proprietors may soon offer double-occupancy guestrooms for about BZ$50.

The **Sam Tillit Hotel & Tours** *($; ☎02-12026)* has a good restaurant in a rustic ambiance. It is separate from the palm-roofed hotel, and is surrounded by hammocks. The menu features original regional cooking: breakfast and lunch for BZ$8, dinner for BZ$14.

 ENTERTAINMENT

Bars and Nightclubs

If you intend to venture out into the city come nightfall, make sure to take the necessary safety precautions.

Located in the southern part of the city right on the sea, **The Bellevue Hotel** *(5 Southern Foreshore)* has an upstairs bar that turns into a popular dance club on the weekend.

The Calypso *(Barrack Rd., ☎02-32670, ⌐02-32660)* bar at the Fiesta Inn Belize hotel is a good place to spend a pleasant night out.

Cultural Activities

The **Mexican Cultural Center** *(Barrack Rd. at Wilson St.)* organizes Mexican cultural activities once a month. The centre also holds concerts, painting exhibitions and folk dancing, and has a collection of pre-Columbian relics.

The **Bliss Institute** *(free admission; Mon to Fri 9am to noon and 2pm to 8pm, Sat 8:30am to noon)* houses the **National Arts Council**, which regularly organizes cultural activities and exhibitions.

 SHOPPING

There are relatively few souvenirs to buy in Belize City besides wooden sculptures of old ships or various kinds of fish. Expect to be approached by street vendors selling these craft items. You can also purchase them in the city's bigger hotels.

A good place to find new books on the culture and history of Belize, **Angelus Press** *(10 Queen St., ☎02-35777)* also carries a wealth of stationery items.

The Cayes

MEXICO

0   10   20km
0   6   12ml

N

Ucum
Juan Sarabla
Sacxán
Ramonal
Patchacan
Yo Chen
Cristo Rey
Louisville
Libertad
Buena Vista
San Estevan
Chetumal
Santa Elena
Chan Chen
Paraíso
Corozal
Cerros
Sarteneja
San Fernando
Chunox
Hill Bank
Progresso
Bahía de Chetumal
Rocky Point
Pta. Calentura
Pta. Jas

Orange Walk
Bird Sanctuary
Honey Camp
Carmelita
Rancho
Crooked Tree Wildlife Sanctuary
Maskall
Chicago
Santana
Altun Ha
Rockstone Pond
Cowhead Creek
Crooked Tree
Crooked Tree Wildlife Sanctuary
Washing Tree
Davis Bank
Salt Creek
Sand Hill
Flowers Bank
Bermudian Landing Community Baboon Sanctuary
Bermudian Landing
Burrell Boom
Lord's Bank
Ladyville
Flour Camp
Bird Sanctuary
Little Guana Caye Bird Sanctuary
Hol Chan Marine Reserve
Cangrejo Caye
Caye Caulker
Caye Chapel
Hick's Cayes
Porto Stuck
Long Caye
Rider Cayes
Montego Caye
Frenchman's Caye
St. George's Caye
Deer Caye
Ambergris Caye
San Pedro
Reef
Shipstern Nature Reserve
Pta. 2 de Abril
Cayo Chelam
Santa Cecilia
Xcalac

Hattieville
Highway
Freetown
Sibun
Western
Bird Sanctuary
Northern Lagoon
Belize City
Swallow Caye
Belize Harbour
Inner
Spanish Lookout Caye
Water Caye
English Caye Channel
Ramsey's Caye
Middle Long Caye
or
Main
Bluefield Range
Alligator Caye
Colson Cayes
Vincent's Lagoon
Northern Lagoon
Cross Cays Central Lagoon
Crayfish Range
Shag Cays
Pelican Caye
Deadman's Cayes
Big Caye Bokel
Crawl Caye
Tree Corner Caye
Pelican Caye
Grassy Caye Range
Turneffe Islands
Blackbird Caye
Calabash Caye
Half Moon Caye Natural Monument Reservation
Lighthouse Reef

Sibun
Forest
Reserve
Southern Lagoon
Gales Point
Channel
Mullins River
Melinda Forest Reserve
Middlesex
Pomona
Alta Vista
Melinda Forest Station
Sarawina
Dangriga
Southern Long Caye
Mosquito Caye
Fly Range
Sandfly Cayes
Columbus Caye
Cross Caye
Garbutt Caye
Barrier
Reef

© ULYSSES

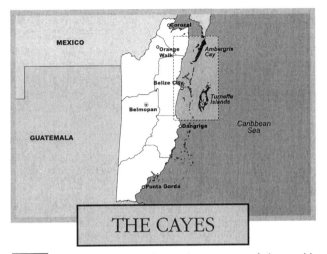

THE CAYES

T he world is slowly discovering a corner of the world that has been scuba divers' best-kept secret for a long time: the Belizean Cayes. It is easy to understand why some guard this pearl of the Caribbean jealously and prefer not to share it with others. The wealth of aquatic flora and fauna that inhabits the second-largest coral reef on the planet, the turquoise, crystalline waters of the Caribbean, the paradisaical little islands speckled with mangroves, palm trees, coconut trees, and bird colonies and the Cayes' friendly, warmhearted people are all well-worth treasuring.

Unlike other Caribbean islands, the Cayes have hardly been developed for tourism. Fortunately, there are still no tourist-mill resorts or seaside skyscrapers here. Instead, the islands offer a gamut of small, friendly establishments suited to every budget.

A favourite destination for travellers, sailors and adventurers from all over the world, **Caye Caulker** remains relatively unaffected by the wave of tourist development that has struck Belize in the last ten years. It is still the friendliest and most laidback island in the country, and its mestizo, black, and Garifuna residents are especially welcoming. Only a handful of automobiles can be seen on its sand streets. Most of the island's population walks around barefoot or in sandals, sending breezy greetings to one another along the way. Caye Caulker never fails to please contemplative visitors.

Ambergris Caye, the largest and most developed island in Belize, is just as appealing as the smaller Caye Caulker. **San Pedro**, Ambergris Caye's only village, has the same relaxed ambience and sandy streets, but with a few more cars, pedestrians, and, most noticeably, art galleries, cultural activities, restaurants, and hotels. Ambergris Caye is home to the best hotels and restaurants in the country, so it will please travellers who appreciate the luxuries of sumptuous dining and upscale accommodations. Ambergris Caye also has a vibrant nightlife and several beaches that are suitable for swimming.

Caye Caulker and Ambergris Caye are both excellent points of departure for excursions to Barrier Reef, where adventurers can see coral colonies and hundreds of species of tropical fish, sharks and rays. For this reason, Belize's two main islands are considered snorkelling and scuba-diving paradises, and the village of San Pedro is replete with dive shops and yachts for deep-sea fishing and diving outings.

 FINDING YOUR WAY AROUND

Caye Caulker

By Plane

Planes to San Pedro will stop over on Caye Caulker upon request when you purchase your ticket.

By Boat

There is a rapid ferry service from Caye Caulker to Belize City and San Pedro.

The offices of the **Caye Caulker Water Taxi Association** *(Front St., ☎02-22992)* are at the foot of the main dock, at the corner of Front Street. It is recommended to make reservations one day in advance for all departures, but especially for those on weekends, when many mainland residents use the service to go to the islands. It is not uncommon for travellers without reservations to have to wait a few hours for a seat on the ferry.

To Belize City: every day at 6:45am, 8am, 10am and 3pm; duration: 40 minutes; fare: BZ$15.

To San Pedro: departure at 10am; duration: 30 minutes; fare: BZ$10.

To St. George's Caye: Take the boat from Belize City to Caye Caulker. Once there, call the Caye Caulker Water Taxi Association *(BZ$20)*.

As there is only one departure a day for San Pedro, an alternative is to go to the Back Pier *(Back St.)*, on the west side of the island, and take one of the **Triple J** *(☎02-33464)* boats, which stop if there are people waiting on the dock. It is also possible to board boats to Belize City from here. The Triple J boats pass by at about 10:30am and 1:30pm.

The only way to visit the **Turneffe Islands** is to join a diving excursion organized by a hotel or a tour agency (see p 115, 123).

On Foot

There is no better way to discover the island than to use one's own two feet! After disembarking at the dock, head to Front Street, Caye Caulker's main street. Most of the hotels and restaurants listed in this chapter are located here, and it is never more than a 10-minute walk to any of the island's attractions.

Ambergris Caye

By Plane

San Pedro's little airport, which is actually just a landing strip with a few kiosks, is very close to the centre of the village.

Tropic Air *(☎02-62012; tropicair@btl.net)*: to **Belize City**, departures every hour; duration: 20 minutes; fare: BZ$60.

Maya Airways and **Island Air** *(☎02-62435)* merged in 1997. They have several flights daily to Belize City, for about the same fare as Tropic Air.

By Boat

Triple J has one departure daily for Caye Caulker *(BZ$15)* and Belize City *(BZ$25)*. Departure from San Pedro at 3pm.

By Taxi

There are usually taxis parked at the airport exit. Visitors can also contact **Mash Taxi** *(Barrier Reef Dr., ☎02-62038)*, which has an office in the centre of San Pedro.

Electric Cart Rental

Palo's Ez-Go Rental *(at the northern end of Barrier Reef Dr., ☎02-63542)* is the best place to rent golf carts: BZ$20 per hour, BZ$50 per half-day (3 hours), BZ$120 per day (24 hours), BZ$300 for 3 days, BZ$500 per week. The rental agency is at the northern end of Barrier Reef Drive, near the cemetery.

Ramon's Wheel Rentals is located across from the airport and offers basically the same rates as Palo's .

Carts can also be rented right at the airport. The **Rental Center** *(☎02-63188)* offers hourly, daily and weekly rates. However, these carts are generally not in very good condition.

On Foot

San Pedro is larger than Caye Caulker, so electric carts are more popular here. However, unless you are staying in a hotel either end of the island, it is possible to get anywhere on foot in under 15 minutes.

PRACTICAL INFORMATION

Caye Caulker

Tourist Information

Tina and Ilna Auxillou are the friendly agents at **Dolphin Bay Travel** *(Front St., north of the dock, ☎02-22214)*. They have the best tips for excursions in the area and always take the time to answer all your questions. Their offices are hard to miss, located just north of the dock on Front Street. These women can inform you about all of the excursions possible on the island, and sell tickets for the same prices you would pay the operators directly. They can even negotiate better rates for groups.

Internet

Island Girl Productions *(9am to noon and 4pm to 7pm; Front St., north of the dock, ☎02-22309; islandgirl@btl.net)* offers e-mail service *(BZ$1 per 2 min use)* and publishes the local biweekly paper, the *Village Voice*, founded in 1997. In addition to island news and gossip, the paper includes useful information for visitors.

Exchange Office

Atlantic Bank *(Mon to Fri 8am to 2pm, Sat 8:30 to noon; Middle St.)* is the best place to exchange currency and to obtain credit card advances.

Post Office

The **Post Office** *(Mon to Thu 8am to noon and 1pm to 5pm, Fri 1pm to 5pm)* is in the southern half of Back Street.

Telephone

The offices of **BTL**, which provides fax and international telephone services, are on Front Street near the dock.

Police

The tiny **Police Station** is on Front Street, near the basketball court.

Hospital

The **Caye Caulker Health Center** *(Mon to Fri 8am to 5pm; Front St., ☎02-22166)* is south of the soccer field.

Ambergris Caye

Tourist Information

Travelling Tours *(across from the airport exit)*, owned by Kevin Gonzales, head of the Belize Tourist Board, is located near the airport. The staff is obliging.

Travellers on limited budgets can make enquiries at **Ruby's Hotel** (see p 127) on Front Street.

Exchange Office

Money can be exchanged at most of the hotels in San Pedro. For currency exchange and credit card advances, head to the **Atlantic Bank** *(Barrier Reef Dr., ☎02-62195)*.

Telephone

The **BTL** office is on Middle Street.

Police

The **Police Station** is on Barrier Reef Drive, near the Atlantic Bank.

Hospital

San Pedro Clinic (☎02-62073) is near the airport.

 EXPLORING

Caye Caulker ★★★

Caye Caulker, situated 34 kilometres northeast of Belize City and 18 kilometres south of Ambergris Caye, is the second-largest island in the Belizean archipelago, even though it is barely seven-kilometres long and the village itself only covers two kilometres. All of the island's attractions can be easily reached on foot. Caye Caulker was once just a small fishing community, whose population was mostly of mestizo origin. In the middle of the 19th century, Mexicans, fleeing the civil war that was raging in the Yucatán Peninsula, came to settle on this desert island. Over the years, the original community grew into a village.

In the 1960s, international tourists began to discover this tranquil paradise. Although Caye Caulker has recently experienced considerable development, especially since the late 1980s, the village is still relatively unaffected by the trend toward mass tourism and is a great place for travellers in search of affordable prices and a relaxed atmosphere. Fishermen are becoming less numerous as they are increasingly giving up their trade to become hotel operators, restaurateurs and reef guides, so only those who knew the little island 20 years ago can attest to the extent of its metamorphosis. One significant result of this process is that the Caye's population has more than doubled in the last 10 years and is now at over 1,000, including many foreigners who have settled here to open hotels and restaurants.

Front Street, the main street, runs through the village. Most shops, hotels, and restaurants are on this street. At its northern end, on the tip of Caye Caulker, is the only public beach that is suitable for swimming. Known as "The Split", this spot marks the division of the island by Hurricane Hattie in 1961. A walkway was heavily damaged in 1996, making access quite difficult, but the water is deep enough for excellent swimming. In all other places, the sea around the island is too shallow for swimming.

Caye Caulker's appeal really lies in its other assets. The little village, with its wood houses and sandy streets, is perfect for taking a stroll or simply to unwind, but few visitors actually spend all day on the island. Most take advantage of their stay here to discover the Barrier Reef on one of the many scuba-diving and snorkelling expeditions that leave from Caye Caulker.

When the sun is at its peak and the tourists are at sea, Caye Caulker's residents emerge. Children play on the basketball court in the middle of the village, fishermen rest in the shade of coconut trees, and hotel and restaurant employees take time out to socialize. Then, in the late afternoon, travellers and residents reunite to enjoy the rhythmic sounds of Caribbean music... and the party begins!

Ambergris Caye ★★

Ambergris Caye, the largest island in Belize, is close to 40-kilometres long, and all evidence suggests that it was inhabited by the Maya as early as 200 BC. Since 1989, archeologists have been studying the "Marco Gonzalez" site, Mayan ruins found in a mangrove on the southeastern tip of the caye. The little enclave definitely prospered, reaching its apex between AD 1150 and 1300. Although it was abandoned by its inhabitants, a few Mayan families still lived on the island when the Spanish arrived in the 16th century.

Pirates and British buccaneers used the island as a hideout in the 17th century. (Who knows – perhaps there is some buried treasure awaiting discovery here!) Colonization of Ambergris Caye, like Caye Caulker, began in the middle of the 19th

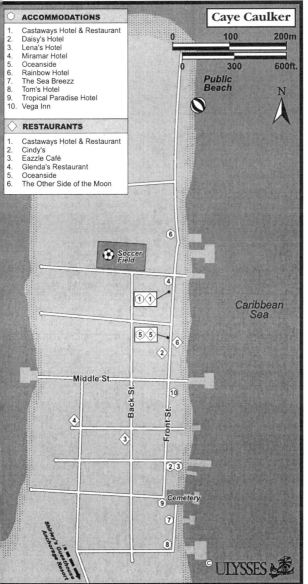

Caye Caulker

○ **ACCOMMODATIONS**

1. Castaways Hotel & Restaurant
2. Daisy's Hotel
3. Lena's Hotel
4. Miramar Hotel
5. Oceanside
6. Rainbow Hotel
7. The Sea Breezz
8. Tom's Hotel
9. Tropical Paradise Hotel
10. Vega Inn

◇ **RESTAURANTS**

1. Castaways Hotel & Restaurant
2. Cindy's
3. Eazzle Café
4. Glenda's Restaurant
5. Oceanside
6. The Other Side of the Moon

Public Beach

Caribbean Sea

Soccer Field

Middle St.

Back St.

Front St.

Cemetery

Shirley's Guesthouse Anchorage Resort

© ULYSSES

century during the civil war in the Yucatán Peninsula, when several mestizo families came to settle here.

Ambergris Caye is named after a grey, waxy substance that comes from the intestines of the sperm whale. The Spanish arrived on the island at a time when many whales spawned here, leaving behind this strange, viscous substance. The word *ambergris* is a combination of the words "amber" and *gris*, Spanish for "grey".

San Pedro is the only hamlet on the island. Once a fishing village, it has become the most popular destination for tourists in Belize, and has managed to accommodate them while still maintaining a manageable size. San Pedro has in fact remained a village of sand streets that are travelled by only the occasional car. The main street, Barrier Reef Drive, runs along the seaside. Parallel to it is Pescador Drive, which is also lined with restaurants and shops, most of which are more affordable than those on Barrier Reef Drive. These two arteries are linked by many perpendicular streets, the busiest of which is Middle Street, the geographic centre of San Pedro.

Barrier Reef Drive is especially lively at dusk. At Fido's Court-yard & Pier, a small interior court is surrounded by restaurants and an art gallery. Because of its waterfront location, Barrier Reef Drive is perfect for long walks.

Like the other Belizean islands, Ambergris Caye does not have very beautiful beaches. However, the beach at Ramon's Village (see p 130) is open to the public and appropriate for swimming, as is the beach at the Banyan Bays hotel (see p 131) on the southeastern part of the island.

The southeastern tip of Ambergris Caye, near the Mayan "Marco González" site, is protected by the **Hol Chan Marine Reserve**, which is located six kilometres from San Pedro and is the destination of many excursions. The reserve covers an area of eight square kilometres that begins at the *quebrada*, a small natural canal between the Barrier Reef and Ambergris Caye.

The reserve protects many species of mangrove and the coral walls that form the canal. It is prohibited to fish, touch the coral, or pick any plants in the reserve. This is an excellent spot for snorkelling and scuba diving.

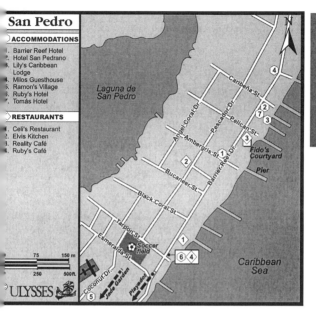

San Pedro

ACCOMMODATIONS

1. Barrier Reef Hotel
2. Hotel San Pedrano
3. Lily's Caribbean Lodge
4. Milos Guesthouse
5. Ramon's Village
6. Ruby's Hotel
7. Tomás Hotel

RESTAURANTS

1. Celi's Restaurant
2. Elvis Kitchen
3. Reality Café
4. Ruby's Café

Laguna de San Pedro

Caribeña St.

Pescador Dr.

Pelican St.

Angel Corial Dr.

Ambergris St.

Barrier Reef Dr.

Fido's Courtyard

Bucaneer St.

Pier

Black Coral St.

Tarpon St.

Esmeralda St.

Soccer field

Caribbean Sea

Coconut Dr.

Jade Garden

Playadot

75   150 m

250   500 ft.

ULYSSES

A Multitude of Little Islands

Aside from the two main islands described in this chapter and **Tobacco Caye** (see p 189) and **Southwater Caye** (see p 189) in the southern part of the country, only a few small islands in the Belizean archipelago offer services for tourists, and access to them is quite limited. Travellers must usually contact the islands' owners to visit them.

Caye Chapel

This island, the closest to Caye Caulker, is five kilometres long and two kilometres wide. It has a little landing strip, and both Maya Airways and Tropic Air can stop over here during flights between Belize City and San Pedro (see p 114), if requested to do so at the time of ticket purchase. Triple J ferries (see p 113) and the Caye Caulker Water Taxi Association (see p 112) also provide transportation to the island.

Spanish Lookout Caye

Located 16 kilometres southwest of Belize City, this island of about 100 hectares is owned by the Spanish Bay Resort (see p 131).

St. George's Caye

About 15 kilometres from Belize City, this island is central to the nation's history because it was the site of the last battle between the British and the Spanish (see p 36). Inhabited by the English from the middle of the 18th century, it became the scene of this legendary battle in 1798. The island was hard-hit by Hurricane Hattie in 1961, so the only remnants of this period are a small cemetery and a windmill.

Turneffe Islands

The Turneffe Islands are a series of little islands about 40 kilometres from Belize City, which are mainly visited by fishers and divers.

Lighthouse Reef

This open-sea reef has become popular because of the **Blue Hole**, a spot that is legendary with divers from all over the world and has been explored by Jacques Cousteau himself. It consists of a series of deep underwater caves on multiple levels.

OUTDOOR ACTIVITIES

THE CAYES

Excursions

Caye Caulker's tour agency, **Dolphin Bay Travel** *(Front St., north of the dock,* ☎*02-22214)* can book you on all excursions. It offers the same rates visitors pay when buying tickets directly from the tour operators.

My favourite guide is **Johnny**, who offers snorkelling outings to the various marine parks in the area. This young Rastafarian native of the island calmly steers a sailboat on which he offers passengers a unique sea experience. It is nice to see other groups arrive at the main diving spots amid the deafening noise of motorboats while you sail peacefully on a silent craft, the quiet broken only by the sound of the wind slapping the sails and the hull cutting through the waves. Of course the timeless voice of Bob Marley rises from the hold... Johnny knows the best spots to see grey sharks and other aquatic plants and animals. Aware of the area's fragile ecological balance, he advises passengers on how to avoid damaging the coral. Very friendly. A unique experience for the open minded...

The best-known guide is **Ras Creek**, who has been leading outings on his motorboat for ages. An excellent guide with a vast knowledge of the region.

The best excursions for the observation of manatees are organized by **Chocolate** *(BZ$55 for the whole day, snorkelling equipment included)*.

Hiking

Daniel Núñez is one of the best guides on Ambergris Caye. He leads expeditions to Lamanaí and Altun Ha from San Pedro, and also offers an excellent nature hike that he designed himself. Very highly recommended. Enquire about his services at your hotel.

Snorkelling

Alfonso Graniel (☎02-62584) is the best guide on Ambergris Caye for sea outings, especially for snorkelling. Enquire about his services at your hotel's reception desk.

Ruby's Hotel (see p 127) rents snorkelling equipment.

 Scuba Diving

Amigos Del Mar Dive Shop (☎02-62706, ⊶02-62648): equipment, excursions, PADI certification courses.

Adventure in Water Sports *(Barrier Reef Dr., corner of Black Coral St.,* ☎02-63706, ⊶02-63707, *advwtrspts@btl.net)*: equipment, excursions, PADI certification courses.

The Dive Shop *(Banyan Bay Hotel,* ☎02-62821*)* offers a variety of scuba-diving and snorkelling excursions.

 Fishing

Most hotels offer fishing trips, either on the high seas or in the coral banks *(BZ$200 for a half-day, BZ$300 per day)*. Night fishing *(BZ$300)* for shark, tarpon and other catches is also possible.

The **Amigos Del Mar Dive Shop** *(7:30am to 6:30pm; Ambergris Caye,* ☎02-62706, ⊶02-62648*)* and **The Dive Shop** *(Banyan Bay Hotel,* ☎02-62821*)* are two outfitters that organize this type of excursion.

 Bird-Watching

Many boating outings visit tiny islands whose only inhabitants are birds. **The Dive Shop** *(Banyan Bay Hotel,* ☎02-62821*)* organizes visits to two ornithological reserves. The price is BZ$50 per person, with a minimum of four people.

ACCOMMODATIONS

Caye Caulker

The most popular establishment with backpackers is the **Miramar Hotel** *(BZ$20; ⊗; Front St.).* This old wooden house has three decent rooms whose main perk is that they are among the least expensive on the island. The upstairs terrace is a favourite meeting place for the globetrotting clientele, and has a beautiful view of the sea. Often full.

Next door, the **Castaways Hotel & Restaurant** *(BZ$22; ⊗; Front St., ☎02-22294)* is one of the most affordable establishments on Caye Caulker. The old wooden house is right in the middle of the village and offers eight relatively comfortable, clean and simple rooms. There is a restaurant on the ground floor.

The famous restaurant-bar **Oceanside** *(BZ$25; Front St.)* (see p 133) has seven upstairs rooms. These are decent and clean, but quite noisy because of the hubbub in the ground-floor bar. If you plan to party during your stay, this is the spot for you!

Tom's Hotel *(BZ$25-BZ$60; ⊗; ☎02-22102)* offers *cabañas* on the beach *(BZ$60)* and affordable conventional rooms *(BZ$25).* Very popular with backpackers who enjoy lounging on the premises, especially on the veranda. A good place to meet fellow travellers. Large shared washrooms.

Daisy's Hotel *(BZ$28; pb, ⊗; Front St., ☎02-22123)* offers about 15 rooms in a typical house. These are large and clean and some have private washrooms. Friendly and generally helpful service.

The two large wooden houses that comprise **Lena's Hotel** *(BZ$30-$53; pb, ⊗; ☎02-22106)* are located right on the seashore, and have many moderately priced rooms with either shared *(BZ$30)* or private *(BZ$53)* washrooms. Although the houses seem a bit unkempt, the rooms are comfortable. There are large patios, a small sand beach, and many palm trees. This

---

Ulysses' Favourites

Accommodations

For wandering spirits: **Ruby's Hotel** (see p 127)
For quality amenities: **Caribbean Villas Hotel** (see p 130)

Restaurants

For fajitas and hot, hot nights: **Oceanside** (see p 133)
For big breakfasts: **Reality Café** (see p 134)
For filet mignon and crab: **Playador Grill** (see p 135)

---

establishment is located on the southern part of the island, in front of the fishing docks. The service is a bit erratic.

The **Vega Inn** *(BZ$50-$120; pb, ⊗; ☎02-22142, ⊷02-22269)* is made up of two buildings. The first is a wooden house with inexpensive upstairs rooms *(BZ$50)*. The concrete building next door has more comfortable rooms with private bathrooms *(BZ$120)*. You can also camp on the grounds *(BZ$15 per person)*. Snorkelling gear can be rented here and some water sports are possible.

The Sea Breezz *(BZ$70; hw, pb, ⊗; ☎02-22176)* is an excellent, charming little hotel. The rooms are laid out in a concrete house on the sea, surrounded by pretty gardens. Situated at the southern end of Front Street near the Tropical Paradise Hotel, it offers the relative tranquillity of this part of the island. Comfortable, practical, well-kept rooms. Good value.

In the centre of Caye Caulker, the **Rainbow Hotel** *(BZ$70-$80; ≡, pb, hw, tv; Front St., ☎02-22123, ⊷02-22172)* offers air-conditioned rooms with televisions. The rooms in this blue concrete building, one of the few of this colour on the island, are pleasant, practical and comfortable, and have private bathrooms. Common terraces on the ground floor and upstairs. The place is very clean and has daily housekeeping. Ocean view. For a worry-free stay.

n the same price category, **Shirley's Guesthouse** *(BZ$80; pb, ; on the shore south of the village, ☎02-22145, ≈02-22264)* rents small rooms in bungalows, which are attractively decorated with exotic-wood floors. They are not, however, the best value for the price in the area. A quiet spot.

The **Tropical Paradise hotel** *(BZ$80-$90; ⊗, pb, hw; southern end of Front St., ☎02-22124, ≈02-22225)* is a rather charming little vacation complex. It offers air-conditioned *cabañas* with televisions and conventional rooms facing the sea. Comfortable and clean. Appealing atmosphere. One of the best bets on the southern part of the island.

Also on the southern part of the island, not far from the landing strip, the **Anchorage Resort** *(BZ$130; ⊗, pb, hw; ☎/≈02-22304; tourism@cayecaulker.org.bz)* rents *cabañas* and rooms in concrete buildings. Comfortable, spacious rooms, and good service. There is a private beach that is appropriate for swimming and has hammocks shaded by coconut trees. You can also participate in a variety of outdoor activities, including windsurfing and excursions to Barrier Reef.

Ambergris Caye

Hotel del Río *(BZ$12-$170; less than 1 km from the village, ☎02-62286)* is located near a beach on the northern part of the island, in the Boca del Río Area. Quieter and less touristy than the rest of the island, this spot is perfect for meeting local residents. Catering to backpackers, the establishment has a room with bunk beds for BZ$12 per person, as well as two *cabañas* with palm-thatched roofs. The largest *cabañas* cost BZ$160 and the others rent for BZ$120; up to three people can stay in a *cabaña*. There are also four air-conditioned double rooms that cost BZ$170. Reduced rates in the off-season. The establishment does not have a restaurant, but does offer continental breakfast. Linda, the owner, is from Louisiana.

Very popular with backpackers, **Ruby's Hotel** *(BZ$26.75-$53.50; pb, ⊗, hw; Barrier Reef Dr., ☎02-62063, ≈02-62434; rubys@btl.net)* is located at the edge of the beach right in downtown San Pedro. The best of the large clean rooms are on the third floor of the wooden house. The service is completely satisfactory, the welcome is warm and, in general, this establishment offers the best value in this price category. There is also a pleasant terrace. A classic.

Above the grocery of the same name in the northern half of Barrier Reef Drive, **Milos Guesthouse** *(BZ$27; ⊗, hw; Barrier Reef Dr., ☎02-62033, 02-62196)* is located across from the cemetery. Nineteen clean rooms face the sea and offer basic comfort. A good option for the price. Close to all of the village activities; friendly staff.

A five-minute walk south of the village centre is a yellow wooden building with a loud blue roof that is hard to miss. The **Hideaway Sports Lodge** *(BZ$40-$90; pb, ⊗, ≡, ≈; Coconut Dr., ☎02-62141)* is an excellent, affordable option on this part of the island, especially for groups sharing a room. In fact, each of the large rooms here can easily accommodate four to six people. You can enjoy the pleasant swimming pool and air conditioning for the same rates charged by hotels that do not offer these amenities, not to mention the tranquil atmosphere and the very inviting dining room equipped with a long bar. Ralf, the establishment's friendly new German owner oversees the service himself. A living room furnished with cable television and a library completes the list of amenities.

The colourful, Spanish-speaking owner of the **Tomás Hotel** *(BZ$50-$70; ⊗, pb, ≡; Barrier Reef Dr., ☎02-62061)* offers excellent rooms and good value for the price. The rooms, some of which are air-conditioned, are equipped with one or two double beds and sometimes with an additional single bed. Very clean and well kept.

Hotel San Pedrano *(BZ$70; pb, ⊗; BZ$90 with ≡; Barrier Reef Dr., corner Caribeña St., ☎02-62054)* offers good value for the money. The clean, well-kept rooms all have private bathrooms. Located right in the centre of San Pedro.

Facing the sea, **Lily's Caribbean Lodge** *(BZ$70; ≡, pb, hw, ⊗; Caribeña St., ☎02-62059)* has about 10 comfortable, practical, air-conditioned rooms. Unpretentious. The rooms are airy, especially the upstairs ones, which offer a view of the sea.

The **Barrier Reef Hotel** *(BZ$100-$140; ≡, pb, ≈, ℜ; Barrier Reef Dr., ☎02-62075 or 02-62049, ≠02-62719;*

barrierreef@btl.net) is in an old Victorian house that has been converted into an inn, though most of the rooms are in an adjacent modern building. The place has all of the amenities, including air conditioning and a small pool behind the hotel. Friendly, and right in the centre of San Pedro.

The small, attractive **Changes in Latitude Bed & Breakfast Inn** *(BZ$100-$160 bkfst incl.; ≡, ⊗, pb, hw; south of the airport on the waterfront, ☎/⊷02-62986; latitudes@btl.net)* belongs to a Canadian woman named Lori Reed. This modern house has been converted into an inn with very small but practical rooms. Well-decorated, they have all of the amenities despite the limited space. Guests will feel right at home in the common room. Although it is set in a quiet area, this establishment is within easy walking distance of San Pedro's centre. There is access to the Yacht Club and its beach, and all sorts of equipment for water sports can be rented.

The very lively **Playador Hotel** *(BZ$105-$400; ≡, ⊗, pb)* offers comfortable lodgings in an atmosphere that often turns into a real party! Set on a pretty stretch of the San Pedro beach with many hammocks and lounge chairs, this establishment also has an excellent restaurant (see p 135) and a bar that is quite popular in the late afternoon. The rooms are especially comfortable for the price and some are even equipped with small refrigerators, microwave ovens and air conditioning. Modern condo-style apartments can also be rented. In front of the hotel there is a dock from which diving excursions leave. The Canadian hosts are welcoming and helpful.

The **Caribe Island Resort** *(BZ$200-$230 and BZ$600-$800; ≡, pb, ⊗, tv, K; south of the airport on the waterfront, ☎02-63233, from the US ☎800-508-5620, ⊷02-63399; ccaribe@btl.net; www.belize.com/chateaucaribe.html)* is one of the luxury establishments on the island. It offers large, American-style condominiums, which are decorated with Caribbean accents, and can accommodate two to nine guests, depending on the layout. Each is equipped with a private veranda and a kitchenette. There is a superb swimming pool on the premises and you can bicycle, kayak and sail free of charge. There is a volleyball court on the beach and a private dock from which scuba-diving and snorkelling excursions depart. On Sundays there are barbecues and concerts on the beach.

Victoria's House *(BZ$200-$1,000; pb, hw, ℜ, ⊛, ≡, ≈, K; south of the airport on the waterfront, ☎02-62067, from the US ☎800-247-5129, ⊷02-62429; victoria@bze.com)* has a whole range of accommodation options, from the conventional room to the luxury three-bedroom villa *(BZ$1,000)*. Set on a magnificent beach, Victoria House offers unparalleled service and an atmosphere that is perfect for a carefree vacation. The complex is a charming architectural ensemble, and the houses are decorated with woodwork and topped by eye-catching red roofs. The apartments are equipped with cable television, small refrigerators, and kitchenettes. Bicycles and a shuttle service to San Pedro are available to guests free of charge. There is also a full-board option.

🌴 Attention to detail makes the **Caribbean Villas Hotel** *(BZ$250-$400; hw, pb, ≡, K, ⊛; south of the airport on the waterfront, ☎02-62715, ⊷02-62885; c-v-hotel@btl.net; www.Ambergriscaye.com/caribbeanvillas)* one of the best establishments in the country. It offers personalized service and a family atmosphere in a sumptuous setting. Its friendly and very environmentally conscious owners, Will and Susan Lala, have kept part of the grounds in its natural state, creating a perfect little grove in which to observe the local flora. There is a tower for bird-watching; almost 200 species have been sighted here. They have also laid out an artificial reef that is home to many species of fish right in front of the hotel, so guests can snorkel from the beach. The owners offer the best guided tours and sea excursions in the area – and for the best prices, since they do not charge any commission. For example, if an excursion normally costs BZ$150, it will only cost guests of the Caribbean Villas Hotel BZ$120. The hotel's apartments and suites are subdued and comfortable, and have a Mediterranean atmosphere. Guests never want to leave this elegant yet practical establishment. The hotel is a 15-minute walk from San Pedro. Bicycles are available to guests free of charge. Reservations are recommended, since this spot is very popular year-round.

The large complex of *cabañas* at **Ramon's Village** *(BZ$260 and up; ☎02-62071, ⊷02-62214)* offers a great variety of rooms. About 50 wooden *cabañas* with palm-thatched roofs are spread about a seaside palm tree grove surrounding the main building. The "village" includes a pretty pool and a long beach that is ppropriate for swimming. Very popular. Many excursions are possible.

Among the establishments that offer condo rental, **The Palms** *(BZ$310 one bedroom, BZ$400 two bedrooms; ≡, pb, ≈; south of the airport on the waterfront, ☎02-63322, ≈02-63601; palms@btl.net)* must be seen to be believed! Its luxury beach-front apartments are attractively decorated and inviting, perfect for lounging and relaxation. Each waterfront condo has its own private terrace. All of the 12 apartments have one or two large bedrooms with double beds. Pleasant pool and well-tended tropical gardens. Long dock. Daily housekeeping.

Each of the modern apartments at **The Villas of Banyan Bay** *(BZ$350; hw, pb, K, ⊛; south of the airport on the waterfront, ☎02-63739, ≈02-62766; banyanbay@btl.net)* offers two bedrooms, a fully equipped kitchen, a living room, and a veranda. A superb swimming pool and a long beach are located on the grounds. The common room is air conditioned and the restaurant is open to hotel guests only. Peaceful and pleasant, this complex is perfect for a carefree vacation in a friendly environment. **The Dive Shop** (see p 124) organizes a variety of sea excursions.

Caye Chapel

The **Pyramid Island Resort** *(BZ$225; ☎02-44409, ≈02-32405)*, which owns the island, is the only hotel on Caye Chapel. The resort was beginning to show its age, so renovations have been undertaken to improve it. There is a dive shop on the premises.

Spanish Lookout Caye

Situated 16 kilometres southeast of Belize City, this island of about 100 hectares belongs to the **Spanish Bay Resort** *(BZ$400 fb; ☎02-72725, ≈02-72797)*, which offers a series of very well-kept, comfortable *cabañas*. A favourite of divers.

St. George's Caye

St. George's Lodge *(BZ$500 and up per pers. fb; diving equipment; ☎02-44190, ⌐02-30461)* offers conventional rooms and *cabañas*. Scuba divers meet up here during their annual descent on the world's reefs.

Lighthouse Reef

Lighthouse Reef Resort *(BZ$2,500 and up per person, per week; ☎800-423-3114).*

 RESTAURANTS

Caye Caulker

Near **Back Pier** *(Back St.)*, on the island's west side, cases of beer can be bought directly from the distributor for the lowest prices – BZ$49 plus a BZ$6.80 deposit for 24 bottles. A relaxing way to spend a few days on the island!

On the southern part of Front Street, the **Eazzle Café** *($)* offers a large terrace under a palm-thatched roof. During the day, the café serves cakes, fudge, chocolate and nut fondants, as well as coffee. This is the ideal spot for an afternoon beer and, come nightfall, for dancing (see p 135).

The Little Kitchen *($; Front St., across from the Vegas Inn)* offers very tasty, traditional meals at affordable prices. Rice and beans with fish or seafood is a staple, and there is also a daily special. The menu features vegetarian and Mexican dishes, including the burritos that are so popular with backpackers. The small restaurant is located in a typical wooden house. Inside, there are picnic tables on a sandy floor. Friendly welcome, and an appealing, unpretentious atmosphere.

The popular **Glenda's Restaurant** *($-$$; Back St., ☎02-22148)* serves a hearty breakfast of eggs, toast and rolls starting at 'am. At noon, it has a good selection of vegetarian and Mexican dishes, including burritos served in generous portions. The establishment is located on Back Street (much less touristy than Front Street) in a charming blue house built on stilts – you can't miss it.

The Other Side of the Moon *($-$$; Front St., ☎02-22930)* is the perfect place to watch the moon rising over the sea, especially when it is a full moon. This restaurant has a good selection of burgers and fries, and also prepares barbecued chicken served with potatoes and salad. It has a superb terrace under the palm trees on the waterfront. The restaurant is right in the heart of Caye Caulker. Good atmosphere at dusk and after dark.

Right in the centre of Caye Caulker, **Castaways Hotel & Restaurant** *($$ Front St., ☎02-22294)* has a mixed menu of American, Chinese and Italian dishes. Thai chicken and lasagna get top billing. Since the portions are very generous, you can also order half-portions or share a full portion with a friend. The Pasta Supreme, pasta in cream sauce topped with two big pieces of lobster, is worth trying. Popular, decent atmosphere. The hotel is located upstairs (see p 125).

Coffee and books go together at **Cindy's** *($$; Front St., across from the basketball court, ☎02-22093)*. With its seaside terrace, this little restaurant is perfect for a healthy breakfast of yogurt, muesli and fruit, or bagels and cream cheese, all of t washed down by a glass of the best café au lait in the area. The portions are relatively small, and the prices slightly high, but what you get is excellent. Cindy, who is originally from British Columbia (Canada), also has a small library that contains donations from travellers who have passed through her café. Books may be borrowed or traded; the collection includes a number of literary classics and reference books. Always packed between 7:30am and 11:30am.

The restaurant-bar **Oceanside** *($$; Front St.)* offers an extremely varied menu in a unique ambiance. Burritos are the house specialty and they are served in large portions. The menu also includes hamburgers and sandwiches. Very lively as of at 9pm, when the karioke sessions begin (see p 135). A meeting place for locals and travellers from every continent!

Ambergris Caye

Cases of beer may be purchased directly from the distributor **Belikin's Distribution** (☎02-62142), and delivered to your hotel or apartment for BZ$50 for 24 beers.

Tasty cakes and pastries can be found at **Ruby's Café** *(Barrier Reef Dr.)*, next door to the hotel of the same name.

Located on the waterfront, **Celi's Restaurant** *($; Front St.,* ☎02-62014) hosts a beach barbecue every Wednesday. Excellent value and pleasant atmosphere all week long. Seafood and the excellent Cheese Stuffed Grouper in Beer Batter are also served. The breakfast menu is offers a lot of variety.

Elvis Kitchen *($$; closed Sun; 14 Pescador Dr.,* ☎02-62176, ☎02-63056) is a classic American-style hamburger joint, although it also has a fish and seafood menu. It is popular for its fruit *licuados*, made with water or milk. Pleasant atmosphere and friendly table service. There is live music from 6:30pm to 10pm on Thursdays and Saturdays.

With a view of the sea, the **Reality Café** *($$; Front St.)*, located in Fido's Courtyard, is a must. It serves delicious espressos and cappuccinos, as well as breakfasts of yogurt, muesli and fruit, or the heartier eggs and toast. Try "The Border": two tortillas, beans, scrambled eggs, cheese and salad. The portions are very generous, so that one dish is often enough for two people. Super fruit juices and banana, mango, or cantaloupe *licuados* are available. A large selection of sandwiches to choose from at lunch. Very good ambience.

The picturesque **Reef Restaurant** *($$; 11am to 2pm and 5:30pm to 10pm; Block 9 Pescador Dr.,* ☎02-63213) is an excellent seafood restaurant that is very popular with locals (who are fish and seafood connoisseurs!). The world of fishing is the theme of the interior decor, and the restaurant has a sand floor. Pleasant atmosphere in the evening. Fresh fish, lobster, and shrimp are prepared with all kinds of sauces. The Reef offers an affordable lunch menu: a fish dish with rice and beans for BZ$35. Since the portions are large, it is not unusual for diners to share one order, especially at lunch.

The **Jade Garden Restaurant** *($$$; every day 11am to 2pm and 6pm to 10pm; Coconut Dr., ☎02-62126 or 02-62506)* serves the best Cantonese cuisine in Belize. The won ton soup is excellent. Various fried rice and chow mein dishes are also served, as well as vegetarian dishes, seafood and steak. A San Pedro classic.

 Thanks to its new chef, the **Playador Grill** *($$$; south of San Pedro, ☎02-63855)* is now an absolute must in San Pedro. The restaurant of the Playador Hotel has a superb seaside terrace furnished with wicker chairs. It offers a wide variety of seafood, and the crab dishes are veritable works of art! The most gourmand diners order the combination crab and filet mignon dish. Every meal is accompanied by fruit. Once a week, *pibil*, a Mayan-inspired barbecue, is featured: stones are heated in an exotic-wood fire in a sand-dug pit; pork is then cooked underground for six hours with orange juice and pineapple slices. A true delight!

ENTERTAINMENT

Caye Caulker

If dancing under the stars is your style, **Eazzle Café** *(Front St.)* is the place for you. This café-bar in the southern half of Front Street has a palm roof and a large open-air terrace. Tropical music. A good place for cake in the daytime (see p 132).

The best parties are organized at the **Oceanside** *(Front St.)* restaurant-bar. Every night at 9pm, locals display their karioke talents to each other. The Oceanside also features a very fun dance floor and jukebox that plays tropical and international music. On Settlement Day, which commemorates the arrival of the first Garifunas, *punta* (the traditional dance of the Garifunas) contests are held here. Two couples are chosen as the winners, one from Belize and one from outside the country. Your humble author had the privilege of meeting a friendly

British traveller, with whom he took first prize in this rather languorous dance.

Ambergris Caye

During the week, most of Ambergris Caye's bars and nightclubs close at about midnight. **Tarzan's Club** *(Barrier Reef Dr.)*, across from a public garden, and nearby **Big Daddy's**, which plays more tropical music than its neighbour, are open later Thursday through Saturday.

Fido's Courtyard *(Front St.)* is always lively after dark.

 SHOPPING

Caye Caulker

There are a few souvenir stands on Front Street, none of which particularly stands out.

Ambergris Caye

Eden Art *(Coconut Dr., ☎02-63149)* is located across from the airport. Kabina Samuels paints most of the vases for sale in this small but very attractive art gallery.

Belizean Art *(Barrier Reef Dr., Fido's Courtyard & Pier)* is a gallery owned by the renowned artist Walter Castillo.

Sea Fan is a pretty shop on Pescador Drive that sells wood sculptures painted with motifs depicting tropical and imaginary landscapes.

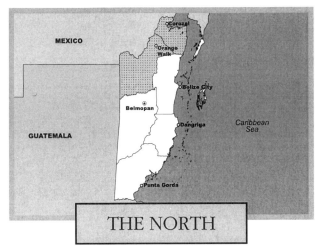

THE NORTH

Northern Belize has some of the most extensive and varied Mayan ruins in the country, though only a few of these will be of real interest to the average traveller. Among them, Lamanaí and Santa Rita are not to be missed. Experts and anyone else curious to see structures that have yet to be excavated should be sure to visit Cuello, Cerros and Nohmul.

This region, bounded by the Yucatán Peninsula to the north, Guatemala to the west and the Belize District to the south, is home to more Mestizo Indians than any other part of the country. With their Mayan and Spanish heritage, Orange Walk and Corozal Town more closely resemble the towns on the Yucatán Peninsula than those in the rest of Belize. If you speak any Spanish, you can put your knowledge into practice; this is sure to win you a smile from local residents who speak the language of Cervantes.

Most of northern Belize's landscape is flat and well-suited to sugar cane and citrus farming, as well as stockbreeding and dairy production. The region's rich soil has been farmed for millennia, starting with the Maya who first settled here some 4,500 years ago. This swampy area is home to flora and fauna found nowhere else in the country, making it a paradise for nature lovers. Although other parts of Belize might be more spectacular at first glance, they do not compare with this region if you want to learn about Mayan civilization in a rich natural setting.

FINDING YOUR WAY AROUND

Crooked Tree

By Car

The entrance to the Crooked Tree Wildlife Sanctuary is at mile 31 of the Northern Highway. The west exit is fairly well indicated. The welcome centre is four kilometres from the Northern Highway.

By Bus

The **Batty Brothers Bus Service** and **Jex Bus Service** provide transportation between the village and Belize City. To get to Orange Walk, Corozal or Chetumal, catch one of the many buses that travel between Belize City and the northern part of the country. They will pick you up where the park entrance meets the Northern Highway.

To Belize City

Batty Brothers Bus Service: BZ$3.50; departures every day at 6am.
Jex Bus Service: departures: BZ$3.50; departures at 5:15am, 6:30am and 7am.

Orange Walk

By Car

Orange Walk is located on the Northern Highway, 93 kilometres from Belize City. The road is in excellent condition and there is generally very little traffic. The Northern Highway runs through

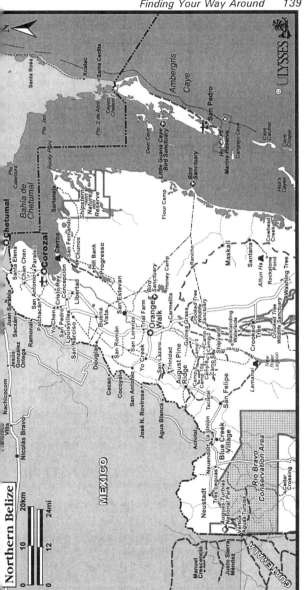

Northern Belize

THE NORTH

Orange Walk, and serves as the town's major artery. Most local hotels, restaurants and public buildings are located along it.

By Bus

All buses to Corozal and Belize City stop at various points along the Northern Highway. A number of companies offer services along this route.

Batty Brothers Bus Service *(Northern Highway, north of Central Park, ☎02-2858)* offers frequent daily service to Belize City and Chetumal (Mexico), via Corozal.

To Belize City

Regular service *(BZ$4.50; several departures daily; travel time: 2 h)*.

Express service *(BZ$6; departures at 1pm and 4pm; travel time: 1 h 15 min)*.

To Corozal

Regular service *(BZ$3; 10 daily departures between 6am and 1pm; travel time: 1 h)*.

Express service *(BZ$4; departures every day at 7:30am and 10:30am; travel time: 40 min)*.

To Chetumal

Regular service *(BZ$4.50; 10 daily departures between 6am and 1pm; travel time: 2 h)*.

Express service *(BZ$6; departures every day at 7:30am and 10:30am; travel time: 1 h 30 min)*.

Local buses offer daily service from the **Banquitas Market** *(Main St.)* to **San Felipe** and **Progresso**. The schedules and fares for these destinations are not fixed, so it is best to go to the market early in the morning or, as soon as you arrive in Orange Walk, to ask about departures.

Taxis

There is a taxi stand in front of the fire station at the corner of San Antonio Road and the Northern Highway, south of Central Park. Taxis can be recognized by their green license plates. The fare to Belize City is about BZ$100; to Corozal, about BZ$75.

You can also get a cab at the **Orange Walk Hospital Taxi Service** (☎02-3705), whose headquarters are in front the hospital.

Cerros

Arrangements for transportation by boat from Corozal to Cerros can be made at the local hotels. You can also reach Cerros by boat from Orange Walk. The latter trip is more scenic, since it takes you down the New River to Corozal Bay, just two kilometres south of Cerros. This route was traditionally used by the Maya. If you would like to experience this memorable excursion first-hand, contact **Jungle River Tours** (20 Lovers' Lane, ☎02-2293, ⌐02-3749) in Orange Walk.

Lamanaí

By Boat

There is no better way to reach Lamanaí than by boat. The scenery is magnificent, and you will get a good overview of the local plant and animal life. The New River was the Maya's communication route back when Lamanaí was a flourishing community. To this day, many local inhabitants use the river as their primary means of transportation.

Several tourist agencies offer day trips to Lamanaí. **Jungle River Tours** (BZ$80; meals and refreshments included; 20 Lovers' Lane, Orange Walk, ☎02-2293, ⌐02-3749), run by the prominent Novelo family, organizes the best excursions and has the most knowledgeable guides, who can give you detailed information about Mayan civilization and the local flora and fauna.

You can also take a boat ride from Orange Walk to the ruins at **Cerros** (see p 141). The New River empties into Corozal Bay just two kilometres from the ruins.

Based in Belize City, **Discovery Expeditions** *(BZ$80; 9:30am to 3pm)* offers boat rides down the New River to Lamanaí. Most of their customers take a day trip from the capital, but you can also embark at their New River welcome centre on the west side of the Northern Highway, just north of the Tower Hill Toll Bridge, at around 9am.

By Car

A dirt road leads from the Northern Highway to Lamanaí and passes through Yo Creek and San Felipe, which is bout 60 kilometres from Orange Walk. This route becomes virtually impassable during the rainy season.

By Bus

There are only two buses a week between Orange Walk and Lamanaí; they depart on Tuesday and Thursday afternoons. If you don't want to stand the whole way, get to the market in Orange Walk a few minutes before departure.

You can also take the bus to the New River and hire a guide once you get there. Just board any bus travelling between Orange Walk to Belize City, and ask the driver to let you off at the Tower Hill Toll Bridge.

Belize City - New River: BZ$5.
Orange Walk - New River: BZ$1.

Corozal Town

Corozal is a small town that is easily explored on foot. It is strongly recommended for travellers arriving from Mexico to exchange their pesos at the border, in Santa Elena, since banks in Corozal and Orange Walk are reluctant to do so. Note that the moneychangers at the border only come on duty at about

8am, and sometimes do not open until 9am. If you are planning to travel early in the morning, exchange your pesos before leaving Chetumal. On the other hand, when leaving Belize, you will have no trouble exchanging your Belizean dollars in Chetumal.

By Car

Corozal Town lies 155 kilometres north of Belize City. To get there, take the Northern Highway, commonly known as "Belize Road", which runs through Corozal. The highway is in good condition, and has few curves and little traffic.

By Bus

Corozal is serviced by two bus companies, that charge the same fares and have similar schedules: **Venus Bus Lines** *(☎02-2132)* and **Batty Brothers Bus Service**.

To Chetumal (Mexico)

The simplest and cheapest way to get to the Mexican border, just 13 kilometres from Corozal, is to take the bus to Chetumal. All buses stop at customs in Santa Elena. From Chetumal, you can easily connect to other towns in the country.

Regular service *(BZ$2; 10 daily departures between 6am and 1pm; travel time: 1 h 15 min)*.

To Belize City

Regular service *(BZ$8; 10 daily departures between 3:30am and 10:30am; travel time: 2 h 30 min)*.

To Orange Walk

Regular service *(BZ$3; 10 daily departures between 3:30am and 10:30am; travel time: 1 h)*.

THE NORTH

By Plane

Although there is a small airport south of Corozal, there are no regular flights between Corozal and Belize City, since there is an excellent bus service between the two towns along the well-maintained Northern Highway. If you decide to fly, you can take one of the regular flights to San Pedro, with a connection to Belize City. If you are travelling in a group and have the means, **Caribee Air Service** *(☎02-4253)* and **Javier's Flying Service** *(☎02-4532)* will take you wherever you want to go aboard a Cessna.

To San Pedro

Tropic Air *(BZ$65; 7:30am, 10:30am and 3:30pm departures; ☎02-2725; Belize City: ☎04-5671)* offers three daily flights to San Pedro.

The San Pedro-based airline **Island Air** *(BZ$60; 8am and 3pm departures; ☎26-2435)* offers two daily flights.

 PRACTICAL INFORMATION

Orange Walk

Tourist Information

Jungle River Tours *(BZ$80; 20 Lovers' Lane, ☎02-2293, ⌐02-3749)*, run by the Novelo family, is the best place in Orange Walk to go for tourist information. Besides offering to take you on a boat ride to the Lamanaí ruins, the Novelos will be happy to tell you about Orange Walk and other parts of the country. It is well worth spending a few minutes at the bar of their restaurant, which is next to the tourist agency.

Post Office

Hospital Crescent St., across from the market;
Mon to Fri 8am to 1pm and 3pm to 5pm.

Currency Exchange

There is a **Belize Bank** on Main Street and a **Scotia Bank** facing Central Park *(both open Mon to Fri 8am to 1pm and 3pm to 6pm)*.

Police

The police station is on Hospital Crescent Street, which leads to the market, and is perpendicular to Main Street.

Corozal Town

Tourist Information

The **Corozal Tourism and Cultural Center** *(BZ\$3; Tue to Sat 9am to noon and 1pm to 4:30pm; 1st Ave. and 2nd St.)* is located on the waterfront, in the old market southeast of Santiago Ricalde Central Park (see p 152). The staff is friendly and generally knowledgeable about the region and the rest of the country. This is a good place to help you organize excursions and obtain practical and cultural information.

Post Office

5th Ave., between 1st St. S. and 1st St. N;
Mon to Fri 8am to 1pm and 3pm to 5pm.

Currency Exchange

The country's three major banks, **Belize Bank**, **Scotia Bank** and **Atlantic Bank**, all have branches on 5th Avenue in Corozal. Their opening hours are the same *(Mon to Fri 8am to 1pm and 3pm to 6pm)*.

If you are arriving from Mexico, it is best to exchange your pesos at the border.

EXPLORING

Orange Walk

Located on the banks of the New River, 105 kilometres north of Belize City, the little town of Orange Walk is the agricultural centre of the district of the same name, but has little to offer in terms of actual tourist attractions. You won't find any museums or cultural centres here; the town is essentially just a stop for agricultural and commercial traffic in northern Belize.

Nevertheless, Orange Walk is an excellent stopping-off place for travellers and archaeologists who are spending a few days in the region. Its residents are of Mestizo descent, and most speak Spanish. Their unique character makes it an interesting place to people-watch, and it is pleasant to stroll through the town and soak up the atmosphere. Farmers and Mennonites can be seen driving their carts through the streets. The latter, who live in the surrounding area and come to Orange Walk to conduct business, can make the town look like a scene from the past.

In the mid-19th century, Orange Walk was at the centre of the Maya's last and most important rebellion against the British. Led by Marcos Canul, troops launched attacks on the logging camps between 1866 and 1872. In 1870, they managed temporarily to take over Corozal. The revolt came to an end in Orange Walk in 1872, when Canul died in combat.

Cuello *(free admission; Mon to Fri 8am to 5pm)* is the oldest known Mayan settlement, dating back to 2500 BC, which was the dawn of Mayan civilization. The ruins are situated on the grounds of a rum distillery five kilometres from Orange Walk. To drive or hitchhike there, take San Antonio Road at the fire station on the Northern Highway. You can also catch an 8am bus at the Banquitas Market (see p 140) then walk or hitchhike back to town. Once you get to Cuello, go to the distillery's entrance and ask permission to visit the ruins. The employees will show you where to go.

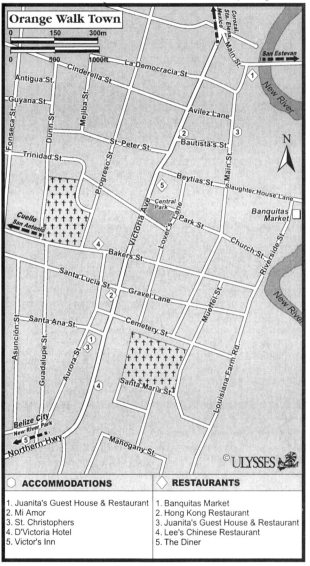

◇ **ACCOMMODATIONS**	◇ **RESTAURANTS**
1. Juanita's Guest House & Restaurant 2. Mi Amor 3. St. Christophers 4. D'Victoria Hotel 5. Victor's Inn	1. Banquitas Market 2. Hong Kong Restaurant 3. Juanita's Guest House & Restaurant 4. Lee's Chinese Restaurant 5. The Diner

Less popular and impressive than the site at Lamanaí, Cuello will be of greater interest to experts than to the casual visitor, since it has not been fully excavated and many of the ruins are covered with dense vegetation. Relatively small, it is made up of two plazas, each with its own little pyramid. It is named after the Cuello family who own the land and the distillery.

Nohmul ("great mound"), another archaeological site, lies on the Northern Highway, 10 kilometres north of Orange Walk and less than two kilometres from the village of San Pablo. These ruins, which stand in the middle of a sugar cane field, are easy to get to. Nohmul enjoyed prominence during the Pre-Classic period, before being abandoned and then reinhabited in the Late Classic era. The largest temple, over 50 metres wide and eight metres high, dates from the latter period.

Unfortunately, this vast settlement, which covers over 20 square kilometres, is blanketed by vegetation and sugar cane fields. The property belongs to Esteban Itzab, and you have to ask his permission before visiting the site. His house is in the village of San Pedro, near the water tower.

Lamanaí ★★★

Located on the banks of the New River, Lamanaí is the major archaeological attraction in the Orange Walk area. The boat ride to the ruins (see p 141) takes you through the enchanting scenery of lush and varied vegetation, including black orchids, the national flower of Belize, and the *cactus du diable*, which attaches itself to trees but does not feed off them, since it is self-sustaining. You will see many different kinds of birds, and with any luck, might even spot some crocodiles, which are protected by environmental laws.

The **Shipyard Mennonite Community** is also located along this winding river, which forms extensive swamplands in places. This group of Mennonite families, of Dutch descent, have refused to adopt a modern lifestyle. They have no electricity or cars, but do use motorized machines for farming, woodcutting and cabinetmaking which, along with stockbreeding and dairy production, are their main economic activities.

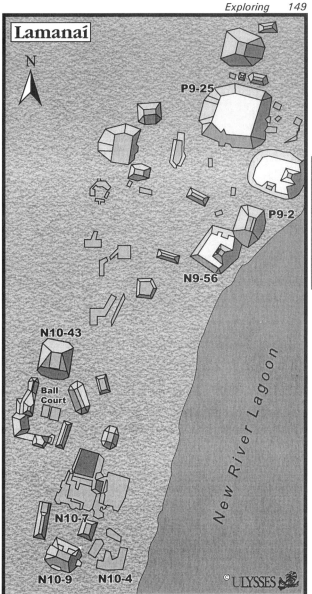

Lamanaí

N

P9-25

P9-2

N9-56

N10-43

Ball
Court

N10-7

N10-9   N10-4

New River Lagoon

THE NORTH

© ULYSSES

Near the ruins of Lamanaí, the river and swamps turn into a large lagoon. Be prepared for a spectacular sight when you see the first hills rising up on the horizon, concealing temples yet to be explored. Further down, you will see the first excavated temples majestically dominating the surrounding landscape.

It is strongly recommended that you enlist the services of a guide to tour the first temple. Not only will you become acquainted with the historical facts, but you will also learn about the vegetation, which is especially diverse in this area.

Lamanaí is the second largest archaeological site in Belize, after Caracol (see p 222). Of its 783 structures, only 70 have been excavated. Its foundations date back to 1500 BC, making them seven centuries older than Tikal's. One of the oldest Mayan sites, Lamanaí is unusual in that was one of the few still occupied by the Maya when the Spanish arrived. Two Spanish missionaries came to Lamanaí regularly between 1544 and 1564, when some 3,500 Maya lived here.

It is thanks to these Franciscan missionaries that the site's original name was preserved: Lamanaí or *lamanay* means "submerged crocodile" in the Mayan language, which explains why there are so many depictions of crocodiles on the various temples here.

Start off your tour at the little museum which displays all sorts of artifacts, including pottery adorned with drawings of birds and snakes. A number of tools, weapons and instruments used in sacrifices, made of obsidian (volcanic glass), are also on exhibit. The Maya carved the obsidian into sharp little spikes which they used to cut themselves, offering up their blood to the gods who protected them.

Following the path running alongside the river, the first temple on your right is **structure N9-56**. Its foundations date from 200 BC, and it was last modified around AD 800, before being abandoned in AD 1100. Archaeologists found four masks inside, one representing a king with a jaguar. Though the top of the temple doesn't offer the best view of the site, climbing up to it is an essential part of any visit to Lamanaí!

The centrepiece of the ruins, **structure N10-43**, was the largest temple in the Mayan world in the first century BC, when

Lamanaí was apparently at its peak. The 32-metre-high structure underwent a number of modifications over the centuries, the last of which date approximately to the year 600.

As you make your way along the paths, you will pass a magnificent stela decorated with a bas-relief of a king's head, and some hieroglyphs. There is also a small ball court, which is, unfortunately, mostly covered with vegetation. All in all, a trip to Lamanaí is a wonderful opportunity to admire the region's natural riches while exploring the vestiges of ancient Mayan civilization.

Corozal Town ★

A relaxed place, Corozal is the only town in northern Belize where you can learn a bit about Belizean culture and history while enjoying a stroll along the waterfront shaded by a row of palm trees. It is well worth spending a day or two in Corozal, even though it has no real beach. You can visit the town's little museum and the ruins of Santa Rita, and take a boat across Corozal Bay to Cerros.

Located on the shores of Corozal Bay, Corozal has a rich and unique history that goes back more than 3,000 years. The Maya settled in the area now occupied by Santa Rita (see p 153), then known as Chetumal. This settlement was an important Mayan trading hub when the Spanish arrived on the Yucatán Peninsula. Alonso Dávila understood the strategic importance of the site and decided to take over the town. Unfortunately for him, another Spaniard, Gonzalo Guerrero, considered the father of the Mestizo population (see p 154), had joined forces with the Maya. The Maya abandoned Chetumal a few years later, and Dávila founded Villa Real on this site. His accomplishment was short-lived, however: after repeated Mayan attacks, he was forced to flee the town in 1532.

It wasn't until several centuries later that Europeans once again began to settle in this area. In the mid-19th century, James Humes Blake, an Englishman from Liverpool, established the first sugar cane plantation on the site of present-day Corozal.

The region's rich soil also continued to attract the Spanish – more so than ever because of the Caste War, when many refugees settled in the area. In 1870, the English built **Fort Barry** to protect their economic interests and to defend the town if the Spanish started launching attacks from Mexico. Four small towers, located east of Central Park, are all that remains of this structure.

Begin your tour of Corozal Town by heading to the waterfront, where the **Corozal Tourism and Cultural Center** ★★ *(BZ$3; Tue to Sat 9am to noon and 1pm to 4:30pm)* is set up inside the old market, built in 1885. Following the construction of a new market in 1969, this iron building had stood empty until 1996. It now houses an excellent tourist information office and a small exhibition space devoted to the history of Belize, with a special focus on Corozal. This charming little museum only presents temporary exhibitions. Anyone interested in the history and culture of Corozal should contact Keila Gonzales, who works at the cultural center and will gladly help you plan your stay in Belize. Inside the building, there is a staircase leading up to a lookout, which has a fantastic view of the town and the sea.

Leaving the cultural center, take 1st Avenue, which runs north along the shore, until you come to **Schofield House**, one of the few traditional wooden houses in Corozal to have survived Hurricane Janet. Built at the turn of the century, it is a good example of English colonial architecture. The history of the Schofield family is closely linked to that of Corozal, since the Schofields owned all the land on which the town now stands. From the beginning of the century until 1955, they rented out plots of land to other families for as little as $5 a month. After the hurricane, ownership of the house was transferred to the government and the land was put up for sale.

Santiago Ricalde Central Park is where the locals gather. It is worth stopping by the **Town Hall** *(6 Calle no. 1; Mon to Thu 8am to noon and 1pm to 5pm)*, on the park's south side, to admire the mural by Manuel Villamor. This painting was inspired by the Mexican muralist movement, and depicts the history of Corozal, beginning with the influx of Mexican refugees during the Caste War (1849). Originally executed in 1953, the mural was repainted in 1986 and restored in 1994.

Corozal Town

0   150   300m

0   500   1000ft.

N

Santa Rita Ruins Mexico

Sta. Rita Rd.

6th Ave.

5th Ave.

4th Ave.

3rd St. North

2nd St. North

1st St. North

1st St. South

2nd St. South

3rd St. South

4th St. South

5th St. South

6th St. South

7th St. South

8th St. S

1st Ave.

4th Ave.

5th Ave.

6th Ave.

7th Ave.

9th Ave.

G-St.-S

9th St.-S

B-St.-S

8th Ave.

©ULYSSES

Consejo →

Corozal Bay

Airstrip, Orange Walk, Belize City

● ATTRACTIONS

1. Corozal Public Library
2. Corozal Tourism and Cultural Center
3. Fort Barry
4. Santiago Ricalde Central Park
5. Schofield House

○ ACCOMMODATIONS

1. Hokol Kin House
2. Hotel Maya
3. Nestor's Hotel Restaurant & Bar
4. Tony's Inn & Beach Resort

◇ RESTAURANTS

1. Hokol Kin House
2. Nestor's Hotel Restaurant & Bar
3. Tony's Inn & Beach Resort

THE NORTH

Also on the park's south side is the **Corozal Public Library** *(Mon to Fri 8am to noon and 1pm to 8pm, Sat 8am to 11:30am)*, a small branch of the National Library Service. It contains some books on Belize, as well as historical documents relating to Corozal.

Located on the Northern Highway, 1.5 kilometres from the centre of Corozal, the ruins of **Santa Rita ★★** *(BZ$5 including guide; every day 8am to 5pm)* are within easy walking distance from town and are not to be missed. It's a good idea to bring along some insect repellent to ward off mosquitoes.

You can easily spend two hours exploring the ruins, which are small but well preserved. They were discovered at the turn of the century by Thomas Gann, a British archaeologist who claimed to have uncovered the foundations of nearly 2,000 houses and 16 temples. These ruins are generally believed to be those of ancient Chetumal, a Mayan trading centre that was attacked by the Spanish *adelantado* Alonso Dávila in the 16th century.

Gonzalo Guerrero – a Spaniard Turned Maya

Considered by many to be the father of Belize's Mestizo population, Gonzalo Guerrero became legendary early in the country's history. His origins are still a mystery: some believe he was a sailor whose ship ran aground near Chetumal, others say he was sent from Yucatán as a peace offering. Whatever the case, he lived in ancient Chetumal, now the ruins of Santa Rita.

Gonzalo Guerrero was apparently assimilated into Mayan culture, had tattoos and according to legend, even married a Mayan princess, which is why he is thought of as the "father of the Mestizos". He was a prominent member of Mayan society in Chetumal before Alonso Dávila, the Spanish *adelantado* who later conquered the city, even came onto the scene.

Guerrero supposedly refused to join the Spanish in their battle against his adopted people and fought on the Mayan side instead. When Dávila withdrew his forces, Guerrero convinced the Maya to leave Chetumal and organize a better defense strategy. When Dávila returned in 1531, Chetumal was a ghost town, so he took possession of it and renamed it Villa Real. However, the Maya, led by a warlord named Nachancan, continued their struggle on the outskirts of town, ambushing the Spanish every time they ventured outside Villa Real. Finding themselves besieged by the Maya once again, the Spanish eventually had to retreat from Villa Real in 1532.

Can Spain's failure to colonize the Corozal Bay be traced back to one man? No one really knows. One thing, however, is certain: the father of Mestizos will remain legendary as the first Westerner to have lived in Belize.

The site dates back to 2000 BC, the dawn of Mayan civilization. That Chetumal, which is also known as Chactahumal, was

a trading hub, is clear, since archaeologists have found numerous artifacts made of jade and obsidian, which are not local materials. Because of Chetumal's strategic location, cacao, *achiote*, honey and vanilla passed through here on their way to or from Petén, as they travelled along the New and Lamanaí rivers, and up the coast to northern Yucatán. Agriculture, particularly cacao cultivation, was the main activity in this area.

Today, the well-preserved **Temple no. 7** is Santa Rita's main attraction, even though the lower floors have yet to be excavated and only the second level is visible. It is a complex structure with numerous rooms, arches, doors and stairways. From the top, there is a lovely view of the area, where scores of Mayan houses used to stand.

Two large tombs were found in the temple, one of which contained the remains of a woman wearing lots of jewellery, surrounded by pieces of pottery. According to archaeologists, she must have been a princess who ruled the city at the beginning of the Classic period, a fairly uncommon occurrence in Mayan civilization. Apparently, her name was X.ZA.ZIL, or "clear water". The second tomb, dating from the 6th century, contained a warlord surrounded by numerous objects symbolizing his power. Curiously, some almost identical objects have been found in Guatemala and Teotihuacán, Mexico, supporting the theory that ancient Chetumal was located on an important trade route.

Unfortunately, many ancient Mayan houses have been destroyed as Corozal developed around the site. In fact, Chetumal residents have used stones from the ruins to build their own houses since the 19th century.

THE NORTH

Cerros ★

Perched atop the hills overlooking the shores of Corozal Bay, Cerros, whose name means "hills" in Spanish, is one of the few Mayan sites that face the sea. It was an important coastal trading centre, particularly for obsidian and jade at the end of the Pre-Classic period (400 BC - AD 250), before it fell into decline. The site now covers an area of over 20 hectares, and includes several plazas, pyramidal structures and ball courts.

The tallest temple is 21 metres high and is adorned with carved masks. Unfortunately, the site has been left largely unexcavated, and most of its structures are still covered with vegetation. Also, a good part of the original site is now under the sea. Nevertheless, in good weather, the boat trip to Cerros is an excellent way to spend a wonderful day at sea, admiring the remarkable natural setting in which the ruins are located.

You can reach Cerros from Corozal or Orange Walk (see p 141).

Jaguar

  PARKS AND BEACHES

Orange Walk

Rio Bravo Conservation Area

Located northwest of Orange Walk, the Rio Bravo Conservation Area was created to preserve the tropical forest. Covering nearly 92,000 hectares, it is the largest expanse of protected forest in Belize, and home to a wide range of animals: tapirs, monkeys, jaguars and many sorts of birds. The Rio Bravo Conservation Area is not accessible by public transportation, but you can get there via San Felipe and Yo Creek in an all-terrain vehicle, or use one of the charter services based in Belize City: **Caribee Air Service** (☎02-4253) or **Javier's Flying Service** (☎02-4532).

Corozal Town

Butterfly-lovers won't want to miss the **Shipstern Nature Reserve** *(BZ$25; Sartaneja Village, ☎03-2046, ⇏03-2046)*, which covers over 8,800 hectares. With a guide leading the way, you can explore some of the many nature trails that wind their way through the wilderness. With a little luck, you will see many different kinds of butterflies: nearly 200 different species can be found in the area. You can also visit a butterfly farm, where 25 species are bred.

THE NORTH

OUTDOOR ACTIVITIES

Canoeing

The areas around Orange Walk and Lamanaí are good places to go paddling. Canoe rentals are available at **Jungle River Tours** *(20 Lovers' Lane, ☎02-2293, ⇏02-3749)*.

Windsurfing

Tony's Inn *(Corozal Town)* rents out windsurfers to its guests (see p 161).

ACCOMMODATIONS

Orange Walk

The hotels in Orange Walk tend to be more family-oriented than Ohose elsewhere in the region. If you are camping, you can pitch your tent on the grounds of the **New River Park** (see p 159) Or **Victor's Inn** (see p below).

Centrally located, **Juanita's Guesthouse & Restaurant** *(US$15, ⌧; 8 Santa Ana St., ☎02-2677)* has four small, relatively clean rooms with shared bathrooms above its popular restaurant (see p 162). The rooms are a bit noisy at certain times of day and the windows do not have screens.

La Enramada *(BZ$40; pb, ℜ, ⌧, #, ≈; 5 Cristock St., ☎02-3894)* comprises small palm wood cabanas, surrounded by tropical gardens. Clean and rustic, the rooms have mosquito screens and a fan, but only one bed, making them most suitable for single travellers and couples. The service is friendly and welcoming. La Enramada has a pleasant little restaurant whose *ceviche* is very popular with local residents (see p 161). This place caters mainly to Belizeans and local couples, attracting few tourists. It is located in a residential neighbourhood south of Orange Walk, two streets west of the Northern Highway, and about a 10-minute walk from the bus station.

Victor's Inn *(BZ$50; pb, #; $15 ⌧; ☎02-0183)*, located 1.6 kilometres east of Orange Walk, is a row of clean, comfortable brick cabanas with thatched roofs and concrete interiors. American archaeologists carrying out excavations in the Honey Camp Lagoon area are regular guests here. You can hang up your hammock in some of the cabanas, which are quiet and safe. The restaurant (see p 163) serves *salpicón*, an excellent smoked meat *ceviche*, and a variety of other traditional dishes. According to the owners, this area is good for toucan-watching in May. To get to the inn, you can call the owners, who will pick you up at the Batty Bus Station or elsewhere in Orange Walk. If you are driving or prefer to walk, cross the San Esteban Bridge behind take Banquitas Market, follow the road, then take the first right.

Ulysses' Favourites

Accommodations

For river tours: **New River Park** (see p 159)

Restaurants

For a traditional cow soup: **Juanita's Guesthouse & Restaurant** (see p 162)

For pub-style ambiance: **Nestor's Hotel Restaurant & Bar** (see p 164)

Located south of town on the banks of the New River, the **New River Park** *(BZ$54 -107; ≡, pb, hw, tv, ℜ, @; Northern Hwy., ☎02-3987)* is the area's most charming place to stay. Built from wood that is typical of the area, it blends in harmoniously with the natural surroundings. Its location is excellent, seven kilometres south of Orange Walk, near the Tower Hill Toll Bridge, which is the point of departure for boat rides to Lamanaí. Easily accessible by bus or by car, this intimate little hotel has only six large rooms, which combine rustic charm with modern comfort. The second-floor rooms have a terrace looking out onto the New River. The friendly English owner, John Foster, welcomes guests at his popular restaurant (see p 163) which is always full of travellers on their way to Lamanaí. If you'd like to take the trip yourself, you can make the necessary arrangements right at the hotel and take advantage of the Novelo brothers' experience (see p 144).

St. Christophers *(BZ$64.50; hw, pb, ≡, ≈, tv; 10 Main St., ☎/≈702-1064)* is a concrete building next to the market and the most comfortable hotel downtown. You can't miss it – it's bright pink! The rooms are decent, having been completely renovated. These have cable TV and brand-new air condition-ers, but the mismatched furniture detracts somewhat from their overall appearance. The hotel is situated on the New River: for a view of the water, ask for a room at the back. The hotel also has a small park with a pavilion, and benches along the river, reserved exclusively for guests. Safe parking is available. The service leaves something to be desired since there is no real lobby, and the reception is in the general store on the ground floor. When the store is closed, go to the small gated entrance opposite the vehicle entrance and call for the concierge.

In a similar category, the centrally located **D'Victoria Hotel** *(BZ$85; ≈, hw, tv, ≈; 40 Northern Hwy.,* ☎*02-2518,* ⊷*702-2847)* has a lovely patio out back. The open architecture makes it possible to fully enjoy the local climate. The rooms have been carefully decorated, and the floors are covered with small ceramic tiles. The rooms at the back are naturally quieter than those facing the Northern Highway.

Right in the centre of town, **Mi Amor** *(BZ$85 with ≈, BZ$55 without ≈, pb, p, hw, tv; 19 Northern Hwy.,* ☎*02-2031,* ⊷*702-462)* is a bit noisy. Clean and well-kept by its friendly owner, Miguel Urbina, this hotel has had the same rather unusual name since 1955. The current building is made of concrete. Live shows are featured every weekend *(BZ$5; 9pm)*.

Lamanaí

The only hotel close to the ruins, **Lamanaí Outpost Lodge** *(BZ$120; hw, pb, ⊗;* ☎*03-3758)* has modern, comfortable cabanas in a lovely setting, facing the lagoon. Excursions available.

Corozal Town

Nestor's Hotel Restaurant & Bar *(BZ$32; ⊗, pb, hw, ℜ, ⊗; 123 5th Ave.,* ☎*04-2354,* ⊷*704-3902)*, run by Montrealer Mark Kramer, is a popular restaurant and bar with several small, clean, functional rooms. This place has the advantage of being centrally located, and is perfect for anyone who can't stand peace and quiet! Karaoke and live music on Friday and Saturday nights.

The **Hotel Maya** *(BZ$45-60; pb, hw, ⊗, ⊗, ℜ; 7th Ave. S.,* ☎*02-2082,* ⊷*702-2827)* has seen better days. Although the rooms could use some freshening up, the attentive service and overall ambiance still lend the place a certain charm. The quietest hotel in this category.

The **Hokol Kin Guesthouse** *(BZ$60-80; pb, hw, ⊗, ⊛, ≈, ♿, ℛ; 4th St. at 4th Ave.,* ☎*02-3329,* ▰*702-3569)* is the best hotel in town, providing modern comfort and a family atmosphere. It is surrounded by hammocks and well tended gardens, and terraces that command a sweeping view of the sea. The Hokol Kin organizes cultural immersion homestays with local Mayan and Garifuna families. There is also a private lounge and a book-lending system. The rooms are spacious and clean, with big wooden beds. They are not air-conditioned, but there is usually a pleasant breeze in this area. The restaurant serves Belizean and international cuisine. You can get all three meals for BZ$26, or an excellent breakfast for BZ$3.50.

Tony's Inn & Beach Resort *(BZ$120; hw, pb, tv, ≡, ℛ, △; BZ$45; pb, hw, ⊗;* ☎*02-2055,* ▰*702-2829)*, the only place right on the shore, meets modern standards of comfort. A worry-free stay awaits you at this excellent hotel, located at the south edge of Corozal. The rooms are spacious and come with two large double beds, and most have a view of the sea. The staff is courteous, efficient and very professional. There is private parking, as well as a private beach and a *paseo* beneath the palm trees in front of the hotel. A good restaurant with a varied menu and attentive service is also on the premises. Tony's organizes all sorts of excursions, including boat trips to Cerros.

RESTAURANTS

Orange Walk

The **Banquitas Market** *(every day 6am to 8pm; Main St.)* serves the cheapest meals in town. Clean and modern, the market stands on stilts, overlooking the New River. Some of the food stalls outside have a stunning view of the water. In addition to a daily menu of traditional dishes, there is usually a good selection of fruits and vegetables.

La Enramada *($; 5 Cristock St.,* ☎*02-3894)* is a modest little restaurant found in the hotel of the same name (see p 158).

THE NORTH

Inside, it is set up like a traditional Belizean house with a thatched roof and wooden tables. Locals come here at any time of day for the excellent *ceviche* (small BZ$5, large BZ$10), as well as other traditional Belizean cuisine, which goes well with a nice cold beer. The restaurant is located in a residential neighbourhood south of Orange Walk, two streets west of the Northern Highway.

Ranking number one with Orange Town residents, the very popular **Juanita's Guesthouse & Restaurant** *($; 6am to 2pm and 6pm to 9pm; 8 Santa Ana St., ☎02-2677)* has a friendly "neighbourhood restaurant" ambiance and a BZ$5 fixed-price menu. This is an excellent place to sample cow soup, a traditional dish made with beef shanks, tripe, potatoes, carrots and pumpkin. Other Belizean specialties are also available. Excellent value.

Hong Kong Restaurant *($; 21 Northern Hwy., next to the Mi Amor hotel, ☎02-2406)* is Lee's Restaurant's most serious competitor when it comes to Chinese food. The ambiance is more inviting here and the Chow Mein and Chop Suey are more popular with locals, but the menu is similar.

An excellent family restaurant, **The Diner** *($$; Northern Hwy., north of Central Park)* is a very friendly, inviting place, thanks to its colourful owner, Terry, who opened it to provide local families with a place to enjoy a quiet, relaxed atmosphere and fine cuisine. Belizean, Mexican and international dishes all appear on the menu. Try the house specialty, "Hawaiian Rib à la Diner" – grilled porkchops with ginger, pineapples and secret spices. Other selections include sautéed shrimp and Lobster Thermidor (broiled lobster with mushrooms, cheese and white wine). The restaurant is located behind the hospital, in the most affluent residential neighbourhood in town. When this guide went to press, Terry was seriously considering opening a second restaurant in downtown Orange Walk, so make sure to inquire about The Diner II!

Like other towns in Belize, Orange Walk has several Chinese restaurants. Among these, **Lee's Chinese Restaurant** *($-$$; 11 San Antonio Rd. ☎02-2174)* is not to be missed. Set up in a rather impersonal modern building, this restaurant is popular with locals not only because of its menu and prices, but also because of the excellent air-conditioning in its big, Chinese-style dining room. The menu features a number of seafood dishes, including garlic shrimp *(BZ$1.50 each)*, lobster cocktails *(BZ$6.50)* and the specialty of the house, baked lobster, which consists of three baked, sliced lobster tails served in a cheese sauce with fresh vegetables *(BZ$28)*. If you're on a tight budget, try one of the many rice and vegetable dishes. The hamburgers *(BZ$3)* are excellent as well.

The **New River Park** *($-$$; Northern Hwy., ☎02-3987, ☞702-3789)* is a very popular restaurant located on the banks of the New River, seven kilometres south of Orange Walk. Because it is near the Tower Hill Toll Bridge, the point of departure for all boat trips to Lamanaí, day-trippers account for a large part of the clientele. The rustic, wood-built dining room fits in perfectly with the spectacular natural setting. There is also a bar. The specialty of the house is Chop Sirloin Steak. Don't forget to try New River Park's most popular dessert, Bananas à la Foster – flambéed in butter and dark rum straight from the Orange Walk distillery.

Victor's Inn *($$; ☎02-0183)* is located 1.6 kilometres east of Orange Walk, at the edge of the woods in the Petville area, and has a big, rustic dining room. The house specialty is *salpicón* – cold smoked meat with onions, tomatoes and lemon. Served with *tostaditas* (fried corn tortillas), it's like *ceviche*, only with meat instead of seafood. The owners will pick you up at the Batty Bus station or anywhere else in Orange Walk. If you are travelling by car or would rather walk, take the San Esteban Bridge behind the Banquitas Market, follow the road, then take the first right.

Corozal Town

Unfortunately, other than hotel restaurants, there aren't many places to eat in Corozal.

Outside of town, next to the ruins of Santa Rita, little **Henessy's Restaurant & Bar** *($; Northern Hwy., Santa Rita)* is a good place to refresh yourself with a soda or a beer after touring the site. If you're hungry, you can snack on simple fare like burgers, fried chicken, sandwiches and fries. The management is very friendly if you care to strike up a conversation.

 Nestor's Hotel Restaurant & Bar *($; 123 5th Ave.
☎04-2354, ⌐704-3902)* is the most popular spot in Corozal for drinking and dining. The colourful owner, Mark Kramer, is from Montreal. Burgers, fried chicken and typical Belizean dishes are served in a pub atmosphere. Breakfast starts at 7am, and the restaurant closes around midnight. There is karaoke and live music on Friday and Saturday nights.

The restaurant at the **Hokol Kin Guesthouse** *($-$$; 4th St. at 4th Ave., ☎04-3329, ⌐704-3569)* is an excellent choice if you want to treat yourself to a good meal without leaving Corozal. The dining room is charming, and near a big patio. Belizean and international cuisine are served in a family atmosphere that invites you to eat, drink and be merry.

Tony's Inn & Beach Resort *($$-$$$)* has an excellent restaurant, which serves Belizean and international cuisine in a modern dining room with a view of the sea. During the daytime, and especially at breakfast, ask for a table outside on the magnificent terrace, which is ideal for daydreaming. Excellent meat and seafood dishes are served, and the service is courteous, with a personal touch.

ENTERTAINMENT

Orange Walk

Mi Amor *(BZ$5; Fri and Sat at 9pm; 19 Northern Hwy., ☎02-2031, ⌐702-3462)* is a large venue in a hotel in downtown Orange Walk. It presents live music every weekend.

Tijuana *(noon to 1am; 2 Bethias St., near Central Park)* is a small, well-kept bar with a regular clientele. There is video poker and the occasional live show on weekends.

Just south of Orange Walk on the Northern Highway, **Tequila Sunrise** *(every day noon to midnight; 137 Northern Hwy., ☎02-0418)* is as popular during the day as it is at night. A

amboo bar with a big thatched roof, it has two pool tables.
he ambiance is generally pleasant, and the music suits the
rowd.

Corozal Town

Nestor's Hotel Restaurant & Bar *($; 123 5th Ave.,* ☎*04-2354,* ☏*704-3902)* hosts karaoke nights and live music on Fridays and
Saturdays.

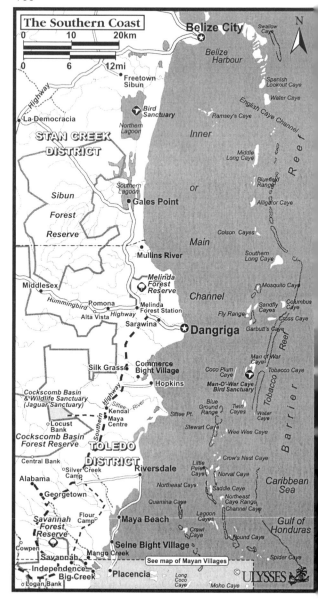

The Southern Coast

| 0 | 10 | 20km |

| 0 | 6 | 12mi |

N

Belize City

Swallow Caye

Belize Harbour

Freetown
Sibun

Spanish Lookout Caye

Water Caye

La Democracia

Bird Sanctuary

Northern Lagoon

English Caye Channel

Ramsey's Caye

STAN CREEK DISTRICT

Inner

Reef

Middle Long Caye

Sibun

Southern Lagoon

Gales Point

Bluefield Range

or

Alligator Caye

Forest

Reserve

Colson Cayes

Main

Southern Long Caye

Mullins River

Melinda Forest Reserve

Mosquito Caye

Middlesex

Hummingbird

Pomona

Alta Vista

Highway

Melinda Forest Station

Channel

Sandfly Cayes

Columbus Caye

Fly Range

Cross Caye

Sarawina

Dangriga

Garbutt's Caye

Man of War Caye

Silk Grass

Commerce Bight Village

Coco Plum Caye

Tobacco Caye

Man-O'-War Caye Bird Sanctuary

Hopkins

Tobacco Reef

Barrier

Cockscomb Basin & Wildlife Sanctuary (Jaguar Sanctuary)

Sittee River

Kendal

Maya Centre

Sittee Pt.

Blue Ground Range

Twin Cayes

Water Caye

Locust Bank

Stewart Caye

Wee Wee Caye

Cockscomb Basin Forest Reserve

TOLEDO DISTRICT

Crow's Nest Caye

Central Bank

Riversdale

Little Peter Caye

Norval Caye

Alabama

Silver Camp

Northeast Caye

Saddle Caye

Northeast Caye Range

Caribbean Sea

Georgetown

Quamina Caye

Channel Caye

Savannah Forest Reserve

Flour Camp

Maya Beach

Lagoon Cayes

Gulf of Honduras

Cowpen

Seine Bight Village

Crawl Caye

Round Caye

Savannah

Mango Creek

Spider Caye

Independence Big Creek

Placencia

See map of Mayan Villages

Logan Bank

Long Coco Caye

Moho Caye

© ULYSSES

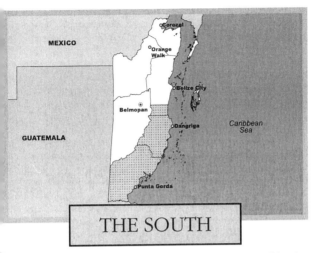

THE SOUTH

Some to the loveliest beaches in the country, Mopán Mayan villages nestled in the Maya Mountains, Garifuna hamlets dotting the coast and vast nature reserves, southern Belize will dazzle even the most seasoned traveller. The **Hummingbird Highway**, which runs through this region, is an adventure in itself: a reddish dirt road, it winds through tree plantations at the foot of the Maya Mountains, which extend to the west, and crosses numerous streams on bridges that are nothing more than a few planks of wood. Though highway's poor condition makes getting around southern Belize something of a challenge, it keeps the region in a relatively pristine state – a real boon to travellers. Thanks to the new **Manatee Highway**, also known as the **Coastal Highway,** which runs south from the **Belize Zoo**, it is now possible to travel south directly, without having to pass through Belmopan. This highway is also a dirt road, and its condition varies with the weather.

Southern Belize is divided into two districts: Stann Creek and Toledo. An agricultural region, the Stann Creek District lies immediately south of Belize City and is a major producer of bananas and other fruits. The first stop on our itinerary is **Gales Point**, popular with nature lovers. Here, you can see lamentins and other animals, and stroll along the streets of this picturesque hamlet. The town of **Dangriga**, the centre of Garifuna zculture, is at the heart of the Settlement Day festivities on November 19, which commemorate the Garifunas' arrival in Belize after being driven off the island of St. Vincent. The town's pier is the point of departure for trips to southern Belize's numerous cayes. The two largest islands in the south lie in the waters off Dangriga. Two little pieces of heaven on Earth, **Southwater Caye** and **Tobacco Caye**, have accommodations for travellers.

Hopkins, south of Dangriga, is one of the few Garifuna villages to have remained unspoiled by the tourist industry. With its magnificent beach, proud and friendly inhabitants and laid-back seaside atmosphere, Hopkins is the best place in the country to get a taste of Garifuna culture. The nearby **Cockscomb Wildlife Sanctuary** is one of the few nature reserves in the world where jaguars can be seen in their natural habitat. There are also the superb beaches of **Placencia Peninsula**, the most common tourist destination in the south and the point of departure for scuba trips to the coral reefs. You can stroll along the now famous "sidewalk" (see p 184) that divides the village in two, bustling with pedestrians and idlers who chat with all the locals.

Toledo is the country's southernmost district. Its major point of interest is **Punta Gorda**, which has a population of about 4000 and is the point of departure for the ferry to Guatemala. In the nearby Maya Mountains, the residents of the Mayan villages of **San Antonio** and **San Pedro Columbia** wear brightly coloured traditional clothing. Visitors can learn about the customs of this thousand-year-old civilization first-hand through the local homestay program. The Mayan ruins of **Lubaantun**, **Nim Li Punit** and **Uxbenka** are all close by.

Have you visited our web site?
www.ulysses.ca

FINDING YOUR WAY AROUND

Gales Point

By Car

Gales Point is located 87 kilometres from Belize City via the Coastal Highway, a dirt road that is in poor condition and gets even worse during the rainy season. You are better off taking an all-terrain vehicle, at any time of year. The scenery is spectacular, with the foothills of the Maya Mountains rising up alongside the road.

By Bus

Ritchies Bus Service and **Z-line** both run to Gales Point from Belize City and Dangriga. The buses stop just long enough to drop passengers off before continuing on their way. When this guide went to press, the Z-line buses were no longer stopping at Gales Point, but three kilometres away, where the Coastal Highway and the road into town meet. If you're backpacking, it's a pleasant walk. If not, you're better off taking Ritchies Bus Service, which stops right in the village.

Ritchies Bus Service

To Belize City: BZ$5; departures: 6am and 9:30am; travel time: 1 h 30 min.
To Dangriga: BZ$5; departures: 3:45pm and 5:30pm; travel time: 1 h.

Dangriga

By Plane

Tropic Air *(☎05-22129)* offers several daily flights to the municipal and international airports of **Belize City**. Departures at 7:40am, 10:10am, 12:40pm and 4:10pm.

THE SOUTH

There is also daily service to **Placencia** and **Punta Gorda** at 8:50am, 11:20am, 2pm and 6:50pm.

By Car

Dangriga lies 24 kilometres south of Gales Point via the Coastal Highway. The town is located on the traffic circle between the Coastal Highway and the Southern Highway.

By Bus

Z-Line *(Commerce St., ☎05-22160).*

Belmopan: BZ$6; departures: 5am, 6am, 8am, 2pm and 5pm; travel time: 2 h. The same bus travels to Belize City on the Hummingbird Highway: BZ$10; travel time: 4 h.

Belize City (via the Coastal Highway): BZ$9; departures: 5:15am and 8:10am; travel time: 2 h.

Placencia: BZ$8; departures: 12:15pm and 4:30pm; travel time: 2 h.

Punta Gorda: BZ$13; departures: 12pm, 4pm and 7pm; travel time: 5 h.

Placencia

By Plane

If you're pressed for time, flying is an excellent way to get to Placencia, given the pitiful state of the roads and limited bus service.

To Belize City

Maya Airways *(☎02-77215)* offers five flights per day to Belize City (BZ$125 to Goldson International Airport and BZ$105 to the municipal airport).

Tropic Air *(☎02-62338)* offers four flights to Belize City (BZ$127 to Goldson International Airport and BZ$107 to the municipal airport).

By Car

The dirt road that runs from one end of the peninsula to the other is in terrible condition. It is strewn with gaping holes, so drive cautiously. During the rainy season, an all-terrain vehicle is strongly recommended.

By Bus

Very few buses travel the road to and from Placencia. **Z-Line** offers two daily departures for Dangriga and Belize City, both before 6am; **Ritchies** has one daily departure for those two towns.

By Boat

It is possible to travel by boat from Independence to Placencia and thus avoid taking the awful road. However, you might not be able to find a boat to take you, and even if you do you, it will probably be expensive.

The **Hokey Pokey Water Taxi** provides regular passenger service from Placencia to Mango Creek *(BZ$10; departure at 10am except Sun, return at 2:30)*.

THE SOUTH

Punta Gorda

By Boat

Contrary to what many maps and tourist brochures indicate, there is no longer a ferry service between Punta Gorda and Puerto Barrios. Instead, a number of charter services take passengers back and forth on small, fast boats. You might be able to take a motorcycle or a bicycle with you, but a car is out of the question.

Requenas Charter Services *(BZ$20; 12 Front St.,* ☎*05-2070)* has one scheduled departure to Puerto Barrios every day at 9am. During the rest of the day, the boat leaves as soon as there are enough passengers aboard. The open-sea crossing takes 45 minutes to an hour. It is best to reserve your seats at least one day in advance. Parking is available for travellers with cars. If you arrive the morning of your departure, go straight to the pier; if you arrive in the afternoon, go to the company's offices at 12 Front Street, two buildings north of the police station.

Private boats are available for those interested in exploring the surrounding islands or going to Livingston, in Guatemala. For more information, stop by **Toledo's Visitors Information Center** (see p 174), located in front of the pier.

By Bus

If you want to take the bus to one of the Mayan villages, wait in front of the Belize Bank *(Main St.)* in Punta Gorda. The buses set out for Punta Gorda from the villages early in the morning, and head back around noon.

Blue Creek: BZ$3; Wed to Sat; leaves Blue Creek at 5:30am; leaves Punta Gorda at noon.

NA Luum Ca: BZ$3; Mon, Wed, Fri and Sat; leaves NA Luum Ca at 3am; leaves Punta Gorda at noon.

San Antonio: BZ$3; Mon, Wed, Fri and Sat; leaves San Antonio at 5am; leaves Punta Gorda at noon.

San José: BZ$3; leaves San José at 3am; leaves Punta Gorda at noon.

San Pedro Columbia: BZ$2.50; leaves San Pedro Columbia at 5am; leaves Punta Gorda at noon.

Santa Cruz: BZ$3.25; leaves Santa Cruz at 4am; leaves Punta Gorda at noon.

Santa Helena: BZ$3.25; leaves Santa Helena at 4am; leaves Punta Gorda at noon.

James Bus Line

Buses north *(in front of the Belize Bank, Main St.)*: Sun 6am, Mon 4:30am, Tue 11am, Wed 4:30am, Sat 4:30am.

Belize City: BZ$22; travel time: 8 h.

Belmopan: BZ$19; travel time: 6 h 30 min.

Dangriga: BZ$13; travel time: 5 h.

Z-Line

This company has three daily departures to Belize City at 4:30am, 9am and noon, and an additional departure at 3:30pm on the weekend.

Taxis

Dwight & Esther Woodye *(8am to noon and 3pm to 5pm; ☎05-2543 or 05-2870)*, whose offices are located right near the pier, offer tours of the Mayan villages and taxi service to archaeological sites in the area.

 PRACTICAL INFORMATION

Dangriga

THE SOUTH

Tourist Information

Although there is no official tourist information office in Dangriga, you'll find all the information you need at the **New River Café** (see p 201).

Post Office

16 Caney Street.

Telephone

Belize Telecommunications Ltd. has a branch on Commerce Street, across from the police station.

Police

Police Station: 107 Commerce Street.

Hospital

On Court House Road, northeast of the bridge.

Punta Gorda

Tourist Information

Alfredo at **Toledo's Visitors Information Center** *(donations appreciated; 7am to 11:30am; ☎07-2470)* is the most reliable person to contact in Punta Gorda. He has accumulated an excellent collection of documents on the region.

Post Office

On Front Street, at the corner of King.

Telephone

Belize Telecommunications Ltd. has a branch on Main Street, one block from Central Park.

Police

Police Station: on Front Street, near King.

Hospital

Right near the bus station.

★ EXPLORING

Gales Point

The little village of Gales Point lies on a four-kilometre peninsula on the Southern Lagoon. It is popular with animals, so you can observe lamentins, birds, crocodiles, sea turtles, iguanas and, if you're lucky, the occasional jaguar or tapir. The Southern Lagoon is also a good place to go sport fishing. There is a small dirt road leading from one end of the peninsula to the other. Along it are a number of houses, several family-run inns and the local church and school. At the northern tip of the peninsula, in one of the area's loveliest settings, is the Manatee Lodge (see p 191), a magnificent wooden home that has been converted into a guesthouse.

Gales Point was a logging camp in the early 19th century. The surrounding landscape is breathtaking. Rising up on the western horizon, are the mountains, separated from the peninsula by a large lagoon that teems with lamentins and mirrors the setting sun each evening. The atmosphere of the village reflects the tranquil lifestyle of its inhabitants.

Though there are no sandy beaches in the village, you can still enjoy a pleasant swim here or partake in any number of water sports, including sea kayaking, sailing and windsurfing.

Dangriga

The village of Dangriga has no tourist attractions per se, but its bustling streets give it a lively atmosphere. Thanks to the markets and all different sorts of stores lining its main street, it is the region's economic hub. You're sure to enjoy mingling with the local population, especially since Dangriga could be called the Garifuna capital of Belize. A large number of Garifunas (see p 179) settled in the area, founding the village around 1823. Their customs have shaped its unique character, and many local restaurants and hotels have a Garifuna flavour.

THE SOUTH

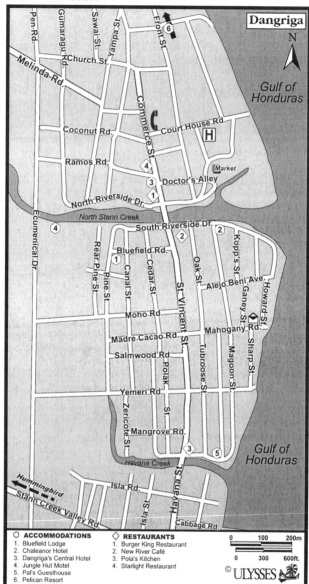

Dangriga

N

Gulf of Honduras

Pen-Rd.
Gumaragu-Rd.
Sawai-St.
Yamgu-St.
Front-St.
Melinda-Rd.
Church-St.
Commerce-St.
Court-House-Rd.
H
Coconut-Rd.
Market
Ramos-Rd.
North-Riverside-Dr.
Doctor's-Alley
Ecumenical-Dr.
North-Stann-Creek
South-Riverside-Dr.
Kopp's-St.
Ganey-St.
Howard-St.
Rear-Pine-St.
Pine-St.
Canal-St.
Cedar-St.
Bluefield-Rd.
St.-Vincent-St.
Oak-St.
Alejo-Beni-Ave.
Magoon-St.
Sharp-St.
Moho-Rd.
Mahogany-Rd.
Madre-Cacao-Rd.
Tubroose-St.
Salmwood-Rd.
Polak-St.
Yemeri-Rd.
Zericote-St.
Mangrove-Rd.
Havana-Creek
Gulf of Honduras
Hummingbird
Stann-Creek-Valley-Rd.
Isla-Rd.
Isla-St.
Havana-St.
Cabbage-Rd.

0   100   200m
0   300   600ft.

© ULYSSES

○ ACCOMMODATIONS
1. Bluefield Lodge
2. Chaleanor Hotel
3. Dangriga's Central Hotel
4. Jungle Hut Motel
5. Pal's Guesthouse
6. Pelican Resort

◇ RESTAURANTS
1. Burger King Restaurant
2. New River Café
3. Pola's Kitchen
4. Starlight Restaurant

Like the rest of Belize, Dangriga is a cultural mosaic. However, the Garifunas take over the streets on November 19, Settlement Day, a national holiday commemorating their ancestors' arrival in Belize. Parades make their way through the streets to the sound of drums in a Mardi Gras atmosphere. Men and women wear traditional dress during the religious and cultural ceremonies, and the festivities go on for days. It seems like night never falls during this period. If you are lucky enough to be visiting Dangriga around Settlement Day, make sure to reserve a room several days in advance, since the town is always packed during the celebrations.

Dangriga used to be called Stand (later corrupted to Stann) because British puritans set up a trading post here. Its present name means "standing waters" in Garifuna. Two rivers, the North Stann Creek and Havana Creek, run through Dangriga, before emptying into the sea. These waterways still serve as communication routes to the hinterland and fertile surrounding area.

Hopkins

A typical little coastal village, Hopkins is truly a haven of peace. Inhabited by Garifunas (see p 179), Hopkins is one of the few villages to have escaped extensive tourist development. Clearly, however, it will not remain this way for long, since it has a magnificent beach that is several kilometres long and perfect for swimming. The beach is lined with little houses, and local residents can be seen sipping a glass of rum with their friends or enjoying their favourite pastime, dominoes, in the shade of the palm trees. If you want to learn about Garifuna culture, Hopkins is an excellent place to do so, since it is easy to mingle with the locals here. A dirt road runs along the south side of town, continuing several kilometres to the Sittee River and its little village. You will find a few inns, most of them run by foreigners, along the way.

Alaska natives Greg and Rita Duke, who moved to Hopkins years ago, run the Hopkins Inn. One day, when the sun was beating down, they served me lemonade on their shady veranda and we got to know each other a bit. While we were chatting, I asked them if they would write a short description

THE SOUTH

of Hopkins for this guide, and they agreed. Here, in their words, is how these two new residents of Hopkins view their adopted home:

"The village of Hopkins (pop. 1100), eight miles south of Dangriga, stretches for about a mile along a gently curving bay. It was settled in 1941 after a hurricane destroyed the site of the old village, New Town, a few miles to the north. Hopkins is a picturesque village; its main road parallels the beach, which is dotted with thousands of coconut palms. Many wood and thatch houses still nestle beneath the palms, but the face of the village is changing as more and more cement houses are being built. In Hopkins people are friendly, they walk or bicycle everywhere, and they always have time for a chat and a laugh. They still meander down the village streets in the evenings after dark to visit with friends. But slowly the modern world is encroaching on the old ways. In the early 1990's water and electricity became available, and in 1996 satellite television and private telephone (and with that e-mail and Internet). But tourism still hasn't had too much impact; the village has yet to be discovered. All hotels, guesthouses, and restaurants in the village are in the low to mid price range. Most are very basic and appeal to the more adventurous traveler. More than half a dozen businesses now offer overnight accommodations; there are numerous restaurants and bars, many small stores, a gas station, a car rental agency (Isuzu Troopers), a post office, and bicycle, sea kayak, and catamaran rentals. Several guides offer boat tours to the cayes and reef for snorkeling, fishing, and sightseeing. There is plenty to do for most visitors. Relaxing, swinging in a hammock reading a good book, enjoying the beach and the water, and observing or participating in local village life are favorite pastimes. Many local women will cook a traditional meal and serve it in their homes (for a fee), if asked to do so by a visitor. Since seeing tourists in the village is not yet a daily occurrence, visitors are treated very politely and locals take the time to talk to them.

The people of Hopkins are called Garifuna. They are a mixture of Carib Indians and black Africans from the islands of St. Vincent and Dominica in the West Indies. They were resettled to the Bay Islands off Honduras. From there they settled all along the coast of Central America, from Honduras to Belize. They established small coastal communities where they fished and farmed for their livelihood. Even today most villagers have

The Story of the Garifunas

The story of the Black Caribs, or Garifunas, begins with the sinking of a slave ship off the coast of St. Vincent. The slaves, who were supposed to be sold in Barbados, thereby escaped this fate. Apparently free men, they settled on the island, which was inhabited by Carib Indians. Though it is unknown whether the Caribs behaved peacefully toward the Africans, a European visitor noted in 1672 that there were about 600 black archers among some thousand Carib warriors.

The Africans adopted some of the Caribs' cultural traits, including their language. Through the intermingling between the two races, Black Caribs became more and more numerous, forming a new, free society. Having had this taste of liberty, they were determined to protect their independence at any cost. This attitude led to frequent conflicts with the English colonizers who took control of the island under the Treaty of Paris (1763), supplanting the French, whose presence had not been strongly felt. Many battles ensued as the English tried to impose their rule on the Garifunas, who struggled to remain independent. The last battle took place in 1796, and resulted in an English victory. Unable to enslave the Garifunas, they deported them to the island of Roatan.

The Garifunas lost their land, but they didn't lose their freedom. Deciding to leave Roatan, they established themselves along the Central American coast, from Honduras to Belize. So begins the second part of the story of this people born of cultural and racial intermingling between Caribs and Africans. In Belize, they founded a number of villages in the Toledo and Stann Creek district.

THE SOUTH

a small plot of land (called farm) along the Hopkins Cut-Off Road where they grow food for their table and also oranges and grapefruit for sale to the juice factories. The locals are proud of their heritage and their language; Hopkins is the only Garifuna settlement left in Belize where Garifuna is the main language spoken. Drumming and dancing are still part of life here, especially on holidays and special occasions, as on

*Settlement Day, November 19, when the landing of the first
Garifunas on the shores of southern Belize is reenacted. Often
the drums don't fall silent all night during the week leading up
to the holiday. Garifuna from all over the country and also from
abroad converge on the settlements in the south to celebrate."*

Maya Center and the
Cockscomb Basin Jaguar Preserve

On the Southern Highway, south of the turn-off for Hopkins, is
the village of **Maya Center** and a dirt road leading to the
Cockscomb Basin Jaguar Preserve, the only jaguar preserve in
Central America. The villagers are Mopán Maya, and still wear
traditional dress. There are usually several Mayan women at the
Jaguar Preserve's little booth at the edge of town. However, if
you don't plan to visit the preserve and just want to spend
some time in the village, you don't have to pay the admission
fee.

A few huts in the forest and along the road to the preserve,
Maya Center is a modern Mayan village. Be sure to stop by the
Hmen Herbal Center & Medicinal Trail *(☎05-2266)*, if only for
a few minutes. It is run by Aurara Saqui, an artist and specialist
in Mayan medicine who studies the secrets and mysteries of
the medicinal herbs used by the Maya. Visitors can tour the
Botanical Garden *(BZ$4, with documentation but no guide,
BZ$20 per group, with guide and documentation)*. Different
types of excursions to the Cockscomb Jaguar Preserve *(BZ$50)*
are also available. In addition to offering accommodations (see
p 195) midway between the village and the park, the Center
has a restaurant and organizes a variety of cultural activities,
including dance performances and traditional Mayan music. It
also has special rates for transportation to other towns in the
area, namely, Dangriga, Hopkins, Sittee River and Placencia.

Funded by the Audubon Society and the World Wildlife Fund,
Cockscomb Basin & Wildlife Sanctuary ★★ *(BZ$10; 7am to
5pm)* is a basin at the foot of the mountains, engulfed by the
jungle. In the 19th century, loggers referred to this area as
"Hell Camp" or *"Sale si puede"* (Leave if You Can). Thanks to
the efforts of environmental groups, it has remained wild and
enigmatic. The Sanctuary is renowned for its jaguars, which are
the third largest members of the feline family, measuring up to

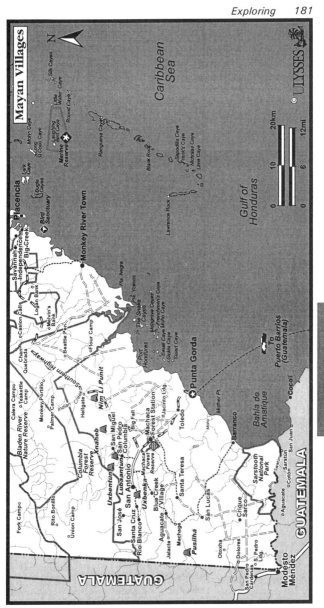

1.8 metres in length and weighing up to 90 kilograms! Pumas also live here, sharing the jaguars' hunting grounds.

In addition to the big cats, visitors can see tapirs, otters, deer and armadillos, to name only a few. More than 290 species of birds have been spotted in the sanctuary, making this a birdwatcher's paradise.

This is without question the most beautiful and unspoiled park in Belize; adventurers, hikers and campers should not miss the opportunity to explore it a little.

The Placencia Peninsula ★★★

The Placencia Peninsula, which only recently got electricity, has been experiencing a slow but steady rise in its tourist industry over the past few years. Although this idyllic peninsula has undergone some development, its laid-back, hospitable spirit has fortunately survived so far. A strip of land stretching 17 kilometres into the Caribbean Sea, it possesses all the elements necessary to become a high-end seaside resort, including the best beaches in the country, especially for swimming, since the coral reef is some distance from the shore. Scuba and snorkelling buffs will also have no trouble organizing excursions out to the reef. Of course, local residents prefer their reef to the one near the cayes where, according to them, there are fewer fish and the coral is not in such pristine condition. It's like asking someone from Bordeaux where the best wine comes from.

The **Placencia Lagoon**, on the west side of the peninsula, is famous for its fabulous sunsets and animal inhabitants – crocodiles, turtles and the odd lamentin. This region's poorer area along the west coast is generally neglected, strewn with failed development projects and rusting piers. The odd ship-wreck is about all there is to inspire poetic thoughts, and even then, you have to be a romantic to start with.

The peninsula has developed fairly quickly, and is now easily accessible thanks to the construction of a landing strip. If you are travelling by car, the Manatee and Hummingbird highways are in quite poor condition, making any trip in the region slow

going. A dirt road runs the length of the peninsula, all the way to the tip. It is lined with hotel complexes, the vast majority of which have been designed to fit in with the natural setting. If you arrive from the north, you will pass through **Seine Bight**, a small Garifuna village.

The village of **Placencia** is just as popular as the beaches on the peninsula. Its little plaza, a patch of hard earth in front of the pier, marks the end of the road that runs the length of the peninsula. Standing on it gives you the strange sensation of having reached the end of the world. To get there, walk past the old wooden supermarket, which is frequented by sailors as well as local residents; the soccer field, which looks like an abandoned lot; and the little houses engulfed by tropical vegetation. In front of the pier are two or three kiosks and a gas station consisting of a single rusted pump in the middle of the plaza. On the shore, colourful little boats lie beneath the palm trees, while local fishermen sit in the shade talking, and a few lost tourists wander around looking for a snack to tide them over until lunchtime, while more seasoned veterans of these sweltering climes chat over a beer in front of one of the stalls. Here, you can still get a sense of just how cut off

Placencia used to be from the modern world, when its only contact with it was the pier and the horizon, where sailing ships would bring good or bad news every now and then. This little square, almost abandoned to nature, seems to be all that has remained of the rustic village of yesteryear.

Placencia's **Main Street**, on the other hand, appears in all the tourist brochures. Running through the village, parallel to the road, Main Street, also known as "the sidewalk", is actually nothing more than a narrow boardwalk built on top of the sand. The perfect place for a stroll, it leads through a cluster of wooden houses on stilts, which have been converted into travel agencies and restaurants; hotels, most consisting of a series of cabanas on the beach, and a few concrete houses, the result of tourist development.

Nim Li Punit

Located on the Southern Highway, 40 kilometres north of Punta Gorda, the Nim Li Punit archaeological site, whose name means "big hat", wasn't discovered until 1976, when oil workers were drilling here. In many ways, the site resembles Lubaantun (see p 186). It has the same kind of stone platforms built without the use of mortar, which were topped with wooden structures that have not survived the passage of time. However, the similarities end there; Lubaantun is much more impressive, both in terms of size and the number of structures.

Nevertheless, Nim Li Punit has its merits. In fact, it has something you won't find at Lubaantun – 25 steles, eight of which are decorated with bas-reliefs. The site also has two plazas and a ball court, as well as pyramidal structures. Though the tallest of these is 12 metres high, the most impressive is a strange structure only three metres high but over 65 metres long.

Nim Li Punit is less than a kilometre's walk from the Southern Highway and is therefore easy to reach if you have a car. In fact, it's an excellent spot to take a little break from driving. If you are travelling by bus, ask the driver to drop you off, but make sure that another bus will be passing by on its way north or to Punta Gorda. The little Mayan village of Indian Creek is right nearby.

Punta Gorda

The little port town of Punta Gorda, the southernmost town in the country, is the starting-off point for boat trips to Guatemala and Honduras. Though there is little to do in Punta Gorda, many travellers spend the day here waiting for their boat to leave. The town has two main streets. The pier where passengers board boats to Guatemala and northern Belize is located on **Front Street**, which runs along the shore. It is right in the middle of town, next to the police station. Before exploring Punta Gorda any further, stop by **Toledo's Visitor's Information Center** *(☎07-2470)*, where you'll find all sorts of documentation on the Toledo District, as well as boat and bus schedules and information on the Mayan village home-stay network (see p 199).

Main Street is lined with restaurants and hotels. There is also a Belize Bank, where you can exchange U.S. currency or get a cash advance on your credit card.

Near Punta Gorda

The village of **San Antonio** is in another world, where borders and countries do not exist. At dawn or dusk, the locals leave this dreamland for their jobs in the more practical Punta Gorda or elsewhere in the area. This is one of those rare places whose soul is immediately felt. Struck by some intangible quality that emanates from this village, which could be anywhere in the world, and seems more like an imagined ideal than anywhere real, I fell in love with this place from the start. San Antonio seems to have a spirit that exists beyond its streets, its inhabitants and their daily concerns. And for two days and one night, I let myself be carried off into this dreamworld.

Perched in the hills, San Antonio is dominated by **San Luis Rey Church**, erected in 1954. A charming school with typical Jesuit architecture stands nearby. You're sure to enjoy strolling along the streets and paths that wind through the village.

THE SOUTH

Not far from San Antonio, the Mayan ruins of **Uxbenka** (whose name means "old place") are located on the road from San Antonio to Santa Cruz, which are less than a kilometre apart. Though this might not be the most impressive archaeological site, it makes for a wonderful excursion, since you pass through the jungle and some cornfields.

Uxbenka is a small ceremonial centre whose central plaza lies on a hill. Several steles overlook the plaza, which is surrounded by six structures, the tallest of which is eight metres high. Other structures and a few smaller plazas lie strewn across the hillsides. The entire site covers nearly three kilometres.

The Mayan village of **San Pedro Columbia** is the most popular destination in the home-stay network, since it is located near the Lubaantun archaeological site. You can also visit the Fallen Stones Butterfly Ranch, which breeds and exports butterflies.

Lubaantun ★, or "the place of fallen stones", lies two and a half kilometres from San Pedro Columbia. A former ceremonial

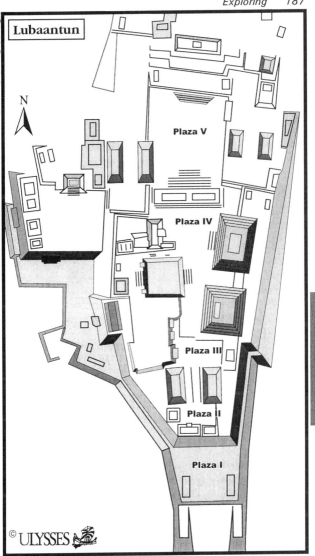

Lubaantun

N

Plaza V

Plaza IV

Plaza III

Plaza II

Plaza I

© ULYSSES

centre, it dates from AD 730 to 850 (Late Classic periods), when its sphere of influence extended from the Maya Mountains to the shores of the Caribbean Sea.

Today, visitors will find five large plazas and 11 pyramidal platforms. Unlike the pyramids at other Mayan archaeological sites, these were topped by wooden structures, which naturally have not withstood the passage of time. Consequently, all that remains are the stone platforms on which the top of the pyramids once sat. The platforms are interesting in their own right, since they were built without the use of mortar. Instead, the stone was carefully cut so that the pieces fit together perfectly.

Unlike those at other Mayan sites, these platforms have no bas-reliefs – all the ornamentation must have been on the wooden parts. Three stone carvings of people playing ball were discovered on the playing field, however.

Unfortunately, there is no public transportation to Lubaantun. Still, the excursion is worth the effort, since the site lies at the edge of a valley formed by one of the rivers that merge with the Columbia River. The dirt path leading there passes through the jungle, and it is only a 20-minute walk from the main road. You can also rent a canoe at San Pedro, paddle across the Columbia River, and walk up the steep little path to the ruins.

The Southern Cayes

The cayes in the southern part of the country are easily accessible from Dangriga. As soon as you approach the town pier, a whole swarm of tour operators will descend on you, offering to take you to one of the local islands.

French Louie Caye

Excursions to this tiny island, home to a few families of fishermen, are organized at **Kitty's Place** (☎06-2327, ⚏06-2326, info@kittysplace.com) in Placencia. You can camp here for BZ$120 a night, which includes a number of activities, such as sea kayaking and snorkelling.

Southwater Caye

This heavenly little island, which covers an area of six hectares and sits atop the barrier reef, is easy to reach from Dangriga (see p 167). There is nothing here but palm trees, white sand, beautiful beaches and direct access to the reef, where you can go snorkelling or simply take a swim. For many years, Southwater Caye was the private domain and refuge of the Sisters of Mercy, who built a big wooden house here. This building and about half the island now belong to the same owners as the **Pelican Resort** in Dangriga. Known as Pelican University, it has been converted into accommodations for university students and travellers (see p 200).

Tobacco Caye

People often camp on this small, sandy island located south of Dangriga, on the barrier reef. There are several places to stay, and it is getting more popular every year. You can go scuba diving or snorkelling straight from the beach.

 OUTDOOR ACTIVITIES

 Sailing

Manatee Lodge *(Gales Point, ☎02-2320, USA 800-334-7942)* offers guests free use of its sailboats and hosts 10 different lamentin-watching excursions *(BZ$100; 7:30am and 8:30am departures; 4 hours long)*.

 Excursions

The **Pelican Resort** *(Dangriga, ☎05-2044, ≠05-2570, pelicanbeach@alt.net, www.belizenet.com/pelican.html)* offers all sorts of excursions in the area – fishing, snorkelling, etc. (see p 200).

THE SOUTH

The **Hopkins Inn** *(in Hopkins, on the waterfront - Sittee)* (see p 194) organizes fishing, scuba and snorkelling trips, river tours and excursions to area parks. You can also rent its catamaran.

The proprietors of **Kitty's Place** *(Placencia, ☎06-2327, ⇴06-2326, info@kittysplace.com)* offer a variety of excursions on the Monkey River, as well as scuba trips. The most popular outing is to **French Louie Caye** (see p 188) *(BZ$90; 8:30am departure)*, which they own. In the morning, you will visit little Laughing Bird Caye before enjoying breakfast on French Louie Caye. The fishermen who live on the island will serve you the best fish of the day, guaranteed. You can camp here for BZ$120, which includes a number of activities, including sea kayaking and snorkelling gear.

Toucan Sittee *(Hopkins - Sittee, ☎05-37039)* lies eight kilometres south of Hopkins on the little trail that leads through the village. Canoe and bicycle rentals are available for BZ$26 per day, and the place also provides fishing equipment.

The travel agency **Hummingbird Adventures** *(on the sidewalk, Placencia, ☎06-2387, ⇴06-2388)* has two 11-metre sailboats for fishing *(BZ$600 per day per boat)*. The manager is from British Columbia.

 Hiking

The **Hmen Herbal Center** *(Cockscomb Basin Jaguar Preserve and Maya Center)* offers guided hiking trips in the wildlife sanctuary.

  Scuba Diving and Snorkelling

The **Placencia Dive Shop** *(every day 7am to noon and 3pm to 6pm, Placencia)*, facing the pier, offers snorkelling and scuba classes and organizes excursions on the Monkey River. Two-tank diving gear is available. During the scuba trips *(BZ$130 per person, lunch included)*, a fisherman finds lobsters to grill on the beach for lunch.

The **Diving Reef Center** *(Southwater Caye, ☎05-2214)* is located at the Blue Marlin Lodge. It offers PADI instruction and is affiliated with the International Zoological Expedition.

 ACCOMMODATIONS

Gales Point

There aren't many places to stay in the little village of Gales Point. If you plan on camping, head to the **Wish Tree Campsite**, located just before the church. There is also **A Jentings** *(BZ$20 bkfst incl.)*, a pleasant, unpretentious little Bed & Breakfast across from the school. Standard level of comfort.

The Shores at Gales Point *(BZ$120; pb, ⊛, ℜ, ≈; ☎/≈02-2023, shores@btl.net)*, a cabana complex near Gales Point, comes recommended. Though modern, it has a rustic ambiance. A variety of activities are available to guests, including scuba, snorkelling and lamentin-watching trips. A family-style restaurant.

Magnificent **Manatee Lodge** *(BZ$362, bkfst. and din. incl.; pb, hw, ⊛, ℜ, ☎USA 800-334-7942, ☎02-2320)* is located on the north tip of the peninsula. A typical Caribbean wooden house, it has a large common room on the third floor, complete with tourist information, games, a large waterfront terrace and hammocks. The large, rustic rooms are well decorated and very comfortable, and the staff is as friendly as can be. Excellent location in a gorgeous natural setting. The hotel has a generator that provides electricity from 8am to 10pm. Sailboats are available to guests at no charge, and the hotel offers some 10 lamentin-watching excursions *(BZ$100; 7:30am and 8:30am departures; 4 hours long)*.

Dangriga

Dangriga's Central Hotel *(BZ$35; 119 Commerce St., ☎05-2008)* is located right downtown. The rooms are not only small and noisy, but they are also poorly ventilated, since the

---

Ulysses' Favourites

Accommodations

Typically Belizean charm: **Pelican Resort** (see p 200)
Modern facilities: **Jaguar Reef Resort** (see p 194)
Inviting atmosphere: **Green Parrot Beach Houses** (see p 195)

Restaurants

Dancing and dominoes: **Swinging Armadillo** (see p 202)
Tropical bar atmosphere: **The Pickled Parrot**
                                   Bar & Grill (see p 203)
Outstanding cuisine: **La Petite Maison** (see p 203)

---

windows are tiny. On the positive side, this is the cheapest place to stay in Dangriga, and has balconies.

Just a bit more expensive but much more comfortable, the inviting **Bluefield Lodge** *(BZ$38; hw, pb, tv; 6 Bluefield Rd., ☎05-2742)* is the best choice for travellers on a tight budget. The rooms are clean, well-ventilated and full of little extras like soap, which make staying here that much more pleasant. Different kinds of rooms are available – with or without a private bath and with one or several beds. In either case, you can cut the cost of your stay by sacrificing a little privacy.

A concrete building on the waterfront, **Pal's Guesthouse** *(BZ$42-64; cb; ☎05-2095)* is in a quiet spot at the centre of town. It used to cater mainly to locals, but is attracting more and more foreign tourists. Very clean and inviting, Pal's is one of the best deals in Dangriga.

The **Chaleanor Hotel** *(BZ$70; pb, ⊗, hw; 35 Magoon St., ☎05-2587, ≈05-3038)* is centrally located and near the sea, just south of the bridge over the river. Clean and comfortable, it has spacious, modern rooms. Good value for the price.

The **Jungle Hut Motel** *(BZ$95; pb, ⊗, hw, ≡; ☎05-3166)* is located near Dangriga's centre, and has the added advantage of being in the upper part of town, on the banks of the North Stann Creek River. The rooms are lovely, clean and spacious.

The cheaper ones cost BZ$50 a night, with private bath and hot water. Though smaller, they are just as comfortable as the more expensive ones. The motel is clean, quiet and safe, but has no restaurant.

The owners of the charming **Pelican Beach Resort** *(BZ$120-240; pb, hw, ℜ, △; ☎05-2044, ⌐05-2570; pelicanbeach@alt.net, www.belize.com/pelican.html)* are clearly proud to be Belizeans. Located in the north part of town, the hotel's setting is extremely secluded and relaxing. The big typically Caribbean wooden houses stand at the edge of the sea. The hospitable local staff, whose love of their country is evident, create a homey atmosphere. There is a large, comfortable common room with cable television and a ping-pong table. In front, you'll find a long veranda, hammocks, the beach, a pier and a basketball court. Everything has been designed to make your stay as pleasant as possible. The rooms are big, with two large beds, a ceiling fan, wall-to-wall carpeting and a balcony with a view of the sea. The place looks a bit dated, but is spotless. Good restaurant. The hotel organizes all sorts of excursions (see p 189) to the surrounding region and nearby islands. It also owns a large portion of Southwater Caye (see p 189) and offers various kinds of accommodations there.

Hopkins

The cheapest place in town is the **Caribbean View Motel** *(BZ$30; on the beach)*, whose name is misleading; it may be right on the beach, but you don't see much of the ocean! Standard rooms with poor ventilation.

Managed by a women's cooperative, the **Sandy Beach Lodge** *(BZ$40; on the beach, ☎05-2560)* is a 20-minute walk south of the village. It has about ten basic but pleasant rooms and an extremely relaxing atmosphere. The food is also good here, and you'll have a chance to sample some Garifuna specialties.

The **Swinging Armadillo** *(BZ$40; on the beach)* is the best place to spend your time in Hopkins, whether you feel like eating, drinking a beer or dancing by the seaside. It also rents out two rooms. Clean, rustic and very charming, they look right down over the sea, since the place is located at the end of a pier.

During the night, you'll be lulled by the sound of the waves; during the day and in the evening, the bar becomes lively and the rooms are noisy. If you'd like to learn more about daily life in the village, the friendly, helpful owners are excellent sources of information.

The **Hopkins Inn** *(BZ$90 bkfst incl.; pb, hw; on the beach; ☎/≈05-7013, hopkinsinn@btl.net, www.hopkinsinn.com)* is run by Greg and Rita Duke, who wrote the description of Hopkins on p 178 Tired of freezing up in Alaska, where they used to live, they decided to move here and set up this seaside inn in the southern part of town, near the church and the basketball court. The red-roofed cabanas are clean and comfortable, with a double bed, coffee machine, bathroom and private veranda with a view of the ocean.

South of the village, the lovely, spacious **Ransoms Cabana** *(BZ$90; on the beach; ☎05-2889)* is available for rent. It is set in a tropical garden, where you can hang up a hammock and drink in the heady fragrances.

Near Hopkins

Toucan Sittee *(BZ$14-BZ$100; pb, hw, ⊗; ☎05-7039)*, located eight kilometres south of Hopkins on the little trail that runs through the village, is a row of charming wooden cabanas on piles, overlooking Sittee River. The grounds are beautifully maintained, but make sure to bring along insect repellent. Several different rates are available, ranging from BZ$14 per person with a shared bath to BZ$100 for a three-room cabana with a private bath. Canoe and bicycle rentals for BZ$26 per day. Fishing equipment is also available for rent.

The **Jaguar Reef Resort** *(BZ$180-300; 3 km south of Hopkins, ☎/≈212041, ☎800-289-5755, jaguarreef@btl.net, www.jaguarreef.com)* is one of the loveliest and most modern seaside resorts in the country. Located right on the water, it has seven large duplex cabanas on a pristine beach near the mouth of Sittee River. The rooms are spacious, very comfortable, attractively decorated, and offer a view of the sea. Every effort has been made to ensure that your stay will be a pleasant one. The resort's main building is a huge thatched cabana with a lounge, restaurant, bar and various services inside. There is a large outdoor patio with hammocks and wicker benches overlooking the sea, the perfect place to relax in the sun or in the shade of a palm tree. The resort organizes a variety of outings, including scuba and snorkelling trips, and excursions to Hopkins and the Cockscomb Wildlife Sanctuary.

Maya Center and Cockscomb Basin Jaguar Preserve

Dormitory-style accommodations are available at the **Cockscomb Basin Jaguar Preserve** for BZ$20 per person. You can also camp there for about BZ$10 per person. However, there are no restaurants or food stalls, so you'll have to bring your own provisions.

Located at the entrance to the wildlife sanctuary, the **Hmen Herbal Center** *(BZ$40; ⊗)* is run by a friendly Mopán Mayan family who perform traditional healing and prayer ceremonies, and are happy to tell you about Mopán music and culture. Marimba concerts are presented here. Each hut has its own Mayan name, and all are simple, clean, comfortable and equipped with mosquito screens.

Maya Beach

There are several places to stay at Maya Beach, in the northern part of the Placencia Peninsula. The **Green Parrot Beach Houses on Maya Beach** *(BZ$170-220 continental bkfst; pb, ⊗, K, ℜ, ⊗, ⌂; ☎06-22488, greenparrot@btl.net, www.belize.com/greenparrot.html)* are charming wooden houses built on stilts along a magnificent section of the beach. Each has a bedroom loft with a large double bed, a sofa-bed on the main floor, a kitchen, a dining table and a private balcony where you can hang up a hammock and enjoy a splendid view of the sea. The rates for the cabanas vary, depending on the number of people per room. If you are travelling in a group, the place is a real bargain for this type of accommodation. Although it is a bit far from the village of Placencia, the two Canadian owners and their staff liven things up. Wonderful overall atmosphere and excellent bar and restaurant. The Green Parrot also organizes tours and has an eight-metre catamaran.

The small, Australian-owned **Singing Sands Inn** *(BZ$158-178; ℛ; ☎/⇌06-2243, ssi@btl.net)* has six traditional, thatched cabanas on Maya Beach. All the rooms have a view of the sea. It has a good restaurant and extremely popular bar, and a pleasant overall ambiance. There is a diving shop, and excursions to the coral reef and the cayes are also available.

The **Placencia Lagoon Resort** *(BZ$180; pb, ℛ, ⊛; Malacate Beach, ☎06-2362, ⇌06-2482, plalagoon@btl.net, http://caribbeancoast.com/hotels/placencia/pics/stm)*, a cluster of cabanas on the shores of Placencia Lagoon, offers all sorts of group activities and excursions in the area. The rustic, thatched cabanas each have a telephone and refrigerator, as well as large, comfortable double beds. Unfortunately, this resort is a little far from Placencia. However, it is in a lovely natural setting near Mango Creek. Camping: BZ$40 per person.

Seine Bight

The **Hotel Seine Bight** *(BZ$80-170; pb, ⊛, ⊛, ℛ; in the centre of the Placencia Peninsula, ☎06-3536, ⇌06-3537)* is a small seaside resort near the last village before Placencia. It has traditional one- and two-story cabanas with thatched roofs. The double rooms are spacious and comfortable, and the place is generally well maintained. The very popular restaurant on the second floor serves good Belizean and international cuisine. Excursions are available.

On the Way into Placencia

Kitty's Place *(BZ$55-BZ$155 bkfst incl.; hw, pb, ⊛; free coffee; ☎06-3227, ⇌06-3226, info@kittysplace.com)*, is a cluster of seaside cabanas with typically Caribbean architecture, located 300 metres south of the airport. Most have private verandas, refrigerators and coffee machines, and some have kitchenettes. The rooms are spacious and rustic, and all face the sea. A trip on the Monkey River and snorkelling excursions for amateurs are offered. The proprietors also own French Louie Caye (see p 188), which you can visit if you feel like organizing an outing (see p 190).

Heading south toward Placencia, you'll pass by a cluster of seaside resorts for travellers with money to spend. **Serenity Resort** *(BZ$170; pb, ⊗, ⊛, ℛ, ≡; ☎06-3232, ⇝06-3231)* is a big, concrete, waterfront hotel with concrete bungalows lining its front garden. Though it is not particularly charming, the units are spacious, modern and comfortable, and are sure to appeal to the practical-minded traveller. Each has a private balcony. Courteous, professional service. The rooms in the main building are air-conditioned, which is their only real advantage over the bungalows.

The peaceful, typically Belizean **Turtle Inn** *(BZ$224; pb, hw, ⊗; 1 km from the airport and 1.6 km from the centre of town, ☎06-3244, ⇝06-3245, turtleinn@btl.net)* rents out wonderful cabanas on the beach. It is also possible to rent a beach house for BZ$2,000 a week. There is a diving shop on the premises. The inn can also arrange for you to stay with a Mayan family in San Pedro Columbia.

The **Rum Point Inn** *(BZ$350-448, all-inclusive; pb, ⊗, ⊛, ℛ; ☎06-2323, ⇝06-2340, USA ☎800-747-7888)*, just north of the landing strip in Placencia, has the largest rooms on the peninsula. Run by an American entomologist, this complex claims to offer the best accommodations in the region. It has an exclusive and laid-back atmosphere, and spacious, comfortable rooms, but this doesn't come cheap! The wooden furniture and overall decor of the concrete cabanas creates a distinctive, intimate atmosphere. The inn has a pleasant restaurant and open-air bar, as well as an inviting lounge with sofas and a library. Numerous fishing and diving trips are available.

Placencia

One of the most economical places in town is the charming **Paradise Vacation Hotel** *(BZ$30-50; pb, ⊗)*, located at the south end of the village. It is a wooden house with several rooms, some with private baths.

In the same category, **Conrad and Lydia's Guesthouse** *(BZ$40-50; ⊗; ☎06-3117)* is a clean, well-maintained and very popular place that feels almost like a home away from home. You can't go wrong with this one.

THE SOUTH

The wonderful, newly renovated little **Cosy Corner Hotel** *(BZ$50 with ocean view, BZ$40 with no ocean view)* has one of the loveliest sites on Placencia beach. A wooden building, its rooms are spotless, well-ventilated and have new furnishings. The atmosphere is relaxed and there are hammocks. Good value for the price.

The **West Wind** *(BZ$110; pb, hw, ⊗, with ocean view, $90 with no ocean view, on the sidewalk, ☎06-3255)* has comfortable, functional rooms and serves a good breakfast. Very well located near the market, where you can buy fruit to snack on in between meals. Good value for the money.

The Barracuda & Jaguar Inn *(BZ$120-180; hw, pb, ⊗; on the sidewalk; ☎06-3166, USA ☎800-991-1969)* has a lovely, inviting wooden cabana surrounded by hibiscus gardens, and a terrace complete with screens and hammocks. The place has a wonderful ambiance and an art gallery. Excellent value for the price.

Whether you are looking for a campsite, a hotel room or a seaside cabana, you'll find it at the **Blue Crab Beach Resort** *(cabanas BZ$150 , rooms BZ$50; RV hook-ups BZ$40 RV; camping BZ$14 per person; ☎06-3544, ⌐06-3543, kerry@btl.net)*, one of the few places with RV hook-ups.

Pallavi's Hotel *(BZ$26-32; pb, hw, ⊗; Main St., ☎07-2414)*, modest but relatively clean, is centrally located and safe. The rooms are decent; those facing the outer side are better ventilated. Same owner as the Grace Restaurant.

The **Wahima** *(BZ$32; ⊗; 11 Front St.)* is run by a friendly local teacher, who you can probe about the town and its history. The rooms are simple but decent. Family atmosphere.

The **St. Charles Inn** *(BZ$60; pb, ⊗, tv; 23 King St., ☎07-2149)* has about 15 rooms, all with cable television, wall-to-wall carpeting and large beds, which makes it a good deal for this area. The service could be better, though, and the place seems a bit run-down.

The **Mira Mar Hotel** *(BZ$70-150; pb, hw, ⊗, tv; 95 Front St., ☎07-2033)* is near the centre of town, and has comfortable, functional rooms. The most expensive ones have air conditioning and cable television. The hotel's concrete building is not exactly charming, but it's a good choice if you're looking for worry-free accommodations.

Toledo

A local home-stay program for travellers wishing to spend some time in the Mayan villages of the Toledo District was launched in 1994. It costs BZ$10 per night per person, and you can join your Mayan hosts for meals for an additional BZ$4. The idea is fairly simple. When you arrive in one of the seven villages involved in the program (San Antonio, Santa Cruz, Santa Elena, San José, Na Luum Ca, San Pedro Columbia and Silver Creek), contact the local *alcalde* (mayor), who will pair you with a family in the network. The *alcalde* will also tell you everything you need to know about your host family, and give you practical advice and tourist information about visiting the area. A portion of the profits go to the village's treasury.

This program is aimed at independent travellers with a taste for adventure. The living conditions in Mayan villages are some-what precarious, so don't expect luxury accommodations. Meals usually consist of corn tortillas with a light soup or some vegetables, and coffee. Meat is served occasionally. Though all the villages have potable water, it is always better to boil water before consumption.

San Antonio

The home-stay program, which is very popular in this area, enables visitors to experience the daily life of the Mopán Maya first-hand.

The **Hilltop Hotel** *(BZ$30)* offers very satisfactory budget accommodations. A Mestizo and Mayan family live on the ground floor. The father is extremely likeable, if you can get him to tear himself away from his newspaper. The rooms, all on the second floor, are small, and the place could use a face-lift, but it has a certain feeling of adventure to it. The toilets and showers are outside on ground level.

THE SOUTH

The Southern Cayes

French Louie Caye

Kitty's Place *(BZ$130; ☎06-3227, ⇌06-3226, info@kittysplace.com)*, in Placencia, offers camping on the island. The rate includes ·transportation to the island, and outdoor activities including sea kayaking and snorkelling. Local fishermen prepare your meals.

Southwater Caye

The **Pelican Beach Resort** *(cottage BZ$242, double room BZ$302, ☎05-2044, ⇌05-2570, pelicanbeach@alt.net, www.belizenet.com/pelican.html)* offers several types of accommodations on the island. The former convent of the Sisters of Mercy, now known as Pelican University, has 16 rooms, each with a fan, private bath and hot water. The common room has satellite television and a kitchenette. The Osprey's Nest, a house with three large bedrooms and a kitchen, can accommodate up to eight people. There are two other, more private houses right near the water, surrounded by palm trees.

At the **Blue Marlin Lodge** *(BZ$450 per week; hw, tv, pb; ≡, ℛ, ≈; ☎05-2243, marlin@btl.net, www.belizenet.com/marlin.net)*, you can stay in one of three private, air-conditioned cabanas or one of nine new rooms in the main building. Modern, well-maintained and efficiently run, the Blue Marlin offers delicious food in its excellent restaurant, and outstanding service all around. There are all sorts of activities for guests to enjoy, including scuba diving and deep-sea fishing.

Tobacco Caye

Tobacco Caye has only a few small, simple places to stay, which gives it place a charming, casual atmosphere. You can easily pitch your tent on the grounds of one of the little hotels on this sandy island.

Island Camps *(BZ$40; ☎/≠05-3433)* has several rustic, comfortable cabanas, some of which have their own bathroom. Good restaurant and friendly service.

At the **Reef's End Lodge** *(all-inclusive; ☎05-2419)*, you can either pitch your tent by the sea or stay in a small cabana. The restaurant and bar are deservedly the most popular on Tobacco Caye.

RESTAURANTS

Dangriga

The town of Dangriga has a lot of little restaurants that offer affordable daily specials and cater to a local clientele. One of the better ones is the **Burger King Restaurant** *($; Commerce St.)* – no relation to the American fast-food chain – located north of the bridge. The menu includes American fare like burgers, as well as rice & beans and other traditional dishes.

The little **Starlight Restaurant** *($; 121 Commerce St.)* serves reasonably priced traditional and regional cuisine. Good ambiance. **Alida's Restaurant** *($; first street south of the Starlight)* is a similar type of place.

For typical Garifuna cuisine, try **Pola's Kitchen** *(Commerce St.)*, which serves fish- and coconut- based dishes.

Whether you go for breakfast or a seafood dinner, you won't be disappointed by the ever-popular **New River Café** *($-$$)*, a traveller's hang-out. Generous servings, and a good selection of sandwiches.

Hopkins-Sittee

The most pleasant and most affordable meals are served at places owned by villagers. **Iris' Restaurant** *($)*, run by a Garifuna woman, serves inexpensive, traditional cuisine – usually fish or chicken with rice & beans – in a family atmo-

THE SOUTH

sphere. This little eatery is located two buildings south of the intersection of Main Street and the road to the highway.

Innie's Restaurant *($)* is similar, serving affordable regional cuisine and cooking up the best breakfasts in town, as well. In addition to fruit, toast and coffee, you can have eggs with rice and beans to start your day off right. Located on Main Street at the south end of Hopkins, just past the Hopkins Inn.

A restaurant and bar, the **Swinging Armadillo** *($-$$)* is the best place in Hopkins to have drinks and a meal on the waterfront. Its clientele consists of some of the most colourful and cheerful folks in town, as well as lots of travellers, who enjoy striking up lively conversations between games of dominos or relaxing in one of the many hammocks suspended practically over the water. American fare, including all kinds of pizza.

An excellent restaurant set up in a traditional thatched cabana perched at the end of a pier, **Over the Waves** *($$; ☎05-7012)* is the best place to go for an intimate dinner at sunset or under the stars. The varied menu includes lobster and other kinds of seafood, turtle steak and assorted meat dishes. One of the best places in Southern Belize for traditional cuisine, Over the Waves is also attractively decorated and has a strong local flavour.

Placencia

If you're having a snack-attack, stop by **John the Baseman** *(7am to 7pm)*, which sells wonderful fresh bread and cinnamon buns.

Anyone who wants to go on a sea excursion or chat with the locals should go to the counter at **Chilies** *($; 8am to midnight)*. John, the owner, serves excellent meals and knows all the best fishermen and guides in the area. The stand is located on the village square next to the gas station, facing the sea, and its menu includes fresh fish to satisfy every palate, and a good selection of sandwiches and salads. You're sure to find something to whet your appetite!

Right nearby, facing the pier, **The End of the Road** *($)* is another little wooden stall, where Bill, a colourful character, will tell you all the best things to see and do in the area. This place serves the most popular pizza in town, as well as burgers and hotdogs. During the high season, fish and other more elaborate dishes are available.

The **Galey Restaurant** *($; 11am to 2pm and 6pm to 9pm)* is run by a local family, and serves the best regional cuisine in the area. The menu features a variety of Garifuna dishes, including fish with coconut. Located south of the soccer field.

It is worth going to the **Pickled Parrot Bar & Grill** *($-$$; noon to 10pm)* just for the atmosphere. This inviting thatched-roof eatery is the perfect place to have a few tropical cocktails before digging into dinner. There are specials every day of the week (for example, pizza gets top billing on Fridays), as well as an extensive à la carte menu complete with vegetarian dishes, excellent salads, seafood, Mexican fare and that old standard rice & beans.

Tentacles Restaurant & Bar *($$; every day 7am to 2:30pm and 6pm to 10pm; ☎06-3156)* is in an appealing thatched house set on piles. The ambiance is especially wonderful at dusk and later in the evening. Whiling away the time on the raised deck is a real treat. The menu is the most extensive in Placencia, whether you're looking for regional or American dishes. Good fish and seafood. The broiled lobster is prepared in many different ways; make sure to try the garlic butter.

When you're travelling, there are times when you really feel like making the most of your vacation time – giving your body a rest, enjoying the presence of a friend or lover, breathing in the fragrant air, treating your palate to a feast. One good way to awaken your senses is to indulge in some topnotch French cuisine, and there can be no better place to this in Belize than **La Petite Maison** *(BZ$48 per person; closed Sun and Mon, open six months out of the year, from Nov to Apr, dinner only; reservations accepted from 2pm on; ☎06-3172)*. Who would have thought that you could find all the subtle flavours and aromas of sophisticated French cuisine in such a remote village? The chef, an American who earned his stripes in the great restaurants of New York, decided to spend his

THE SOUTH

golden years here in Placencia with his wife. For six months, their little wooden house is transformed into a restaurant at nightfall. Once the candles are lit and the three tables set, the few lucky guests who had reserved well in advance are ready to be seated. The itinerary: a five-course table d'hôte, home-made French bread and a good selection of French wine. The menu changes daily and usually includes a choice of appetizers, then fish or meat for the main course.

Punta Gorda

Idolly's Café *($; 25 Main St.)* serves one daily special, rice & beans with meat or fish, and great breakfasts, starting at 6am (dinner BZ$6, breakfast BZ$5). The place is well-decorated in tropical hues and has a laid-back atmosphere. Good choice for Belizean cuisine. **Verdi's Comedor**, right nearby, owned by the same family, has a similar menu and prices.

Grace Restaurant *($; 6:30am to 9:30pm; ☎07-2414)* is very popular with local residents. A lovely little terrace faces the BTT company. Breakfast served. A la carte menu and BZ$7 daily special. Traditional and international fare, including fish and seafood. Good atmosphere.

Just south of the market, the **charming Morning Glory Café** *($-$$; 59 Front St., ☎07-2484)* faces the sea. Good place for breakfast. Starting at 7am, buttered toast with jam and American-style bacon and eggs are served. Good place for lunchtime sandwiches.

 ENTERTAINMENT

Placencia

Popular **Dockside Bar** is a cabana at the end of the pier where Tentacles Restaurant is located. Good place to listen to the soothing sound of the ocean.

Cosy Corner is a beach bar run by a Frenchman. Meals served. Good atmosphere and a terrific waterfront terrace.

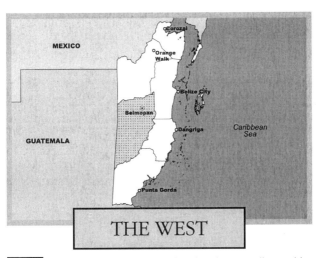

THE WEST

With its waterfalls, caves, jungle, rivers, valleys, this region of the country is paradise for nature-lovers. Not only is the Cayo District a favourite place for ecotourism, it is also home to many Mayan ruins, including those at Caracol, the largest site in Belize which is almost three times the size of Tikal. Although they are not as well-known as the latter (serious excavations only really began in 1985), they are becoming increasingly popular.

Many travellers take the Western Highway to reach the ruins, on their way to Guatemala. They also stop in San Ignacio for a few days to explore the tourist Mecca of Belize's interior. This border town is bustling day and night: travellers sit at one of a few café-terraces to read or to write to friends, while others set off to discover the numerous rivers, Mayan ruins and mountains.

Western Belize is also home to the nation's official political capital: Belmopan. The city was built primarily for the political elite after the country's independence and devastation following Hurricane Hattie. Thus, it is rather a city of bureaucrats who return home to Belize City after a day of work, and is of little interest to visitors.

FINDING YOUR WAY AROUND

Belmopan

By Car

Belmopan, the capital, is easily reached by car via the Western Highway, the best road in the country. Belmopan is also on Hummingbird Highway, which runs to southern Belize. This road is in poorer condition; it is therefore best to drive slowly, because the highway is full of stones, which can puncture your tires. Yours truly had three flat tires during the two-hour drive to Punta Gorda!

By Bus

If all roads lead to Rome, it is fair to say that all buses pass through Belmopan. Buses coming from Belize City, southern Belize or San Ignacio make a stop in the capital before continuing to their destinations. You should therefore have no trouble finding a bus.

Because Belmopan is merely a transfer point, bus timetables vary considerably and it is difficult to pinpoint the exact time of departures. Go to the market and board the first waiting bus.

The **Novelo's Bus** company has a passenger station in the market.

To **Belize City**: departures every half-hour; fare: BZ$3.50; travel time: 1 hour, 30 minutes.

To **San Ignacio** *(BZ$2)* and the Guatemalan border *(BZ$2.50)*: departures every hour; travel time: 1 hour, 30 minutes.

Batty Bros. also offers departures every half-hour to San Ignacio (same fare).

Z-Line offers frequent but irregular departures to the southern part of the country, because its buses must first arrive from

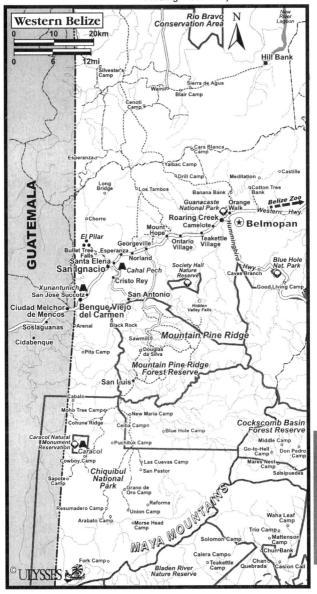

Belize City. You can stop at the Blue Hole National Park on the way.

Taxis

There are many taxis at the market. The fare is a flat rate of BZ$5 for trips within the city. To Guanacaste National Park, BZ$6; to Blue Hole National Park, BZ$50 due to the bad road conditions (It's better to take the Z-Line bus south for BZ$1).

On Foot

Belmopan's urban layout is very simple. Ring Road, the capital's main thoroughfare, encircles the city and its main attractions. Unless you have arranged to meet people, you will not really need to go beyond the market, which is also where the bus station is.

San Ignacio

By Car

The town of San Ignacio is on the Western Highway, 35 kilometres from Belmopan.

It is strongly recommended to rent an all-terrain vehicle to reach the surrounding areas, including the Mountain Pine Ridge Forest Reserve, especially in the rainy season.

By Bus

From noon on, **Batty Bros.** Leaves every half-hour to Belmopan *(BZ$2)* and Belize City *(BZ$5)*.

To reach the southern part of the country, you must transfer at Belmopan.

Buses leave every half-hour for the Guatemalan border (Melchor), starting at 7:30am *(BZ$1.50)*.

Taxis

Taxis wait at the bus station, right in the centre of town. This is a good way of getting to the hotels outside San Ignacio. Negotiate the fare before getting in. If you are staying in town, you can reach your hotel on foot.

The fare to the Guatemalan border, in Melchor, is about BZ$20.

On Foot

The town of San Ignacio can easily be explored on foot. Burns Avenue is the town's commercial street with plenty of restaurants and shops, and several hotels. As for the outskirts, Santa Elena, San Ignacio's small twin town, is east of the suspension bridge. You can get there quite safely, even at night.

The Guatemalan Border

Expect to pay a BZ$7 border tax to leave Belize and $5 US to enter Guatemala, payable in American funds, Belize dollars or Guatemalan quetzals.

If you are travelling by bus, you can take one of the private minibuses at the border to your destination. **Mini Trasporte Miaita** *(☎09-22253)* leaves for Tikal at 10am ($12 US, $20 US return) and returns to the border at 4pm.

Hitchhiking is also a fairly reliable option, if you get there early in the morning.

Most travellers organize their transfers from Belize City or San Ignacio to Tikal directly from their hotel or with a travel agency. This will save you time at the border and ensure your safe arrival in Tikal or Flores.

On the Guatemalan side, the road is unpaved but in good condition. Though it was once the scene of carjackings, the situation has greatly improved. The Guatemalan authorities have tightened security and the thugs have moved on.

THE WEST

If you are driving there by yourself, take the usual precautions. Do not travel by night and be sure to have a full tank of gas and good spare tires.

 PRACTICAL INFORMATION

Belmopan

Tourist Office

Unfortunately, there are no official tourist information offices in Belmopan, so you will have to glean what information you can at hotels or Novelo's bus station.

Post Office

The **Post Office** *(Mon to Fri, 8am to noon and 1pm to 4pm)* is on Independence Plaza, north of the market.

Telephone

BTL *(Mon to Fri, 8am to noon and 1pm to 4pm)* has offices on Bliss Parade, south of the market.

Police

The **Police Station** is on Independence Plaza, next to the post office.

Hospital

The **Hospital** *(☎08-22518)* is on Ring Road, north of the market.

San Ignacio

Tourist Office

Original Eva's Restaurant *(22 Burns Ave.)*, is the best place to get all the information you'll need about the region: its walls are covered with maps and flyers. A popular meeting point for travellers, Eva's also provides Internet access.

Foreign Exchange Office

At **Atlantic Bank** *(Mon to Fri, 8am to 1pm and 3pm to 6pm; Burns Ave.)*, you can get a cash advance on your credit card and exchange foreign currency. Most hotels and restaurants do the same for American currency.

If you are arriving from Guatemala, it is best to exchange your quetzals at the border.

 EXPLORING

If you are arriving from Belize City, be sure to stop at the **Belize Zoo** (see p 97), on the Western Highway. If you are making the trip by car, you can make a stop at the **Jaguar Paw** (see p 226), a resort that offers numerous river-tubing and caving excursions.

Guanacaste Park (see p 212) is a pleasant stop along the way, located right where the Western Highway meets the Hummingbird Highway, which leads to the southern part of the country and Belmopan.

If you are travelling from southern Belize via the Hummingbird Highway, be sure to stop at the **Blue Hole National Park** (see p 213), a few kilometres before Belmopan.

THE WEST

Belmopan

Belmopan is the country's fabricated capital, a city that has not succeeded in becoming what its founders in the 1960's dreamed of. You might even get a bad first impression of it. The small government buildings, not more than two or three stories tall and of typical sixties' architecture, give Belmopan the look of a North American university campus. Instead of students, masses of lax civil servants mix with a few hawkers. The market is the city's hub and also serves as a bus station. Amidst the throng of the unemployed, formally dressed young women and men await the next bus home to Belize City or San Ignacio. Despite the tempting offers of low-priced land, civil servants prefer to live in Belize City rather than the completely artificial new capital. Belmopan was built after Hurricane Hattie devastated Belize City in 1961. Thus, what was once nothing more than a wasteland became the nation's capital, sheltered from the onslaught of hurricanes.

Not a very popular tourist destination, the capital is a stopover for travellers heading to the southern part of the country.

There are very few places to visit in the city itself. For those keen on archaeology, the **Belize Department of Archeology** *(Mon, Wed and Fri, 1:30pm to 4:30pm; ☎08-22106, ⇌08-23345)* grants entry to the various archaeological sites that do not have visitor centres. The construction of a museum has been slated for ages. In the meantime, you can visit their vault, but you must reserve in advance by making an appointment.

Guanacaste Park ★ *(BZ$5; every day 8am to 4:30pm)* is right on the Western Highway, at the junction of Hummingbird Highway, and makes for an ideal excursion of a half day or more. Founded in 1990, the national park is a 22-square-hectare (50-acre) nature reserve right near the nation's capital between the Belize River and Roaring Creek. The park is named after the 150-year-old *guanacaste* tree located inside.

Managed by the Belize Audubon Society, the park is very well laid-out, with many interpretive nature trails leading to the

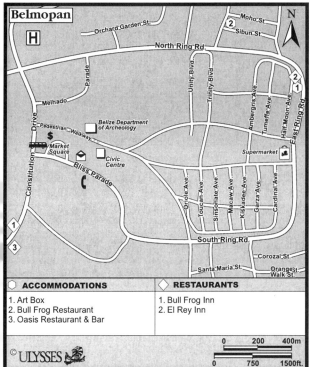

Belmopan

○ ACCOMMODATIONS	◇ RESTAURANTS
1. Art Box 2. Bull Frog Restaurant 3. Oasis Restaurant & Bar	1. Bull Frog Inn 2. El Rey Inn

© ULYSSES

0	200	400m
0	750	1500ft.

brook and the river. This is a great place to enjoy a swim, a picnic or a stroll to see lovely clusters of orchids and observe numerous species of animals, including jaguarondis, kinkajous, pacas, armadillos, iguanas, deer and opossums. The park is also home to approximately 125 bird species.

The price of admission includes a fifteen-minute guided tour. You can even spot howler monkeys from the Momot Trail, which takes about 90 minutes to cover.

THE WEST

Blue Hole National Park ★

Less than 20 kilometres south of Belmopan, on Hummingbird Highway, the **Blue Hole National Park** *(every day 8am to 4pm)* is a must for anyone passing through this part of the country. The Blue Hole is an 8-metre-deep rock formation that creates a basin of fresh water into which a brook flows. Deep in the jungle, the cerulean blue pool is the perfect place for a dip.

Opposite the park is **Ian Anderson's Jungle Lodge ★★** (see p 227), which is the starting point for the best caving expeditions in Central America (see p 224). The place is easily accessible on foot from the Blue Hole.

San Ignacio

With just over 10,000 inhabitants, the town of San Ignacio is described in many tourist brochures as a border town. You'll either love it or hate it, depending on what you make of it from the literature. For some reason, travellers from Guatemala are more often disappointed than those from the coast. Perhaps their familiarity with the Spanish language makes the place seem less exotic. Anyone who goes to San Ignacio and its surroundings – the Caracol ruins, the Hidden Valley Falls or the Macal River, which runs through town – will tell other travellers: *"Definitely stop in San Ignacio."*

A border town, a cowboy town, the starting point of ecotourism – all describe San Ignacio. However, there is more to it than this. There is something special in the air, something that makes you feel like you're in a real American frontier town of the Wild West, where different cultures and races are struggling to survive this barren land. A mere walk is simply not enough to breathe in this mysterious air that is so typical of the early settlement of the American West. Yes, that may be it, an air of unfinished conquest, as if the people here were still battling the natural elements, the rivers and the mountains, to create the town of their dreams, or simply find a bit of freedom away from civilization.

You will become even more aware of this by meeting the local residents. Very few people were actually born in San Ignacio. It seems that they are all either former British soldiers, Hindus seeking a better life, Cubans on the run, Americans fleeing their own dream or winter-weary Canadians seeking better climes.

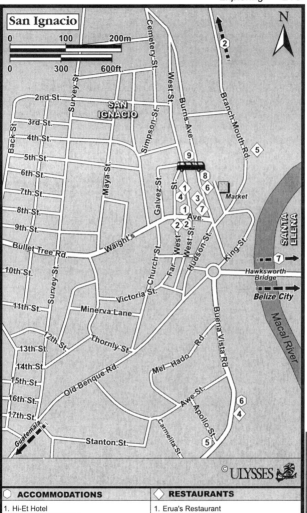

San Ignacio

○ ACCOMMODATIONS

1. Hi-Et Hotel
2. Martha's Guesthouse
3. Midas Resort
4. Pacz Hotel
5. Piache Hotel
6. San Ignacio Resort Hotel
7. Snooty Fox Guest House
8. The Budget Hotel
9. Tropicool Hotel

◇ RESTAURANTS

1. Erua's Restaurant
2. Martha's Kitchen
3. Original Eva's Restaurant
4. Running Steak House and Restaurant
5. Sand Castle
6. Serendi Restaurant
7. Yesteryear Café

© ULYSSES

All have settled in San Ignacio, running a hotel or restaurant here, offering travellers excursions and, come nightfall, sitting down for a drink with the locals who, all the same, still populate the town!

There are also sloping streets that criss-cross the town and can become a small confusing maze at night for anyone who is slightly drunk. You can also cross the suspension bridge, known as the Hawksworth Bridge, over the river that separates the twin towns of Santa Elena and San Ignacio, which are really one save for the fact that they bear different names and that the first is much smaller than the second. Then there are taxi drivers, who take a malicious pleasure in zooming right past you before you can flag them down.

And of course, there are the holiday resorts outside town, most of which are over-priced because of a few property developers who are trying to cash in on the ecotourism trade which is lucrative, if late in coming. Though these superb places are found in breathtaking natural surroundings, some come off as a little too trendy.

Only 24 kilometres from the Guatemalan border, San Ignacio is a town, a village, a region and a nature reserve, all wrapped up in one. To explore every corner of San Ignacio, you will undoubtedly have to spend a few days here before setting off to other parts. As the saying goes, if you love something, set it free.

Located above the Macal River Valley, near San Ignacio, the **Cahal Pech Visitor Center ★** *(BZ$5; Tue to Sat 9am to noon and 1pm to 4:30pm, Sun 9am to noon)* allows you access to the Cahal Pech ruins and its museum. This archaeological site constitutes an excellent half-day excursion. To get there, take the Western Highway toward Guatemala. You can make the journey to Cahal Pech on foot or by bus with Batty Bros. or Novelo's, which continue to the Guatemalan border. By taxi, residents usually pay BZ$5, but tourists are charged BZ$7, so you might want to bargain down the price.

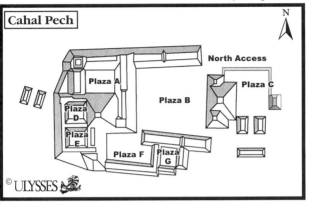

The name Cahal Pech is the combination of Yucatec and Mopán Maya words. Cahal Pech means "Place (or City) of Ticks"; Cahal means "city" in Yucatec, while Pech means "tick" in Mopán Maya. This name was given to the place in the 1950s, when the ruins were found in the midst of a livestock-breeding area.

This archaeological site is one of the few in Belize to boast an on-site museum. Managed by the Belize Tourist Board, it opened its doors in 1997 and features a fine collection of relics, most of which come from excavations carried out at Cahal Pech. The collection is made up of ceramics (pottery, dishes, plates, ocarinas), including a superb piece of pottery painted with two birds. According to famous American archaeologist Thompson, this piece depicts an ancient Mopán and K'eckchi myth. There are also pieces carved out of obsidian and jade, as well as seashells and funeral urns. The museum's crowning glory is a jade-and-shell mosaic mask, rebuilt from original pieces found in a tomb inside the main pyramid of Cahal Pech's central plaza. The mask was undoubtedly part of an elite Maya's wardrobe, most likely the centrepiece of a ceremonial belt. It was found by a Mexican archaeologist by the name of Peter Schmidt. The museum has explanatory texts in English

The site of Cahal Pech itself *(BZ$5; every day 6am to 7pm)* extends over a one-hectare area and the ceremonial centre is composed of 34 structures, two ball courts and five steles. You will be able to explore about a third of the entire city, because the rest has not yet been restored.

The structures are very well-preserved and consist of several small passages and stairs. Walking through the site is a pleasure, especially because of its magnificent views of San Ignacio and the valley.

The excavations carried out at Cahal Pech seem to indicate that it was occupied by the Maya from the Pre-Classic Period (1,000 to 600 BC) to the Late Classic Period (AD 800 to 900). Like the surrounding Maya cities, it was probably abandoned around that time.

El Pilar

The ruins of El Pilar are among the few in Belize that have not been subjected to excavation and restructuring work. So, if you want to feel like a real archaeologist discovering ruins, head to El Pilar, situated about twenty kilometres northwest of San Ignacio. Hotels in the area organize excursions – the most enjoyable way of getting there is on horseback.

The city of El Pilar, which was under Mayan occupation from 500 BC to AD 1,000, is about three times the size of Xunantunich, the site of El Castillo temple. El Pilar has over 25 plazas still buried beneath the tropical vegetation. The region is magnificent, and the site is over 300 metres above the Belize River.

Medicinal Trail

A popular interpretive nature trail on medicinal plants and herbs used by the Maya was developed by the late Mayan healer, Doctor Eligio Pantí, and his apprentice, American doctor Rosita Arvigo.

The trail allows you to discover over 4,000 species of plants and their medicinal properties. The price of admission to the site is BZ$10. Excursions are organized from San Ignacio and the Chaa Creek Cottages hotel (see p 233).

Xunantunich and San José Succotz

Located about 12 kilometres west of San Ignacio, Xunantunich is the most frequented Mayan city in the country. The first archaeological site to be open to the public, Xunantunich has been the subject of excavations since the late 19th century, and boasts 'El Castillo', an impressive 40-metre-high temple.

To get there by public transport, take the local bus *(BZ$1)*, which leaves the San Ignacio station regularly. It will drop you off on the Western Highway (which leads all the way to Guatemala) across from the village of **San José Succotz** and the pier from which you take a small ferry across the rapids of the Mopán River. Then it's a 1.6-kilometre walk uphill, which is wonderful provided you brought water! This trail is also open to cars. Whether you head toward the border or return to San Ignacio, buses pass by on the road every hour, the last one leaving for San Ignacio at 4:30pm. Excursions to Xunantunich can also be easily arranged through travel agencies in Belize City and hotels in San Ignacio.

Xunantunich, which means "Maiden of the Rock", is a ceremonial centre dating from the Classic Period. Its name, however, is more recent and was bestowed upon it by present-day Maya. At the site's epicentre are three plazas surrounded by tropical vegetation. The ruins' main attraction is a 40-metre-high temple, which is the second highest in the country after that at Caracol. This pyramid, called 'El Castillo' is made up of several levels and terraces. The lower part of the temple is famous for the stucco frieze that used to extend all around its perimeter, but of which the archaeologists were only able to preserve and restore one side. This impressive frieze depicts a carved mask with large ears. The ears are adorned with symbols that represent the sun god.

The climb to the top of El Castillo is phenomenal, not only for the many terraces of the temple but for the panoramic view of the region past the Guatemalan border. Various types of birds can be observed, including toucans and parrots that breed in

THE WEST

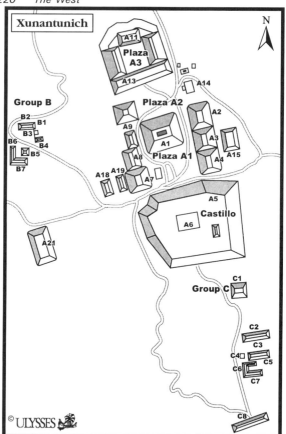

one of the last bits of jungle in the area which have not been touched by farmers thanks to the presence of the ruins.

The winding and sloping roads of San José Succotz are also worth exploring on foot.

Mountain Pine Ridge

Ecotourism is centred in the region of Mountain Pine Ridge, a nature reserve that has an ecosystem unlike any other in

Central America. The 480-square-kilometre-plus forest reserve abounds in rivers, waterfalls and underground caves that offer nature lovers a taste of adventure. You will be able to observe a host of animal species here and find a few comfortable but rather expensive hotels. Budget-conscious travellers should sooner stay in San Ignacio and make one-day excursions to the region.

To get there by car, take the Western Highway to the Georgeville intersection.

Hidden Valley Falls

About 15 kilometres from the entrance to the nature reserve are the highest waterfalls in Central America. The Hidden Valley Falls are inarguably one of the country's most prized natural wonders. The trip there is an experience in itself, as the dirt road runs through one of the wildest regions. Once there, you'll want to slip into a bathing suit, or, if you are more daring, go nude! The waterfall, also known as the Thousand-Foot Falls, is 495 metres tall and rushes down into a deep basin. It is an ideal place for a swim, though the water is rather rough in parts.

Numerous hiking trails lead through the surrounding area and to the top of the valley, where there are breathtaking views.

The Hidden Valley Institute for Environmental Studies is on the way to the falls. Its researchers study the region's ecosystem and protect the local environment.

Rio On Pools

Thirteen kilometres from the Hidden Valley Falls are the smaller waterfalls and rapids collectively known as Rio On Pools. Here, you can swim in a series of small natural pools, a real treat after coming all the way from the top of Hidden Valley Falls.

From here, you can make your way to the country's largest river cave, the **Rio Frio Cave** (which can also be reached more easily from the road). The river flows through the cave for close

THE WEST

to a kilometre. Bring a miner's lamp and non-skid shoes. A good part of the cave can be covered on foot.

Caracol ★★

Caracol is the largest Mayan city in Belize. Still partially buried, its ruins consist of over 35,000 structures, or three times the number at Tikal, Guatemala. With over 150,000 inhabitants in its heyday and an area over 8 square kilometres, Caracol is becoming one of the more popular Mayan sites for archaeologists and tourists alike.

Reaching Caracol is always an adventure. It is located some 40 kilometres from the Mountain Pine Ridge Forest Reserve, and the dirt road that goes there runs deep into the jungle. The surrounding vegetation is dense and magnificent, and home to numerous animal species, including howler monkeys and birds. You may also be fortunate enough to spot felines such as the jaguar. To get there, you will have to either rent an all-terrain vehicle or take part in an excursion organized by travel agencies in San Ignacio and Belize City. If you set off on your own, make sure to have an adequate supply of gas, especially in the rainy season, because gas stations are scarce in this very remote region. But first, you must obtain a permit to visit the ruins from the Department of Archaeology, in Belmopan.

Although the ruins were discovered in 1936 by *chicleros*, archaeological excavation efforts only really began in 1985. The following year, an altar bearing a hieroglyphic inscription denoting the military victory of the Caracol Water God over his Tikal rivals was found in a ball court. The evidence shows that Caracol defeated the city of Tikal circa 562, and dominated the entire region for over a century.

Surprisingly, the Caracol site is not situated near a waterway. But how their foremost deity got the name "Water God" is no mystery: Caracol has a complex irrigation system whose main water reservoir is an astounding feat of engineering that still works today.

Most structures and pyramids at Caracol date from the Early Classic era and were expanded throughout this period. A large

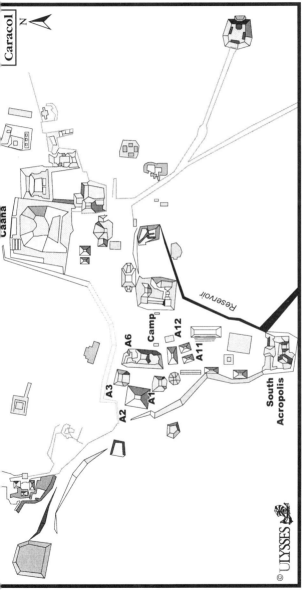

Caracol

N

Caana

Reservoir

Camp

A6

A3

A2

A1

A12

A11

South
Acropolis

ceremonial centre covers a surface area of about 1.5 square kilometres and the largest structure on site stands 42 metres tall, making it the highest Mayan pyramid in Belize. Other structures surrounding the ceremonial centre cover an area of more than three square kilometres.

The digs carried out by Arlen and Diane Chase, the two resident archaeologists at Caracol, have led them to believe that the downfall of the Mayan Empire resulted from the fact that the war between the cities was no longer limited to conflicts between the elites, but involved all inhabitants. The Mayan population probably fled the cities to seek shelter from these armed conflicts.

Beyond the speculations over the downfall of the Mayan Empire, the Chases have brought many archaeological discoveries to light, including royal tombs in which female bodies were buried. This led them to conclude that women played a much greater role in Mayan society than was once commonly believed.

 OUTDOOR ACTIVITIES

Caving

In the vicinity of Belmopan, the ever-popular underground river-caving expeditions led by Canadian-born **Ian Anderson** (☎/≈08-22800) are among the most exhilarating adventures. Excursions to the Caves Branch grottos are custom-made for every level, and are very safe. Ian Anderson offers some ten different expeditions. Anyone travelling to Belize should take a day to explore the country's underground world with the best guides in Central America! This way you can discover both natural wonders and Mayan archaeological remains. Several caves were used for ceremonial purposes by the Maya, who left behind vases and ashes. Sheltered from the outside world, even the Maya's footsteps have left their mark in the ground for hundreds of years! The Caves Branch River flows through the caves. You can navigate it in an inner tube, but you will have to go alternately with or against the current.

Ian Anderson also runs an excellent hotel (see p 227) on Hummingbird Highway, opposite the Blue Hole National Park, from which the excursions start off.

The **Jaguar Paw** (see p 226) resort also offers an excursion on the Caves Branch River.

Excursions

Most of the hotels in the San Ignacio area offer outdoor excursions. The best place to get information about them is at Original Eva's Restaurant, on Burns Avenue (see p 235). Shop around for the excursion that best suits you!

Canoeing

Several hotels around San Ignacio have canoes at their guests' disposal.

In Santa Elena, the **Snooty Fox Guest House** *(64 George Price Ave.; ☎09-22150, ⌐09-23556)* rents out canoes and organizes outings up river (BZ$70 for a two-person canoe).

Horseback Riding

From San Ignacio, **Easy Rider** leads horseback riding excursions along the Macal River and to various Mayan ruins in the area. Full-day excursions are BZ$40 per person and BZ$25 for a half-day. Information at Original Eva's Restaurant (see p 235).

If you prefer renting a horse by the hour, **Macal Adventure** *(Belizean Handicraft Center, 2 West St., ☎09-23902)* offers the best service. They also organize excursions to Cahal Pech, Ix Chel Farm, Chaa Creek and Duploy's. One-day outing: BZ$70; half-day outing: BZ$40.

The **Parrot's Nest** (see p 231) and **Crystal Paradise Resort** (see p 232) hotels offer horseback-riding excursions and rent out horses.

ACCOMMODATIONS

On the road to Belize City, the stunning and luxurious **Jaguar Paw** *(BZ$260 -$300; ≡, hw, ℜ, pb, ≈; Mile 37, Western Hwy.; ☎08-13023; USA ☎800-233-JUNGLE, ⌐08-13024; cyoung@btl.net)* resort is nestled deep in the jungle, by the Caves Branch River. The superb main lodge was built to look like an ancient Mayan temple. The lobby features a huge mural, measuring about 3 metres in height by 15 metres in length. It is a reproduction of a mural found in the Mayan ruins of Bonampak depicting kings and warriors in ceremonial dress. The hotel mural was painted by Pam Braun, an American who has been living in Belize for some fifteen years. The magnificent restaurant set up at the foot of the mural offers very attentive service and delicious meals.

The rooms are in eclectically decorated *cabañas*. Each of them is styled after a different era, from the Victorian room to the "Western" room.

The place also organizes various excursions on the Caves Branch River, which runs above and below ground. These include tubing in the caves. The river is safe for everyone and some natural wonders can be seen along its course, including almost virgin beaches.

Belmopan

The most inexpensive establishment in Belmopan, the **El Rey Inn** *(BZ$45; pb, ⊗; 23 Moho St., ☎08-23438)* is quite popular with hikers, especially if they are staying in the capital for a day or two. The hotel is easily reached on foot from the bus station – the walk takes about fifteen minutes. The rooms are clean and even large for a small hotel of this category. Moreover, the hotel is run by a K'eckchi family, so you can learn a bit more about contemporary Mayan culture.

Located on the bypass that surrounds the city, the **Bull Frog Inn** *(BZ$125; ≡, pb, tv; 25 Halfmoon Ave., ☎08-22111, ⌐08-23155)* is one of the best hotels in the capital. There are two kinds of rooms: the conventional ones are spacious, well-kept, modern and comfortable, while the studios are smaller and don't have telephones, but offer very decent comfort. The service is attentive. The clientele consists primarily of businesspeople and civil servants. Excellent restaurant (see p 234).

Blue Hole National Park

Ian Anderson's Jungle Lodge (☎/⌐08-22800) is one of the best jungle hotels in the country. Rustic yet comfortable, it offers a very pleasant ambiance and a truly unique experience. People who have come to spend the night have been known to stay for over a week! The wooden *cabañas* fit perfectly into the deep jungle surroundings, but they are also very comfortable, clean and well-decorated. Prices vary. The more economical shared *cabaña* is also available. Excellent meals for hotel guests.

Guests will also be treated to the colourful tales of Ian Anderson, the Canadian-born proprietor with a gift for storytelling. Passionately interested in archaeology and speleology, Ian knows the country's many secrets. As you enjoy your evening meal with him under the stars, he will regale you with one of his numerous stories, which fill the night air along with the glow of the torchlight and the sounds of the waking nocturnal creatures.

THE WEST

San Ignacio

As its name indicates, **The Budget Hotel** *(BZ$20; ⊗, hw,* 17 Burns Ave., ☎09-22024) is one of the lowest-priced establishments in San Ignacio. Run by the same management as The New Belmoral Hotel, it has two shared bathrooms. Clean and centrally located, The Budget Hotel is only a stone's throw from the bus station. The place can be a little noisy in the morning, however.

In the same price category, the **Tropicool Hotel** *(BZ$25; hw, ⊗* 30 Burns Ave., ☎09-23052) is also right in the heart of town. It has seven rooms, all of which are safe and very clean, the whole in a family ambiance, this is unarguably one of the best choices for discount rooms in San Ignacio.

Family-oriented and charming, the **Hi-Et Hotel** *(BZ$30; 12 West* St. at Waight St.) is in an old house in the region's typical style. The rooms are clean and the service is very decent. The place is quiet, unpretentious and simply good (for the price)!

With only three rooms, **Martha's Guesthouse** *(BZ$30; ⊗, hw,* 10 West St., ☎09-23647) is one of the most prized places in San Ignacio. There is a lovely and comfortable common room with high ceilings, sofas, tables, a terrace and fireplaces. You can also use the kitchen. The rooms are rather small but very clean and practical. Very friendly ambiance, and good service all around.

The very pleasant and popular **Pacz Hotel** *(BZ$35; ⊗, hw; Far* West St., ☎09-22010, ⊶09-22972; pacz@btl.net) is one of the few hotels not located on Burns Avenue, which makes it one of the quietest. The rooms are fairly large, clean and safe. You can also relax in the comfortable living room with large windows, a communal refrigerator and cable television. Diane manages the place, while Peter organizes excursions. Both are obliging and very familiar with the region. There are only five rooms, and they are almost always occupied, so reserve in advance. Very good ambiance.

Still unknown to international visitors, but much prized by Belizean businesspeople and travellers, **The Aguada** *(BZ$40,* *b, hw, ⊗, tv, ⌨, ℜ; 2 km north of the bridge)* has both *cabañas* and conventional rooms. The rooms are comfortable, and the *cabañas* offer excellent value for the money. Located in Santa Elena, the hotel is nonetheless a little far from San Ignacio, though within easy walking distance or a short taxi ride away *(BZ$5)*. The place boasts a family-oriented common room with a piano, comfortable sofas and cable television, as well as the best restaurant in Santa Elena, which is a local favourite (see p 236). The owners reside in the main house and are very hospitable.

Iguana

In Santa Elena, on the other side of the suspension bridge from San Ignacio, the **Snooty Fox Guest House** *(BZ$40 -$70; ob, hw, tv, ⊗; 64 George Price Ave., ☎09-22150, ⌨09-23556)* has something a little sly about it. The superb terrace, which has one of the best views of the whole region, including spectacular sunsets, has a very pleasant bar with a pool table and a festive ambiance. The hotel is 20 metres above the river and can be reached on foot via a little trail where iguanas and toucans nest. The establishment rents out canoes and organizes canoe trips up river at BZ$70 for two people. The Snooty Fox is about 10-minutes walking distance from San Ignacio, in a safe Santa Elena neighbourhood. The *cabañas (BZ$70)* are very well-equipped, with refrigerator, cable television and private bathroom. A real bargain for the price. Budget rooms *(BZ$40)* with shared baths are also available. Warm and pleasant welcome.

The pleasant **Piache Hotel** *(BZ$70-$100; pb, hw, ⊗, ≡ 18 Buena Vista Rd., ☎09-22032, ⬱09-22685)* is something between a downtown hotel and a jungle hideaway. Situated between San Ignacio and Cahal Pech, this establishment offers thatched-roof *cabañas*. Even though it is close to the city, it feels like you are out in the country. Good lay-out and well-kept grounds. Comfortable rooms and good value for the price for this region.

The **San Ignacio Resort Hotel** *($70-$80 US; ≡, pb, ⊗, ≈, hw, Buena Vista St.; ☎09-22034, 22125 or 22220, ⬱09-22134 sanighot@btl.net; www.belizenet.com/sanighot.html)* is the only upscale hotel in the centre of town. The staff likes to boast that Queen Elizabeth had lunch here during her visit to Belize in 1984. Room no. 31 has since become The Royal Suite – even though she did not spend the night there! The swimming pool and terraces with tables and deckchairs are very relaxing. You can take a trail through the Macal Valley all the way to the river. You are sure to spot many iguanas along the way, as the hotel is involved in the Green Iguana Conservation Project, the goal of which is to protect these endangered lizards in their natural habitat. The hotel's only weak point is the rooms, which are rather second-rate for the price. Nevertheless they offer all modern conveniences and a balcony with a view of the valley. Moreover, the establishment houses one of the best restaurants in town (see p 236).

Near the ruins of the same name, **Cahal Pech Village** *(BZ$90, pb, hw, ≡, ℛ, ≈; ☎09-23740, ⬱09-22225; daniels@btl.net)* has excellent customer service and a superb view of the valley. The establishment consists of a large, three-story wooden hotel that fits very well into the surrounding natural environment. A secluded ambiance has been successfully created for rest and relaxation – the main building's architecture and the swimming pool contribute to this atmosphere. You can choose between one of the rooms in the hotel proper or one of 14 typical *cabañas*. The latter are built of wood and palm fronds and are very comfortable. You can enjoy magnificent views of San

Ignacio and the mountains in Guatemala from anywhere on the grounds, especially at night when the city lights up. In the morning, a light fog slowly dissipates over the valley and the air is fresher, a real blessing in hot weather. Pleasant dining room. Lunch and dinner meals range in price from BZ$10 to BZ$30. The hotel also organizes tours.

Located right at the entrance to the museum and the ruins, **Cahal Pech Tavern & Cabañas** *(BZ$90; pb, hw, tv; ☎09-23380)* offers excursions and pleasant wooden *cabañas*. There is no restaurant, so you'll have to find a bite in San Ignacio or at the Cahal Pech Village, which is cheaper.

Around San Ignacio

The affordably priced **Midas Resort** *(BZ$45; pb, hw, ⊗; BZ$7 per person for camping; Branch Rd.; ☎09-23172 or 09-23845)* offers a series of *cabañas* and allows camping on the grounds which are located two-minutes walking distance from the Macal River. Good, fairly large and comfortable *cabañas*. Patrick Lind, the manager, offers numerous excursions in the area, including outings to Pine Ridge, Gallon Jug and Tikal.

The popular **Parrot's Nest** *(BZ$45; hw; ☎09-37008; parrot@btl.net; www.netspaway.com/parrotsnest/parrot)* is in the village of Bullet Tree Falls, only 5 minutes from San Ignacio. The place has five "tree cabins" and the best rates outside San Ignacio. The treehouses, the only ones in Central America according to the owner, are particularly charming and rustic, and fit harmoniously into the natural environment. The grounds are in the midst of dense vegetation, and are an excellent place to observe the region's flora and fauna and swing in one of the hammocks to the sounds of the birds while writing in your journal or reading. You can also take a little trail to the river, where most guests go swimming. A ten-minute walk will lead you to the Bullet Tree Falls. Finally, you can walk all the way to the El Pilar ruins, located 11 kilometres from the hotel, which makes for a great one-day excursion. Hotel guests are offered breakfast *(BZ$6)* and dinner *(BZ$12)*, a daily menu with a main dish (seafood or chicken) served with big salads and wholewheat bread. To get there, you must take a taxi *(BZ$10)*. Otherwise, tell Bob at Eva's Restaurant that you would like to meet Fred Prost, the owner of the Parrot's Nest. Fred is in town almost every day until 11:30am. He leaves his establishment for San Ignacio at around 8:30am to drop off his guests and run errands. You have to reserve your room in advance, because the Parrot's Nest rarely has vacancies.

On the road leading to the Guatemalan border, the **Clarissa Falls Hotel** *(BZ$50-$80; pb, hw in the* cabañas; *BZ$15 per person for a standard room; BZ$7.50 for camping)* is an excellent choice for anyone with a car or seeking simple and low-cost accommodation outside the city. Warm welcome and very affable owners. Good ambiance and right near the river, where you can rent canoes or go tubing. Comfortable rooms.

In Benque Viejo, **Maxim's Palace Hotel & Restaurant** *(BZ$65; pb, hw, tv, ⊗, ℜ; 41 Churchill St., ☎09-32360, ⊷09-32259)* is a four-story hotel with several rooms. Despite its lack of charm, it is practical good value for the price. Friendly owner. Good Chinese restaurant on the main floor.

Right near the bridge leading to the village of Bullet Tree Falls is the **Riverside Resort** *(BZ$70; pb, hw, ℜ, ⊗, ⊛)*, with large, modern, clean and comfortable *cabañas*. Conveniently located near the road and by the river, the place has a lovely terrace with a restaurant and bar that, unfortunately, can get noisy when the music is too loud. The thatched-roof dining room is open for all three meals.

On the road to Mountain Pine Ridge, near the village of Christo Rey and by the Macal River, is the magnificent **Crystal Paradise Resort** *(BZ$70-$200; pb, hw, ℜ, ☎09-22772)*. Managed by the friendly and colourful native-born Victor, this family-run establishment has something for everyone and offers an excellent view over the Macal River Valley. The service is particularly efficient and hospitable. There are two types of *cabañas*, some with palm-thatched roofs *(BZ$200)* and others with zinc roofs *(BZ$150)*. Rates include two meals (breakfast and dinner). Without dinner, the rate is BZ$70. The place also offers numerous excursions in the area and rents out horses. Transfers to Goldson International Airport in Belize City. The Crystal Paradise Resort has offices at the San Ignacio bus station, where you can make reservations for accommodation, the excursions or for the transfer to the hotel or the international airport in Belize City.

The following tourist facilities are accessible via a (southbound) junction leading to the Macal River, on the Western Highway, west of San Ignacio:

The most competitive establishment in the area, **duPlooy's** *(BZ$100-$300 fb; hw, pb, ℜ; ☎09-23101, ⇝09-23301; judy@btl.net)* has conventional rooms and *cabañas*. The rooms are less expensive but don't have private bathrooms. The *cabañas* have all the modern conveniences. The accommodations are located by the Macal River, so they are right on the beach. The service is courteous and the overall ambiance one of the friendliest.

The **Windy Hill Resort** *(BZ$125; hw, pb, tv, ≈, ℜ, ≡; ☎09-22017, ⇝09-23080)* provides very well-decorated *cabañas* with all the modern conveniences, including air conditioning and cable television. In addition to its *cabañas* of unrivalled quality, the establishment is popular with travel agencies across the country because of its courteous and professional service. Moreover, it has a swimming pool and beautiful terraces, and organizes many excursions in the area.

Property of the famous American film director Francis Ford Coppola, the very select **Blancaneaux Lodge** *(BZ$225-$450; hw, pb, ℜ, ⊗; ☎09-23878, USA ☎800-746-3743, ⇝09-23919)* has some fifteen rooms and a series of luxury *cabañas*. It is set in beautiful natural surroundings close to towering waterfalls.

The first hotel in the region to spearhead ecotourism, **Chaa Creek Cottages** *($260B; pb, hw, ℜ; ☎09-22037, ⇝09-22501; chaacreek@btl.net)* is located on a 120-hectare-plus private nature reserve. The jungle hideaway boasts superb, comfortable and tastefully decorated *cabañas* and serves excellent meals. The complex is right near the Ix Chel farm and the interpretive nature trail, which introduces you to the medicinal plants and herbs of the region (see p 218). The place is worth visiting if only to take a look.

THE WEST

RESTAURANTS

Belmopan

For inexpensive meals, head to the market or to **Fried Chicken** *($; 22 Moho St.)*, a small neighbourhood food stand right across from the El Rey Inn, about a fifteen-minute walk from the market. This unpretentious place serves traditional rice & beans, fries and, of course, fried chicken.

On Hummingbird Highway, right near the junction of the Western Highway, the **Oasis Restaurant & Bar** *($$; Mon to Sat 7am to 9pm; ☎08-23548)* is an excellent place to sample the country's traditional cuisine in a rustic setting. Rice & beans are served with beef, chicken or pork in very generous portions. Very popular with civil servants in the capital. Various soups are also on the menu. The ambiance is warm and friendly in this typical thatched-roof house with its rural decor. If the weather is good, why not ask for a take-out and have a picnic by the little river? It is common practice and well worth it!

Unquestionably the most original restaurant in the country, **Art Box** *($$-$$$; Mon to Thu 11am to 2pm and 5pm to 10pm, Fri to Sun 11am to 10pm)* is a veritable Jack-in-the-box! This very stylized restaurant, is also an art gallery and seems like something right out of Manhattan. The brightly coloured walls are so completely covered with modern paintings that I even thought the waiters and clientele were part of a huge painting! Featured on the round menu, whose shape and design change every year (it could well be in the shape of a triangle when you visit), are excellent Taiwanese-style Chinese food and Belizean fare. This restaurant is a must for anyone wishing to stretch all their senses to the limit. There is also a "gift" shop, and the paintings are up for sale. Art Box is located on Hummingbird Highway, right near the junction of the Western Highway.

The unique interior decor of the popular **Bull Frog Restaurant** *($$-$$$; 25 Halfmoon Ave., ☎08-22111, ⬲08-23155)*, with its wooden arches and terracotta tiles, creates a typically Spanish ambiance. The menu is varied, featuring rice & beans served with grilled meats, fish or seafood. The service is courteous and attentive.

San Ignacio

Very popular for its pleasant terrace, **Martha's Kitchen** *($; 10 West St., ☎09-23647)* serves typical Belizean dishes as well as sandwiches and burritos. It is an excellent place in which to relax at lunchtime or at dusk after spending the day in the sun. Vegetarian dishes are also served here.

On Burns Avenue, you can't miss **Original Eva's Restaurant** *($; 22 Burns Ave., ☎09-22267; evas@btl.net)*. More than a mere restaurant and bar, Eva's is both the meeting point for travellers and the best tourist information centre in the Cayo District. Its walls are covered with maps, advertisements for excursions, timetables and establishments worth checking out. The ever-popular place has a varied and low-priced menu, featuring traditional Belizean dishes and American-style fast food, sandwiches and vegetarian meals alike. The daily menu is chicken- or fish-based. Good breakfast selection. It is also a great place to simply sip a beer or enjoy an excellent espresso. Eva's also offers fax, telephone and E-mail service.

Also on Burns Avenue is the excellent **Serendi Restaurant** *($-$$; Mon to Sat 9:30am to 3pm and 6:30pm to 11pm; 27 Burns Ave., ☎09-22312)*, which will take you on a delightful culinary escapade to eastern and western Sri Lanka. Open for some ten years now, the restaurant has become a neighbourhood institution. Several vegetarian dishes are featured here, curry rice being among the most popular, served with potatoes and salad. Also offered are Belizean and international dishes, including surf n' turf. If you want to try something different, sample the Savoury Rice, a concoction of rice sautéed with chicken and ham and seasoned with curry. During my visit, the owners were building a terrace out back. Looks promising! Tea lovers will find a good selection of Sri Lankan brews here as well. These are also sold in boxes so that you can stock up for the rest of your trip.

Right nearby, the **Yesteryear Café** *($-$$; 30 Burns Ave., ☎09-23209)* serves excellent Mexican food and great cakes.

THE WEST

Try the very generous portion of chicken *fajitas*. The Mexican-style breakfasts are particularly lavish and offered all day long. The decor is very pleasant, with old-style double booths and walls with period photographs. Very clean.

Inarguably the best restaurant in Santa Elena and very popular with the locals, **The Aguada** *($-$$)* offers a daily special and has a very varied menu. American-style breaded seafood is the house specialty. The ambiance is made pleasant by the locals who come to sit at the precious-wood bar. Excellent, hospitable service. Located in a residential district, it is part of a hotel with conventional rooms and *cabañas* (see p 228).

Erua's Restaurant *($-$$; Mon to Sat 6:30am to 10pm, Sun 6am to 10pm; 4 Far West St., ☎09-22821)* is located below the Pacz Hotel and the restaurant owners prepare meals for the excursionists at the hotel. Decent food; cafeteria ambiance. Good selection of breakfasts, including omelettes and oatmeal. Also served here are rice & beans as well as vegetarian dishes, good pizza, *fajitas*, steak and lobster.

The **Sand Castle** restaurant *($-$$; Waight St., behind the bus station toward the river)* has a terrace on the sand – hence the name. It is a pleasant place, but can get noisy quickly if the television is turned up at full volume. Traditional dishes are served here. Art gallery upstairs.

The restaurant of the San Ignacio Resort Hotel, the **Running "W" Steak House and Restaurant** *($$$; 12 Buena Vista St., ☎09-22034, 09-22125 or 09-22220, ≈09-22134; sanighot@btl.net; www.belizenet.com/sanighot.html)*, is without doubt the best restaurant in San Ignacio. Meat eaters will be in seventh heaven here, because the place prepares the best filet mignon in Belize, served with potatoes, mushrooms and vegetables in season. Since this establishment belongs to a family of stock breeders, you will understand why particular attention is paid to the meats! Need we say more? Also worth sampling are the smoke-cured pork chops. Less carnivorous types can enjoy seafood here, as well.

ENTERTAINMENT

Bars and Nightclubs

Belmopan

For a night on the town, head to the **Bull Frog Inn** (see p 234) or the **Art Box** restaurant (see p 234).

San Ignacio

The **Blue Angel** nightclub, located in downtown San Ignacio near the roundabout, is open Fridays, Saturdays and Sundays. Women get in for free, while men pay a BZ$5 cover charge. Tropical music concerts are held here. A good place to test your ability to *punta*, the traditional dance of the Garifunas!

Opposite the bus station, the **Sports Bar** is always a popular local nightspot for having a drink on the terrace. A big-screen television broadcasts sports and favourite soap operas.

The popular **Stork Club** in the San Ignacio Resort Hotel is a good place for happy hour. "Western" decor and air conditioned. The place also serves different kinds of steak.

SHOPPING

Belmopan

Art Box *(Mon to Thu 11am to 2pm and 5pm to 10pm, Fri to Sun 11am to 10pm)* has an excellent "gift" shop. On Hummingbird Highway, right near the junction of the Western Highway. Sample one of the house specialties while you're there (see p 234).

THE WEST

San Ignacio

Arts & Crafts of Central America *(Mon to Sat 8am to 6pm;* *28 Burns Ave.,* ☎*09-22253)* boasts a good selection of arts & crafts, maps, cassettes and books about Belize.

The **Black Rock Girl Shop** *(every day 8am to 9pm;* *30 Burns Ave.,* ☎*09-23770)* specializes in Belizean woodwork.

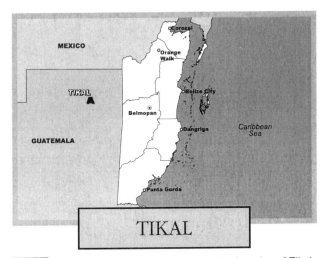

TIKAL

Nestled in lush flora deep in the jungle, the ruins of Tikal stand in the middle of the forest of El Petén, a vast flat region in northern Guatemala. Tikal's setting, with the omnipresent jungle presiding over the site, is as impressive as the ruins themselves. The Parque Nacional de Tikal, which covers over 17 square kilometres of tropical rainforest, is one of the most incredible nature reserves in the world, sheltering more than 260 species of birds and numerous other animals, including the howler monkey, the fox, the puma and the tapir. Tikal offers a complete introduction to the world of the Maya, enabling you to experience its architectural and artistic achievements, as well as the natural environment into which it was seamlessly integrated, just like the animal and plant life.

Tikal is undoubtedly one of the most fascinating places on earth. The flight of toucans, the captivating cries of howler monkeys and the indefinable rustlings of the jungle, will mesmerize you as you experience them from atop a stepped pyramid. Although this ceremonial centre was abandoned more than a thousand years ago, Tikal remains singularly intact. You cannot help but commune with the spirit of the ancient Maya, or that of all of humankind, which seems to be present in the space between you and the scene before you, in the silence during your ascent toward the pyramid's summit and in the exhilaration of reaching the top. Tikal almost seems to transcend the Maya's specific history, taking us beyond culture, race and borders.

You will want to spend at least two days (one night) in Tikal to fully appreciate it. Because Tikal is in Guatemala, it is best to change your money into quetzals, the Guatemalan currency, or use American money, which is accepted throughout the site. All prices in this chapter are given in American dollars.

FINDING YOUR WAY AROUND

By Plane

Flights

The airport of Santa Elena is increasingly busy due to the growing popularity of Tikal. Numerous daily flights from Belize City, Guatemala City and even Cancún and Merida, in Mexico, land here.

Tropic Air *(☎02-4567, ⌐02-62338; USA and Canada ☎800-22-3435; tropicair@btl.net)* and **Aerovias de Guatemala** offer daily flights to **Belize City**.

Shuttle Services to Tikal

Numerous tour operators provide shuttle services between the Santa Elena airport and Tikal. The fare is about $3.50 US per person, or $7 US return.

By Car

Though unpaved, the road between **Melchor de Menchos**, a Guatemalan village on the Belizean border, and Tikal is in good condition. For safety reasons, it is best to avoid taking this road after dark: many carjackings targeting tourists were reported between 1994 and 1996. Since then, Guatemalan authorities have increased police presence considerably on this road and

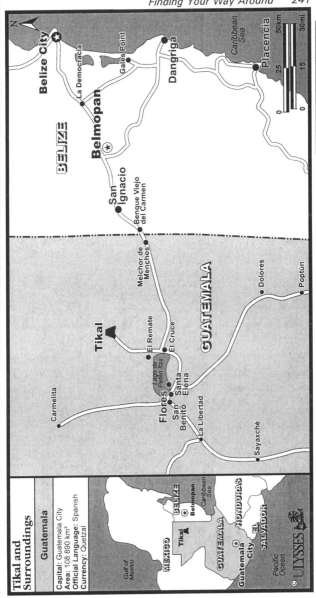

carried out a successful "clean-up" operation, making the road much safer than it was in the past.

By Bus

Every hotel in the region offers mini-bus shuttles to the Santa Elena airport, San Ignacio, Belize City and Chetumal (Mexico). The fare to Belize City for four people is about $150 US, and $200 US to Chetumal. Anyone travelling to **Melchor de Menchos** should not pay more than $12 US for a one-way fare (per person).

 PRACTICAL INFORMATION

Tourist Information

The **Centro de Visitantes** has a tourist information office *(every day 8:30am to 5pm)*.

Exchanging Money

American and Belize dollars are accepted everywhere in Tikal. To exchange currency, head to one of two change kiosks at the Centro de Visitantes, or to one of Tikal's three hotels. Currency can also be readily exchanged at the border at Melchor de Menchos.

Be sure to bring enough ready cash with you. Visa is the only credit card that is universally accepted here! MasterCard is useless in Tikal, even to pay your hotel bill. Should you need a cash advance on your credit card, head to the small shops in the Centro de Visitantes; however, a commission of at least 10% is charged.

Telephone

There is only one telephone in Tikal, at the Centro de Visitantes. However, this phone is not always in working order! The hotels get around this by using CB radio communications. Therefore, do not expect to be able to call your family from Tikal!

 EXPLORING

Tikal ★★★ is built on a slightly elevated natural platform, protecting it from the marshes that form in the lowlands of El Petén during the rainy season. The first traces of human

Tick-Tock Tikal!

Some temples are better appreciated at certain times of day. Here are some tips on how to see the wonders of Tikal at their very best.

At Dawn
At 5 o'clock in the morning, when the jungle is still shrouded in darkness, you can see flashlights pierce the gloom, heading to **Temple IV** (see p 251). Arrange for someone to accompany you, or at least make sure you know the way before venturing onto the site in the dead of night, since you can hardly see a thing at that time. This pilgrimage is one of the most magical ways to experience Tikal, whose mysteries will enthral you. Cautiously climb Temple IV, then patiently await one of the most spectacular sunrises you will ever see!

Early Morning
At about 8 o'clock in the morning, using binoculars, you will be able to make out the frieze of masks on the upper part of the façade of **Temple II** (see p 250), also known as the Temple of the Masks, on Plaza Mayor.

Late Afternoon
The frieze on the summit of **Temple I** (see p 249), also on Plaza Mayor, can only be clearly seen late in the afternoon, when you can behold the huge figure of a sovereign surrounded by what appear to be serpents.

At Dusk
The summit of the **Mundo Perdido** Pyramid (see p 252) is the best place to witness the sun setting beneath the canopy of the jungle and the Tikal ruins. From this lofty height, you can also observe numerous toucans, and the occasional monkey swinging from branch to branch at the foot of the temple.

presence at the site date back to about 800 BC, and the most recent structures date from approximately AD 900. During these 1,500-odd years of Mayan occupation, Tikal became one of the most important urban and ceremonial centres in the Americas. The site also boasts the most impressive structures in the Mayan world, whose gigantic size is unequalled.

The construction of temples on the site began in 200 BC. Although Tikal was not among the first ceremonial centres of Mayan civilization, it was the first seat of its political power. Tikal's economy was probably based on farming corn, beans and squash. As part of the trade network between Mayan cities, Tikal undoubtedly exported exotic goods such as jaguar pelts and toucan, parrot and hummingbird feathers to the highlands.

The Ruins

The beginning of the road leading to the Tikal ruins is easily recognizable by its gate, set up beneath a large tree at the junction of the trail leading to the Jungle Lodge hotel. On this westbound road, you will notice a large *ceiba*, the national tree of Guatemala, on your right. The *ceiba* was sacred to the Maya: the lower part of the tree, where the roots begin, represented night; its trunk symbolized human life as well as day; and, ultimately, its branches were said to signify the sky. This special tree has parasitic plants wrapped around its branches.

The checkpoint to access the site is a few metres beyond the *ceiba*. Since most visitors obtain their ticket at the border, they can simply present it to the guard here. If you remain on the site for more than a day, however, you must pay additional charges for each extra day of your stay *($8 US; 5am to 8pm)*.

Once past the checkpoint, you fill find yourself at the starting point of an overwhelming maze of trails that criss-cross the park. The first trail, to the south, is a long path that leads to Temple VI, known as the Temple of the Inscriptions. The middle trail (southwest) leads to Calzada Méndez and to Temple VI, then to Plaza Mayor. Finally, the trail on the right runs to Complexes Q and R, as well as to Plaza Mayor.

The shortest way to Plaza Mayor, the "Great Plaza", is the middle trail, which runs through Complex F. If you only have one day to visit the ruins, however, the trail that begins on your right is the best one to take. This route will lead you to **Complex Q** (AD 771), which boasts a very well-preserved pyramid made up of five terraces, and with a perfect east-west

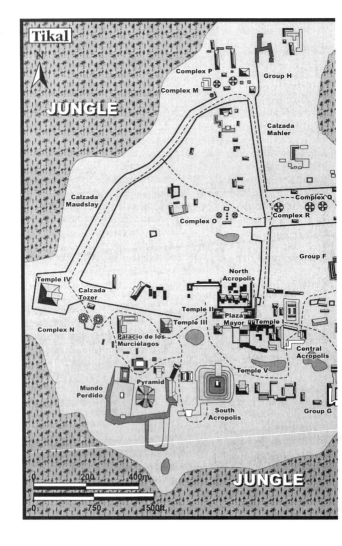

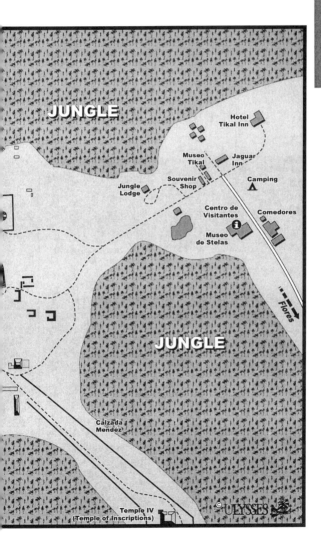

JUNGLE

Hotel
Tikal Inn

Museo
Tikal

Jaguar
Inn

Jungle
Lodge

Souvenir
Shop

Camping

Centro de
Visitantes

Comedores

Museo
de Stelas

Flores

JUNGLE

Calzada
Mendez

Temple IV
(Temple of Inscriptions)

© ULYSSES

alignment. Most complexes consist of twin pyramids facing each other across vast plazas. In Complex Q, however, only one of the two pyramids has been unearthed; the second, farther west, remains buried beneath vegetation. Standing before the uncovered pyramid are nine smooth, upright steles; at the foot of each is an oval stone altar on which animals and humans were sacrificed. Like the lime-coated steles, these altars, on which the priests painted complete descriptions of the traditional ceremonies, were primarily used to celebrate the end of the Catún (20-year period) and the beginning of a new temporal cycle.

South of Complex Q stands a nine-entrance structure that used to shelter members of the elite from the sun during the ceremonies. To the north, an enclosure contains a carved stele depicting a god or ruler. There is also an interesting Mayan arch marking the enclosure's entrance.

Stele 22 and **Altar 10** are found inside the structure. Stele 22 boasts a bas relief depicting the god of the forest or corn. The figure, whose hand is depositing what appear to be kernels of corn, carries a scepter, the symbol of power. The hieroglyphs that adorn the stele have not been deciphered. At the foot of Stele 22 is Altar 10, whose flat surface depicts a sacrifice in bas relief.

Head west between the two pyramids. A few metres to your left stands the first pyramid of **Complex R**. This complex has not been touched by archaeologists, so you can see what all of Tikal looked like when it was discovered in 1878: the steles lie on the ground, covered in tree roots, and the pyramid (AD 790) has yet to be restored.

Go up the short slope to **Calzada Maler**, a causeway that runs between Plaza Mayor and groups P and H. This road dates from the time of the ancient Maya. During this period, it was 40 metres wide and used for commercial and ceremonial purposes. Turn left onto the Calzada Maler, and proceed about 500 metres to Plaza Mayor.

Plaza Mayor

Plaza Mayor, or the central plaza, is the very centre of Tikal. You can reach it from both the south (Calzada Maler) and the northeast (Calzada Méndez).

Temple I, also known as "Gran Jaguar", marks the east end of Plaza Mayor, and the view of the plaza from its 45-metre-high summit is spectacular. Across from it, to the west, is **Temple II**, also called the "Temple of the Masks." Four strata of mortar that have accumulated over time can be found under the central plaza; the last most probably dates from about AD 700.

Temple I (Temple of the Great Jaguar)

The consummate symbol of Tikal and, by extension, of all Guatemala, Temple I towers 45 metres above the plaza level and dates from AD 700 (Classic Period). At the time of its construction, Tikal was ruled by Ha Cacau, whose tomb was discovered by American archaeologist Aubrey S. Trik. It was found at the same level as the temple's first terrace, close to 6 metres below the surface of the plaza. A replica of this magnificent relic (Tomb 116) can be viewed at the Museo Tikal (see p 253).

The temple consists of nine platforms, at the top of which a group of Mayan vaults and arches connect three chambers. Its summit is also carved with of a sovereign surrounded by what appear to be serpents, though this can only be discerned in late afternoon, when the light creates shadows on the bas relief.

Archaeologists have found magnificent wood-carved lintels here, including one depicting Ha Cacau sitting on his throne with the figure of a crawling jaguar, the ruler's protector, at his feet. These pieces were all taken from Guatemala to Basel, London and New York.

Temple II (Temple of the Masks)

Temple II, which stands 38 metres tall, is in several respects a reduced version of Temple I, its twin across the plaza. Built in the same period (AD 700) and by order of the same ruler, it has three terraces topped by a smaller one that supports the crest. Much like Temple I, it has three chambers, one of which features a mural depicting a ceremony in which an arrow flies toward a sacrificial victim. The temple is nicknamed the "Temple of the Masks" because of the masks on its façade. They can be viewed through binoculars at about 8 o'clock in the morning, when the light is good.

North Acropolis

The North Acropolis encompasses three main structures and seems to have served mainly as a cemetery; it contains numerous mausoleums, undoubtedly erected for the ruling class. This part has the most masks sculpted in high relief, including that of Chac, the rain god, and Kinitch Acau, the Sun God, as well as a zoomorphic sculpture.

After climbing to the first level, go down one story to the **Mask of Chac** beneath the thatched roof. You will recognize it by its large nose and ears. Human sacrifices by decapitation were performed at its feet; the victim's blood was sprinkled onto the mask, after which the body was burned on the spot. From here, take the small tunnel to the east, which leads to another mask of Chac. A little higher is the **Mask of the Sun God**, with a the serpent emerging from its ears. The zoomorphic high reliefs are on the next terrace.

Central Acropolis

Located on the south side of Plaza Mayor, and more than 210 metres long, the Central Acropolis is so named because it stands between Temple V and Temple I. Six small courtyards surrounded by one- to two-story buildings are found at its summit.

Behind Temple II (to the west) is a **rest area** with public washrooms and a refreshment stand. Head west (to the left) along the path to Temple III, then on to Temple IV.

Temple III (Temple of the Jaguar Priest)

The highlight of this temple, built in AD 810 and close to 55 metres tall, is the frieze on its summit. At the foot of the temple lies **Stele 24**, whose inscriptions mark the year of the temple's construction. Although it is in a bad state of disrepair, **Altar 6**, before the stele, depicts a goddess reclining on a three-legged pedestal.

The climb to the temple's summit is rather difficult, so be cautious. If you persevere, however, you will be amply rewarded! One of the two skylit chambers contains a carved lintel depicting a priest clothed in a jaguar pelt — hence the temple's name.

On the way to Temple IV, the path skirts around Temple III, then crosses the **Palacio de las Ventanas** (Palace of Windows), also known as the **Palacio de los Murciélagos** (Palace of Bats). The various chambers of the unexcavated two-story temple all lead into each other, and feature numerous period inscriptions.

Midway between the "Palace of Bats" and Temple IV are the twin pyramids of **Complex N**. Dating from AD 711, these rectangular-shaped pyramids each have two side stairways, but no structures on their summits. They are separated by a plaza graced with numerous steles, including **Stele 16**, which stands out for its very well-preserved inscriptions. The base of **Altar 5**, is also magnificent.

Temple IV (Temple of the Two-Headed Serpent)

Built in AD 741, Temple IV rises to a height of 65 metres and ranks among the tallest structures in the Mayan world; it is surpassed only by that of Caracol, in Belize. It is estimated that close to 90,000 cubic metres of building materials were used to construct this towering pyramid.

TIKAL

To reach the top of the temple, you have to climb a series of wooden ladders on the north side of the pyramid (those on the south side have been blocked off). Once, visitors could climb onto the crest itself, but it is now off-limits, to protect it from further decay. You can, however, walk around the temple on the last terrace of the upper level, and admire the crest from up close. This temple affords the best views of the entire Tikal ruins at sunrise.

Built for the ruler Ha Cacau, the god of cocoa, Temple IV is also called "Temple of the Two-Headed Serpent," because a lintel depicting a throne resting on a two-headed serpent was discovered here. The wooden figures once found in the chambers of Temple IV are now in Basel, London and New York.

Temple IV also has three chambers similar to those of Temples I, II and III. Archaeologists believe that the last chamber was used to store the priest's ceremonial instruments, notably sacred objects such as censers and obsidian blades.

Retrace your steps and take the path to the ruins of the Mundo Perdido.

The Lost World

Climb the large Mundo Perdido (Lost World) pyramid for a magnificent view of the most beautiful sunsets over Tikal and the surrounding jungle. This 30-metre-high pyramid was built around AD 600 (Late Classic Period). It was likely one of the largest in the Mayan world at the time, and it is similar in construction to the pyramid in Teotihuacán, Mexico.

Temple V

Measuring 57 metres in height, Temple V was built circa AD 700 and has but one small chamber at its summit. At the time of our visit, this pyramid was undergoing major restoration work by the Spanish government, and was closed to visitors.

Temple VI (Temple of the Inscriptions)

This temple, which stands at the end of Calzada Méndez, was built in AD 766 by the ruler Yaxkin Caan Chac. It boasts the longest glyph in Tikal, inscribed in its 12-metre-high crest. There are two chambers at the summit, and at its base stand **Stele 21** and **Altar 9**. Although both monuments are rather damaged, their glyphs can still be discerned. The figure of a prisoner lying on his back is engraved on the upper part of the altar.

The Museums

The Parque Nacional de Tikal has two museums that display archaeological artifacts found at the site, and explain the history of the Maya, the discovery of the Tikal ruins and the work carried out by archaeologists over the years. Both are worth visiting, even if you have only a day.

In the **Centro de Visitantes** is the **Museo de Stelas** *(Mon to Fri 9am to 5pm, Sat and Sun 9am to 4pm)*. This museum features various steles found at the site, as well as texts and photographs describing the excavation of Tikal from its discovery to the most recent archaeological efforts. Unfortunately, the texts explaining the historical photographs are in Spanish only. Nevertheless, many of the photos successfully illustrate the sad state of the temples when they were first discovered, and the outcome of the restoration work.

The **Museo Tikal**, or **Museo Siluanus G. Morley** *($3 US; Mon to Fri 9am to 5pm, Sat and Sun 9am to 4pm)*, features a collection of pottery found at Tikal. There are also jade artifacts and bone carvings uncovered in the site's tombs. The explanatory texts are in both Spanish and English. This small museum is in a traditional colonial-style house with an interior courtyard.

The museum's crowning glory is a replica of **Tumba 116**, which was found behind the first terrace of Temple I, or Templo Jaguar Gigante, by American archaeologist and architect Aubrey S. Trik in 1962. Inside it were the remains of Ha Cacau, the god of cocoa. He was 1.80 metres (six feet) tall, ruled Tikal for over half a century (AD 682 to 734) and died between the 3rd and 4th Catún.

The tomb in the museum is an exact replica of the original one at 1.20 metres deep, 2.4 metres wide and 4 metres high. Artifacts inside include jade necklaces, bracelets, shells and pottery.

 OUTDOOR ACTIVITIES

 Hiking

Most guides at Tikal offer two-hour jungle excursions ($10 US per person). Go to the checkpoint at the entrance of the ruins, where the guides usually wait for visitors.

 ACCOMMODATIONS

It is not uncommon for hotels in Tikal to lose reservations. Confirming your reservation on the day of your arrival, or the day before, is thus strongly recommended.

Jaguar Inn *($5-$48 US; pb, sb, ℜ, ⊗, ≡; ☎502-926-0002)* is popular with hikers and offers several different types of accommodation. The most expensive rooms have private bathrooms and air conditioning, similar to those of the Jungle Lodge (see p 255). The hotel also has *cabañas* with a shared bathroom available for $25 US. You can also camp on the property and sleep in a hammock with mosquito netting for $5 US per person. The Jaguar Inn has a relaxed family ambiance. The common room and the wood-built restaurant (see p 255) fit harmoniously into the park's environment; what is more, this restaurant is inexpensive and is the most inviting in Tikal.

The **Hotel Tikal Inn** *($55 US; pb, ⊗, ≈, ℜ; ☎/≠502-926-0065)* is inarguably the best establishment in Tikal. Smaller than the Jungle Lodge, it is both quieter and more enjoyable. The inn offers beautiful traditional thatched-roof *cabañas* with large rooms and bedrooms, all in wood. It is very clean and well-kept, and has a lovely swimming pool. The restaurant (see below) has a fixed-price menu, but the quality of the meals is not outstanding.

The biggest hotel in Tikal, **Jungle Lodge** *($60 US; pb, sb, ℜ, ⊗, ≈, ≡, hw; ⊗ $25 US; ☎04-768775, ⌐04-760294)* rents out very attractive, comfortable and air-conditioned rooms. Those in the lower price range have shared bathrooms. There is a pleasant living room and delightful terrace, as well as a lovely swimming pool with bar. The hotel, however, is often full and the service is rather rushed at times. Make sure your reservation is really and truly confirmed prior to your arrival. Large restaurant (see p 256).

RESTAURANTS

Unfortunately, the calibre of local restaurants leaves something to be desired, and meals are relatively expensive. There are nevertheless several *comedores* opposite the information centre which are somewhat less expensive than hotel restaurants. The **Comedor la Jungla Tikal** *($-$$)* offers an original rice and beans daily menu with meat, accompanied by good tortillas.

Comedor Tikal *($-$$)* offers a fairly varied à-la-carte menu, featuring typical rice and beans dishes. Take-out sandwiches are also available here. The place is decent, but definitely not exceptional.

The restaurant of the **Jaguar Inn** *($-$$; 6am to 9pm)* has a varied and lower-priced menu than the other hotel restaurants in Tikal. The thatched-roof restaurant stands out for its pleasant and relaxed ambiance created by candlelight dinners. Try the spaghetti with bolognese or cream sauce, which is quite decent considering the general quality of the food in Tikal (sample the grated cheese before sprinkling it onto your dish; its taste is very distinctive). Excellent fresh bread and butter always accompany the meals. There is an extensive breakfast menu that includes peanut butter!

The **Hotel Tikal Inn** *($$$)* has a pleasant restaurant that offers a fixed-price dinner menu, with a choice of three dishes. The meals are decent, but not outstanding. Breakfasts are more interesting because of their variety, and are especially popular with the hotel's guests (see p 254). Good table service.

The restaurant of the **Jungle Lodge** *($$$)* offers a fixed-price dinner menu and an à-la-carte lunch menu. At dinner, you can choose among four main dishes: fish, chicken, pork or beef. The pork dish is generally the best choice at this very crowded restaurant where the overly busy kitchen tends to translate into rather bland food. The ambiance may be elegant, but don't get your hopes up about the food! The restaurant provides "box lunches" (sandwich, juice, etc.) the day before you visit the ruins. The quality of the service is erratic.

INDEX

INDEX

INDEX

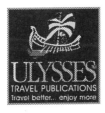

Enjoy more...

ULYSSES
TRAVEL PUBLICATIONS

**Travel better...
enjoy more**

OTHER ULYSSES GUIDES

Acapulco (Mexico)
Ulysses Due South guide offers a fresh look at Acapulco, the most famous Mexican resort: Acapulco Bay, its beaches, restaurants and captivating nightlife are all in there, but so are the neighbouring mountains, as well as an enlightened look at the people and history of this spot.
Marc Rigole, Claude-Victor Langlois   150 pages, 5 maps
$14.95 CAN $9.95 US   £6.99
2-89464-062-5

The Islands Of The Bahamas
Vacationers will find extensive coverage of the big favourites of New Providence (Nassau) and Grand Bahama (Freeport) with their spectacular beaches, glittering casinos and great scuba diving, but they will also find the most extensive coverage of the Out Islands. Here island-hoppers enjoy world-class fishing, scuba diving and boating, friendly people and pristine deserted beaches.
Jennifer McMorran   288 pages, 25 maps
8 pages of colour photos
$24.95 CAN $17.95 US   £12.99
2-89464-123-0

Belize
This tiny Central American country encompasses part of the ancient Ruta Maya and is rimmed by spectacular coral reefs. Its archaeological and natural treasures make it an explorer's paradise. Practical and cultural information will help you make the most of your vacation.
Carlos Soldevila   208 pages, 10 maps
$12.95 US
2-89464-179-6

Cancún & Cozumel (Mexico)
The entirely man-made resort of Cancún on the Yucatán Peninsula attracts visitors from the world-over. They come to enjoy a unique travelling experience with fabulous archaeological sites, the last remnants of the Mayan civilization, and the island of Cozumel, a scuba-diver's paradise, both close by.
Caroline Vien, Alain Théroux   200 pages, 20 maps
$17.95 CAN $12.95 US   £8.99
2-89464-040-4

Cartagena, 2nd edition
Here is the new edition on this colonial jewel. Declared a World Heritage Site by UNESCO, Cartagena boasts historic charm, cultural riches, luxurious hotels, beautiful beaches and the possibility of exciting excursions, all the ingredients for an extraordinary vacation.
Marc Rigole   128 pages, 10 maps
$12.95 CAN $9.95 US   £6.50
2-89464-018-8

Costa Rica

This fresh look at Costa Rica provides travellers with the most extensive choice of practical addresses, no matter what their budget while also placing special emphasis on eco-tourism, independent travel and the culture, history and natural wonders of this Central American gem.

Francis Giguère, Yves Séguin   368 pages, 35 maps
8 pages of colour photos
$27.95 CAN $19.95 US   £13.99
2-89464-144-3

Cuba, 2nd edition

Already a second edition for this unique guide to Cuba. The island's spirit is revealed, from colonial Havana, to the world-heritage site of Trinidad and to Santiago with it Afro-Cuban culture. The guide also covers the famous beaches and provides travellers with countless shortcuts and tips for independent travel in Cuba.

Carlos Soldevila   336 pages, 40 maps
8 pages of colour photos
$24.95 CAN $17.95 US   £12.99
2-89464-143-5

Dominican Republic

The most complete reference to this Caribbean hot spot: excursions, historical information, cultural details, addresses of restaurants, shops and hotels, road maps and city plans.

Pascale Couture, Benoit Prieur
250 pages, 20 maps
8 pages of colour photos
$24.95 CAN $17.95 US   £12.99
2-89464-064-1

Ecuador and the Galápagos Islands

All the major sites of this South American country are explored including extensive coverage of the capital city, Quito, but also the extraordinary Galapagos Islands. Hundreds of addresses for all budgets as well as countless useful hints for discovering this fascinating and ancient land of the Incas.

Alain Legault   300 pages, 25 maps
8 pages of colour photos
$24.95 CAN $17.95 US   £12.99
2-89464-059-5

El Salvador

This guide provides everything the traveller needs to discover this fascinating Central American country: explanation of cultural and political contexts, advice on how to travel in the area, descriptions of the various attractions, detailed lists of accommodation, restaurants, entertainment.

Eric Hamovitch   152 pages, 7 maps
$22.95 CAN $14.95 US   £11.50
2-921444-89-5

Guadeloupe, 3rd edition

This is the only guide to provide such extensive cultural and practical coverage of this destination. The charm of this dramatically beautiful Caribbean island is revealed along winding picturesque roads through typical villages and towns. Magnificent colour plates help to identify Guadeloupe's birds and plants.

Pascale Couture   208 pages, 15 maps
8 pages of colour photos
$24.95 CAN $17.95 US £12.99
2-89464-135-4

Guatemala

Historic peace talks have once again allowed tourism to develop in Guatemala, providing a spectacular glimpse at a country whose native traditions are so strong and omnipresent.

Carlos Soldevila, Denis Faubert   336 pages, 30 maps
$24.95 CAN $17.95 US £12.99
2-89464-175-3

Honduras, 2nd edition

The prospects for tourism in Honduras are among the brightest – promising travellers a first-rate vacation, whether they are in search of spectacular deserted beaches, fascinating archaeological sites or supreme diving locations. This guide offers numerous suggestions for outdoor adventure plus practical tips and information on everything from A to Z.

Eric Hamovitch   224 pages, 20 maps
$24.95 CAN $17.95 US £12.99
2-89464-132-X

Martinique, 3rd edition

A perfect marriage of cultural and practical information provides the best coverage of Martinique. Numerous tours lead across the island of flowers, from Fort-de-France to Saint-Pierre, with stops in Grande Anse and Montagne Pelée. Everything you need to know about hiking and water sports. Magnificent colour plates help to identify birds and plants.

Claude Morneau   256 pages, 18 maps
8 pages of colour photos
$24.95 CAN $17.95 US £12.99
2-89464-136-2

Nicaragua

Once a headline-maker the world over, Nicaragua is more often featured in the "Travel" section these days. Besides the capital city of Managua and the popular resort of Montelimar, this guide traverses the whole country, discovering the touching cities of León and Granada, among other places, along the way.

Carol Wood   224 pages, 15 maps
$24.95 CAN $16.95 US   £11.50
2-89464-034-X

ORDER FORM

ULYSSES TRAVEL GUIDES

☐ Affordable B&Bs in Québec	$12.95 CAN / $9.95 US	☐ Lisbon	$18.95 CAN / $13.95 US
☐ Atlantic Canada	$24.95 CAN / $17.95 US	☐ Louisiana	$29.95 CAN / $21.95 US
☐ Beaches of Maine	$12.95 CAN / $9.95 US	☐ Martinique	$24.95 CAN / $17.95 US
☐ Bahamas	$24.95 CAN / $17.95 US	☐ Montréal	$19.95 CAN / $14.95 US
☐ Belize	$16.95 CAN / $12.95 US	☐ New Orleans	$17.95 CAN / $12.95 US
☐ Calgary	$17.95 CAN / $12.95 US	☐ New York City	$19.95 CAN / $14.95 US
☐ Canada	$29.95 CAN / $21.95 US	☐ Nicaragua	$24.95 CAN / $16.95 US
☐ Chicago	$19.95 CAN / $14.95 US	☐ Ontario	$24.95 CAN / $14.95US
☐ Chile	$27.95 CAN / $17.95 US	☐ Ottawa	$17.95 CAN / $12.95 US
☐ Costa Rica	$27.95 CAN / $19.95 US	☐ Panamá	$24.95 CAN / $16.95 US
☐ Cuba	$24.95 CAN / $17.95 US	☐ Portugal	$24.95 CAN / $16.95 US
☐ Dominican Republic	$24.95 CAN / $17.95 US	☐ Provence - Côte d'Azur	$29.95 CAN / $21.95US
☐ Ecuador and Galapagos Islands	$24.95 CAN / $17.95 US	☐ Québec	$29.95 CAN / $21.95 US
☐ El Salvador	$22.95 CAN / $14.95 US	☐ Québec and Ontario with Via	$9.95 CAN / $7.95 US
☐ Guadeloupe	$24.95 CAN / $17.95 US	☐ Toronto	$18.95 CAN / $13.95 US
☐ Guatemala	$24.95 CAN / $17.95 US	☐ Vancouver	$17.95 CAN / $12.95 US
☐ Honduras	$24.95 CAN / $17.95 US	☐ Washington D.C.	$18.95 CAN / $13.95 US
☐ Jamaica	$24.95 CAN / $17.95 US	☐ Western Canada	$29.95 CAN / $21.95 US

ULYSSES DUE SOUTH

☐ Acapulco	$14.95 CAN / $9.95 US	☐ Cartagena (Colombia)	$12.95 CAN / $9.95 US
☐ Belize	$16.95 CAN / $12.95 US	☐ Cancun Cozumel	$17.95 CAN / $12.95 US

| □ Puerto Vallarta | $14.95 CAN
$9.95 US | □ St. Martin and
St. Barts | $16.95 CAN
$12.95 US |

ULYSSES TRAVEL JOURNAL

□ Ulysses Travel Journal . . . . $9.95 CAN
(Blue, Red, Green, Yellow, Sextant) $7.95 US

ULYSSES GREEN ESCAPES

□ Cycling in France	$22.95 CAN $16.95 US	□ Hiking in Québec	$19.95 CAN $13.95 US
□ Hiking in the . .	$19.95 CAN		
Northeastern U.S.	$13.95 US		

TITLE	QUANTITY	PRICE	TOTAL

Name _____	Sub-total	
Address _____	Postage & Handling	$8.00*
_____	Sub-total	
Payment : □ Money Order □ Visa □ MasterCard	G.S.T. in Canada 7%	
Card Number _____		
Signature _____	TOTAL	

ULYSSES TRAVEL PUBLICATIONS
4176 St-Denis,
Montréal, Québec, H2W 2M5
(514) 843-9447 fax (514) 843-9448
www.ulysses.ca
* $15 for overseas orders

U.S. ORDERS: **GLOBE PEQUOT PRESS**
P.O. Box 833, 6 Business Park Road,
Old Saybrook, CT 06475-0833
1-800-243-0495 fax 1-800-820-2329
www.globe-pequot.com